ORGANIZE!

Organize!

MY LIFE AS A UNION MAN

BY WYNDHAM MORTIMER

EDITED BY LEO FENSTER

BEACON PRESS BOSTON

Library of Congress catalog card number: 73-136233

International Standard Book Number: 0-8070-5438-0 (casebound)
0-8070-5439-9 (paperback)

First published as a Beacon Paperback in 1972

Beacon Press books are published under the auspices of the Unitarian Universalist Association

Published simultaneously in Canada
by Saunders of Toronto, Ltd.

Printed in the United States of America

This book is dedicated to

HENRY KRAUS, *whose services to the UAW, much of it without pay, were greater than many in the union's top leadership, and*

ROBERT TRAVIS, *the real leader of the 1937 GM sitdown strike, and the most brilliant strike strategist the UAW ever had.*

Two rare individuals who consistently placed principle above personal gain. The automobile workers owe them a debt of gratitude it will be hard to pay.

CONTENTS

INTRODUCTION: AN ASSESSMENT —HE TOOK THE HIGH ROAD

ven when I jog my memory and calculate, it appears that I could not have been with Wyndham Mortimer on more than ten or so occasions over a span of almost thirty-three years. This is odd because we were intimate friends and behaved as such when we were together. I especially recall five times when we met. The first may have been late in 1933 or early in 1934. I was an officer in an AFL union. Some of the other officers and active members, left wing in their political inclinations, persuaded me to attend a meeting of AFL people concerned with enacting an unemployment insurance law. The meeting was proscribed by the AFL leadership because, unbelievably, at the height of the Depression with its universal unemployment, these leaders rejected the idea of unemployment compensation. They said that it was a dole which American workers would never accept, and forbade involvement of AFL members.

The meeting was addressed by Louis Weinstock who was head of the New York painters; Ralph Rhymus, an officer among Cleveland painters; and Wyndham Mortimer, president of the White Motor Local, a federal AFL local union of auto workers. Mortimer was becoming known in the city because his union was the first in Cleveland's auto industry which had achieved recognition and an agreement.

The other two union officials spoke about jobless pay: Mortimer told us how important it was to organize the auto industry. I remember him as dramatically as a color photo caught in suspended motion and impressed forever on the retina of the eye. He stood in sort of a semi-gloom of grays, browns, and blacks. He spoke slowly and squinted as he spoke and punctuated his emphases with a squint. He spoke, thinking aloud with his audience, framing his thoughts with their thoughts. It was this simultaneous arrival at conclusions which was the center of his persuasive powers. I spoke to him briefly after the meeting and I was hooked on the eternal pilgrimage of the auto union toward the economic sunlight.

I was at all but one of the conventions of the United Auto Workers (UAW) from 1943 through 1966. Mort must generally have been present. Yet, for the most part I have no clear pictures of meeting with him. In 1961, however, I bought a brand new Renault in Milan and drove through Italy, then east through Austria, Czechoslovakia, and Poland to Moscow. In Moscow, by one of those miraculous accidents which make this such a small world, I bumped into Mort. We arranged for him to come up to my hotel apartment with two youthful leaders of the Soviet trade unions who spoke English. One of them had just finished squiring Joe Curran, president of the National Maritime Union, through the USSR.

Mort was one of those people completely involved in his "thing." He accepted the conventions for everyday living because they were laid out for him. But he made one concession to vanity: his hats. He always had a sharp one, nattily blocked, perched suavely at the back of his head. That afternoon, with his hat set back, he expounded for hours to his Soviet listeners on the birth of the CIO, the North American strike, and the personalities of certain American trade union leaders. At the end of the afternoon one of them remarked, "We have learned more this afternoon about your American trade union movement than in all of our books." They had.

On February 10, 1962, our local union arranged a celebration of the twenty-fifth anniversary of the signing of that first contract with General Motors. The local union put on a dramatic presentation of the sit-down strike. The two speakers for the occasion were Leonard Woodcock, at that time an International Vice President in charge of the union's GM department, and, quite properly, Wyndham Mortimer. There was a message from John L. Lewis. Both speakers paid scant attention to the events twenty-five years past; they almost bypassed the UAW, seeing it only in the ambit of the world scene, world problems, the future. Leonard was in his late forties, Mort was pushing his four-score years; but the past was a bucket of ashes unless it lighted the future.

Sometime before his eighty-second birthday Mort's good health broke down. He suffered a stroke, but with fierce application to his therapy, he overcame all but a minimum of the original paralysis. The 1966 Convention of the UAW was held in Long Beach, California, and Mort was in the balcony every day. The stream of delegates, staff members, and friends to greet him and talk to him was unending.

As the Convention neared its last day Joe Ditzel of Toledo GM Local 14 and an early organizer of the UAW went to the platform and asked Walter Reuther to introduce Mort from the stage. Reuther flatly refused. Joe went back to his seat and stewed. He shouted for a point of special privilege which had to be granted. In two brief sentences he told the Convention about Mort and pointed to him sitting in the balcony. The delegates cheered and leaped applauding to their feet in an ovation. Reuther glowered on the platform. "Other people have made contributions to this union," he said. It was a churlishly graceless public performance.

For Mort it was a sundown vindication of all the purposes of his life. Yet when John DeVito, myself, and our wives had dinner with him that night he refused to be drawn into discussion of the event. It had happened, and he must have been glad, but he wanted to talk about what the Convention ought to be accomplishing.

Later that year, in August, Mort came East to visit his sister and friends in the Cleveland area. But almost on the first day of his visit he was overtaken by a painful prostate condition. The doctors said that surgery was imperative. Mort insisted he would feel more comfortable with the medical people he knew back in Los Angeles. The illness had confined him to a wheelchair so his daughter Irma called John DeVito and me and we got him out to the airport, a trip of more than thirty miles. But the airlines had been struck nationally by the IAM and only American Airlines was being permitted to fly. The airport was deep with people waiting on a stand-by basis. The waiting period was six to eight hours at least, and here was a man who had lost control of vital functions and who must have been in misery. He was utterly calm and casual; he was in the hands of his daughter and his good friends and they would do whatever was necessary. John and I went to talk with the American Airlines manager. In the midst of the frantic ado he was graciously cooperative and arranged for Mort to be put on a plane within half an hour. While we waited we all went for some lunch, and I noticed that Mort was using orinase. He was diabetic. "I used to use six a day," he said, "but two weeks ago for the first time in years I had negative readings. I only take one for each meal now. It looks like I may be licking it." We got Mort and his daughter on the plane. But he did not survive the surgery.

Throughout his book Mort refers insistently to the rank and file. It was neither a pose nor a fetish. He did not idealize the rank and file nor endow it with glamour. Rather he understood it as a reality. If workers in a shop could have their intuitions and their basic self-interests translated into a reasoned construction and a viable program, then they were capable of powerful, persistent actions and the almost limitless sacrifices which made victories possible.

On occasion Mort was unable to convince other leaders, especially if they were encrusted with pure self-interest and a desire to appear compatible to the establishment. But he almost never lost an argument to the rank and file. Until he was well into middle age, Mort spent his life with them shoulder-to-shoulder in the shops. And while he was different from them in that he spent all his waking moments thinking about unions, the unions he conjured up were constructed of these very shop-mates, convinced to join and to act. The knowledge of how to convince them was in the marrow of his bones. He did not fear them; he loved them. He was aware of and undisturbed by their vacillations, and he was infinitely impressed by the potential of their strength.

The ifs and buts of history are as tantalizing as the events which actually occurred. It is so tempting to indulge a few fantasies, especially where Mort is concerned. What if it were known at the right time that the Hillman–Murray team did not represent the thinking of John L. Lewis in respect to UAW leadership? What if the Browder-led Communist Party had not plugged so zealously for R. J. Thomas? That party had strong balance-of-power influence at that time. What if the delegates had rejected both outside influences? They were marching through the downtown Cleveland streets bitterly singing, "Addes is our leader, Thomas gets our votes." What if? Well, Addes would have been elected and it would have been a different ball game. Yet these futile speculations, while they may have a momentary nostalgic balm for the participants, tend to block out the solid achievement of Wyndham Mortimer.

Events of some significance occur daily; our newspapers record them. Events of greater importance are less frequent. But they happen, and they are conversation pieces for a longer or shorter time. But a different measure has to be applied to events which become turning points in history. The coming to power of Mussolini, of Hitler? Were those turning points? Not really. These events and everything they implied were reversed. But the building of the Panama Canal was a turning point. It staked out the United States claim to Latin America which the Monroe Doctrine had so prematurely and feebly advanced. It gave burgeoning American industry and finance the large outlet it so obviously needed. It made possible our emergence as the world's great private enterprise power. Some of us may not like the mechanics but we cannot doubt the results.

The Russians have supplied two turning points—in 1917

with their revolution, and again in 1942–43 with the Battle of Stalingrad. The last was the retrogressive turning point for fascism.

Turning points in history must be irreversible. They must change the path of peoples and of history. When Martin Luther King stood firm at Montgomery, Alabama, he may have created a turning point. The Negro people had chosen a new direction for freedom. The Bay of Pigs may have been a turning point, for it kindled the viability of a new road for Latin America. The road may diverge into many paths, but all with the goal of economic and national independence. The Tet offensive of 1968 may have dashed forever the hopes of military subjugation of Asian insurgency. But all these events are only candidates for historic turning points. They are too close; the aftermaths are still in gestation; they will have to be judged in fuller perspective.

Within the American scene, the General Motors strike of 1936–37 and the signing of that first agreement was a turning point in our domestic history. Nothing that the UAW had done before, nothing that it has done since, had that kind of impact on events. The UAW has since, to a considerable extent, taken care of many of the problems of its members. But it has done so within the routine of the status quo, an adjustment there, a correction here, all within the perspective of the establishment, and easily within their ability to afford and to accept. But this was the one occasion when the status quo was wrenched loose from those who would cling to it, when the establishment was yanked from its moorings, when the sacred, inviolable, indispensable open shop was turned into its opposite—the union shop.

General Motors was the battlement of industry and Big Business. You could pick along the fringes and nothing decisive would happen. But if you stormed the bastion you were playing for keeps. This was the essence of the Mortimer–Lewis strategy. Workers who took part in the sit-downs coined the expression, "We were too dumb to know what we were doing." The enormity of their effrontery, the magnitude of their task, the historic nature of their effort, all this escaped them. But

Mortimer knew. He was keenly aware of each facet. And he planned it all—from minutiae to grand strategy.

Read his story; reread the relevant passages. See how carefully he planned each step, how delicately he evaluated each problem. And observe that he was involved with every detail of execution. Watch those eyes squint behind those spectacles as he thinks, thinks, thinks. He talks with hundreds of people, listens to them, answers them. Out of their melding comes the grand strategy. The assault can be made, the victory is won.

It was a victory which fertilized an era of profound changes in American life. When General Motors gave in, the door was wide open. Not without struggle, but inevitably, the basic industries were organized. No longer was the worker a cringing organic entity in the production process. He had a right to express himself, both on the job and politically. He had a right to his job. No longer could he be capriciously dismissed. He had a right to fight for wages, hours, conditions. He had a right to secure his future. And a thousand contracts plus public legislation has insured him in sickness and in health, on the job and in joblessness, in his working days and in his retirement. And he has the possibility openly, demonstratively, to forge a political road.

But the nation changed also. The Great Depression, despite apprehension, has not reappeared. Recessions, yes, and more to come. But the economy has built-in safeguards against depression. And the general continuity of income has made the good life, materially speaking, possible for tens of millions. Nothing that happens is forever. The new problems are piling up, and solutions are being too long delayed by the same establishment manipulators who still think that you can turn off an atomic explosion by adjusting an innocuous screw.

Not a few bemoan the fact that Mortimer's career was cut short even before he was sixty. But a look backward would show that within the framework of the realities he could have helped to build only a somewhat more efficient UAW, perhaps a small sector of the labor movement that was somewhat more receptive. But as for another creative mutation, the dice were loaded against that.

Today's new problems, more ominous, really, even than the depression, will have to find new solutions and new leaders fully equipped in all the dimensions of stature. But the future will come out of the present, a present which the Mortimers supplied out of the past.

For Mortimer the time and the man had coincided in the mid-thirties. And he pushed all the right buttons.

Leo Fenster

ACKNOWLEDGMENTS

To Henry Kraus, Wyndham Mortimer's close friend of more than thirty years, must go major credit for the completion of this work. Mort was, after all, not a writer and he recognized his own literary limitations. From the beginning Mort mailed section after section of the manuscript to Henry in Paris for critical comments and corrections. For Henry, as for many of us, this book has been a labor of love. He has been a most valuable friend.

Special recognition must also be given to another friend of more than thirty years, Robert Travis, whose frequent visits were always helpful.

The list of those who helped in other ways would be very long, but a few deserve special mention: Tom Bledsoe, a fine writer and editor whose untimely death saddened us all; Thelma J. Pettit, Helen Travis, Dorothy Kraus, Mary Volz, John and Babs Anderson, Len De Caux, and especially my daughter Jeryl, who worked with me tirelessly to complete the job.

To all who helped my father, and to those who helped me in putting it all together . . . . my sincere thanks.

Irma Mortimer Stewart

PREFACE

Important men are sometimes almost strangers to their wives and children. Through the years, I have known men who maintained a public image quite different from the one their families knew. Their smiling "public" faces turned to stone when they were at home and not impressing strangers and newsmen. But my father, Wyndham Mortimer, never had two faces. It is important, I think, that I write some of the little stories so typical of him, and express some thoughts on the countless ways in which this great man affected the lives of those who knew him well, and those who loved him most.

It has been a while since my father's death, but his presence is still felt in our daily lives, and in the lives of his many friends. We quote him repeatedly—his little jokes, and his homespun wisdom. Bob Travis expressed it this way, "Mort still lives: in you, in me, and in all of us who knew and loved him." So long as any of us remain I am sure it can truly be said that he will never die. His autobiography, which he worked on during the final years of his life, is a fascinating story of a man whose life was devoted to his fellowman, a hero in the eyes of thousands, who never thought of himself as heroic or self-sacrificing. And since he never saw himself as a hero he could not be expected to glorify himself when writing the story of his life or the history of his favorite union.

He was a man to whom all men really were "brothers." Long ago he argued in favor of adding Negro union brothers to the International Executive Board of the United Auto Workers (UAW) and was told it was "reverse racism." But he felt they needed *special* representation. Black workers themselves are now demanding the same thing, and roughly twenty-five years later the same men who coined the meaningless phrase "reverse racism" have reversed their own positions in the light of these demands.

He responded to several names throughout his life. As a child he was always "Wyn" and my mother called him by that name. When he worked in the factory at White Motor he was called "Bill" for some unaccountable reason. To my sister and me he was always "Papa." As the union became a reality and he became more widely known, he suddenly was "Mort." John L. Lewis was the only one who ever called him by his full given name, and Lewis seemed to enjoy saying the Welsh-sounding name of "Wyndham." The only other name he ever earned after that was "Grandpa," which he wore proudly. His grandchildren were a source of great pleasure and pride to him. He was always interested in their numerous triumphs and little tragedies. They made his final years worthwhile and in them he placed great hope for the future.

Those who knew him intimately will perhaps notice that he mentions my mother very little throughout his story, even though she was the single most important person in the world to him. He wrote this story after her death, and at first he found it impossible to mention her at all. He loved my mother more than life itself. While he could struggle with giants like General Motors Corporation and never be at a loss for words, my mother had to tell him which shirt to wear—had to restrain him from wearing a plaid tie with a clashing plaid shirt! He just didn't care about such little things as proper dress, and should really have been a young man in these times of psychedelic colors. He would have loved wearing orange and red at the same time, but it was unthinkable in his generation. Mama managed him in all the myriad of details that kept him fed, clothed, and just generally well-cared-for, and her word was final so far as he was concerned. He loved her so devotedly that he never needed to go around expressing it in public displays. It just radiated from his eyes whenever he looked at her. It was typical of him, however, that when I urged him to write more about my mother in his book, he had great difficulty in doing so. It took many re-writings before he managed to say the things that he did. She was too precious to him and he could not talk about it to anyone. As a matter of fact, he mentions members of his immediate family hardly at all, and knowing him, we all realize that he considered us as part of himself, and he assumed that anyone would know we were all involved wherever he was.

While I was growing up I never realized that my home was different from many others. I was unaware that most children did not have the kind of family I had. My parents never fought, and seldom had even a minor argument, and then it was only when my mother, the perfectionist, would try to get perfection out of my father. But he never seriously argued with her. He would just be amused at her insistence and try to do the job to please her.

Every afternoon when he had washed up from his work, Papa would come into the kitchen and put his powerful arms around her while she was cooking the supper. She was always freshly combed and pretty when he came home and never failed to put on a fresh dress and "get cleaned up" before he arrived. He would tease her and pretend he was going to strangle her if she did not hurry the supper, and Mama would laugh happily.

My mother was a tiny woman, a most fastidious housekeeper, and true to the traditions of her Scottish father, was as thrifty as anyone I have ever known. She could make a meal of stewed tomatoes with bread and butter sound like a real banquet. When we would ask, "What's for supper?" she would answer with exaggerated emphasis, "Why, tonight we are having Mock Duck!" Of course it was never even remotely like duck, but we loved her teasing. My sister and I never realized that lots of other people had much more to eat than we did. We were thoroughly contented.

Today most fathers want nothing more than to be let alone when they come home from work. The little ones must get out of Daddy's way. My father worked long and hard under conditions that would be unthinkable today, and yet he never asked that I not bother him, never let me know that he was exhausted when I raced down the street to meet him and hung on his arm so he would "swing me" as he came home from the shop. In the evenings, tired as he was, he always read long stories to me before I went to bed, or when we got our first radio, a crystal set, he would give me one half of the headset so I could listen while sitting on his lap. I must have been a terrible pest, but I never ever had an inkling of that from him. Even on Sunday afternoons, when he took his weekly long walks, he patiently took me along to badger him with questions.

His patience with us was endless, his love for us knew no bounds. In my entire lifetime I can never recall a time when my father was ever anything but gentle, kind, fair, and loving to me and to every member of our family. He never refused to do any favor we asked of him, and could be counted upon always to go out of his way to do the simplest of tasks or the most difficult, with never a grumble.

Papa had an exceptionally fine singing voice when he was younger, and he continued to sing as long as he lived. Around the house he always sang or whistled his many favorite old tunes. "When You and I Were Young, Maggie" was one of his favorites. (My mother had always been called "Maggie" as a child.) My sister and I were always awakened on Sunday morning by the sound of Papa playing the piano and singing. We would crawl out of bed and hurry to join him. It was our favorite time of the week. He taught us many songs, and one of my earliest memories is of sitting on the piano bench beside him and singing "Uncle Ned." He had a special way of playing, a special "touch" that I can hear quite clearly even yet. He played beautifully—but only simple tunes.

My father's sister, Sue, has told me many stories of their childhood. Sue was six years younger, and remembers many of the funny things her big brothers did.

My father took his first music lessons from a widow woman

who lived at the foot of the mountain, in Westport, when they lived in Bitumen. Every Saturday night after he got off work and had his bath, he would walk down the mountain for his piano lesson. On the way home, about halfway up the mountain, he would walk out onto a big rock that jutted out from the side of the mountain. He would face the big valley below and the hills all around and pretend he was standing on a gigantic stage and that he had a tremendous audience. He would sing the many songs he knew and would perform a whole concert as though to a big opera house, letting his voice fill the valleys. Then he would bow with the sound of imaginary applause in his ears and continue on home, thinking no one knew about it. He confided in his little sister, however, and showed her the rock where he sang each week. When he was about sixteen years old he was sent away to school because of his health, and the people down in Westport started asking what had happened to the boy who always sang on the mountain on Saturday night. He had not known that every Saturday night the neighbors, traveling salesmen, and hotel guests would gather on the porch of the little roadside inn to listen to him sing. It was a weekly event in their otherwise uneventful lives, and they missed him when he went away.

The many young men of today who find themselves running away from home and feeling guilty about it, will be surprised to know that my father also ran away from home when in his late teens.

Around the coal mines there were three days a year when the men didn't have to work: Christmas, the Fourth of July, and Election Day. On election day the bosses made it a point to see that everyone went to the polls, and voted right, or else. But the Fourth of July was really a day for pleasure. On that morning, everyone got up bright and early, walked down to Westport and caught the train to Renovo. Renovo was the only town of any size where there was any entertainment, and so all the young people went down there to spend the day. They had a carnival with a merry-go-round and a big display of fireworks in the evening.

My father and his older brother, Tom, left early one Fourth

of July morning to go to Renovo with all the others from their town. Late in the evening when the train came back, their mother and sister Sue were waiting at the gate, watching the tired crowd returning from the holiday. When Tom came trudging up the hill, his mother said, "Where's Wyn?" Tom said he hadn't seen him all day. Another friend passed by and again she asked, "Did you see anything of Wyn?" The young man said, "Oh, yes, Mrs. Mortimer, he didn't get off the train at Renovo this morning. He told me to tell you he was going on to Williamsport."

The whole family was upset. But a few days later they got a letter from him saying that he had not gone to Williamsport, but had stopped off at a little town called Jersey Shore and had taken a job on the railroad. He said he wanted to try something else besides coal mining.

There was much consternation at home. His mother was worried and shed many tears. His father said, "Well, he has chosen to do this, and we must not let him know we are troubled. We will write and tell him to let us know where he will be staying, and that his mother is getting his clothes ready to send to him. We must not tell him how much we miss him."

After about two weeks had passed, one evening as the family was sitting down to supper, their wandering son walked in and sat down at the supper table as though nothing had happened. Nobody mentioned his absence and neither did he. After supper he put on his old clothes and went out in the garden and worked with his brothers, hoeing and planting potatoes. He seemed very happy to be back home.

After supper it was Sue's job to get all the dinner pails ready for the next day and line them up at one end of the big kitchen table so her mother could pack them in the morning. While she and her mother were working in the kitchen that evening, they heard him in the parlor playing the piano. They exchanged the happiest of smiles. He was home again, and life was good again; the family was together.

When he was a young man, nearing twenty, he played for the Saturday night dances at the YMCA in the little town of

Winburne. He also played for the church social affairs. That was how he met my mother.

My mother, a beautiful little blonde girl of about seventeen, had come to visit her cousin Nora Gray, who lived in Winburne. She went with Nora to the Young People's meeting at church. My father wandered in, and she thought the tall dark-haired boy was quite the handsomest fellow she had ever seen. He went straight to the piano. The little blonde visitor was thoroughly entranced. He kept glancing in her direction all the time but never came near. When she and Nora finally had to leave, she was very disappointed that she had not met him, but was too shy to do anything about it. But he wasn't so slow as to let her get away without meeting her, and as soon as they left, he suddenly had to leave, too.

It was with real joy and relief that she saw him coming along, as he "just happened" to be going the long way home past Nora's house—just in time to stop for a few words of greeting. However, the few words dragged on into a long conversation, and she didn't leave for her home in Ginter without his having asked for her address so he could write to her.

From that moment on there was never anyone else for either of them. They were complete unto themselves. It was love at first sight—and it lasted until death.

Their happiness together was able to survive many hardships—little food, no money, joblessness—but the death of my sister was their hardest blow. Neither of them ever really got over the loss of their first-born, beautiful, twenty-two-year-old daughter.

During later years, when my father became an officer of the UAW and was on the front pages of most newspapers, he remained the same family man that he had always been. No matter how late the union meetings lasted, no matter how difficult to get there, he would go straight home to his beloved Margaret. He was often teased by some of the fellows who were finding union meetings a good excuse to stay out nights.

Papa never wasted any time in getting home, and if possible, he took Mama with him to the meetings. She became involved in many of the tasks and was in the thick of it all. Many of the caucuses and early board meetings were held in their living room in Detroit, with Mama serving various delicious cakes and breads that she baked herself. Halfway through any meeting, Papa would ask her the same question, "Say, Honey, how about putting the kettle on for a cup of tea?" And, of course, she was expecting it and was ready with something special for his sweet tooth.

What I'm trying to say, I suppose, is that I realize I have been very fortunate to have had such wonderful parents. My father and mother had the kind of marriage that I used to read about in fairy tales.

That is why I never doubted the stories that ended, ". . . , and they lived happily ever after." At my house it really *was* that way.

Irma Mortimer Stewart

Margaret Hunter, Mortimer's bride to be, at age 19.
Wyndham Mortimer in 1906 at age 22.

As worker at White Motor (Cleveland, 1923).

It was the night after Christmas and not a Press was stirring (Cleveland plant of Fisher Body).

Newsmen getting the inside story . . . UPI

while strikers get the news inside (GM strike, December, 1936). UPI

Some won't shave for the duration . . .

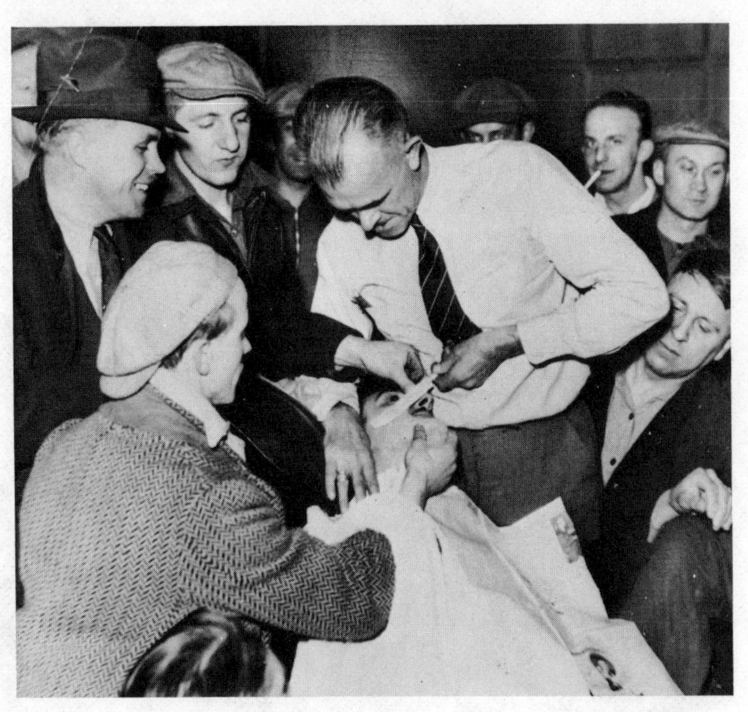

while others are shaved by improvised methods (GM strike, January, 1937).

Injunction is impotent and troops pack to leave (GM strike, January, 1937). UPI

Mortimer with pen that did the signing. Knudsen and Lewis had to borrow Mort's pen since he was the only one who had one on him (GM strikers' victory, February, 1937). Photo Spencer & Wyckoff

Martin's "goons" at play (Martin-Lovestone conspiracy, 1939). UPI

The Five. (l. to r.) *Mortimer, George Addes, Richard Frankensteen, Walter Welles, Ed Hall (Union expulsion, Detroit, 1938). UPI*

North American Aviation picket lines before troops' arrival (June, 1941).

Troops supervise return to work, 1941.

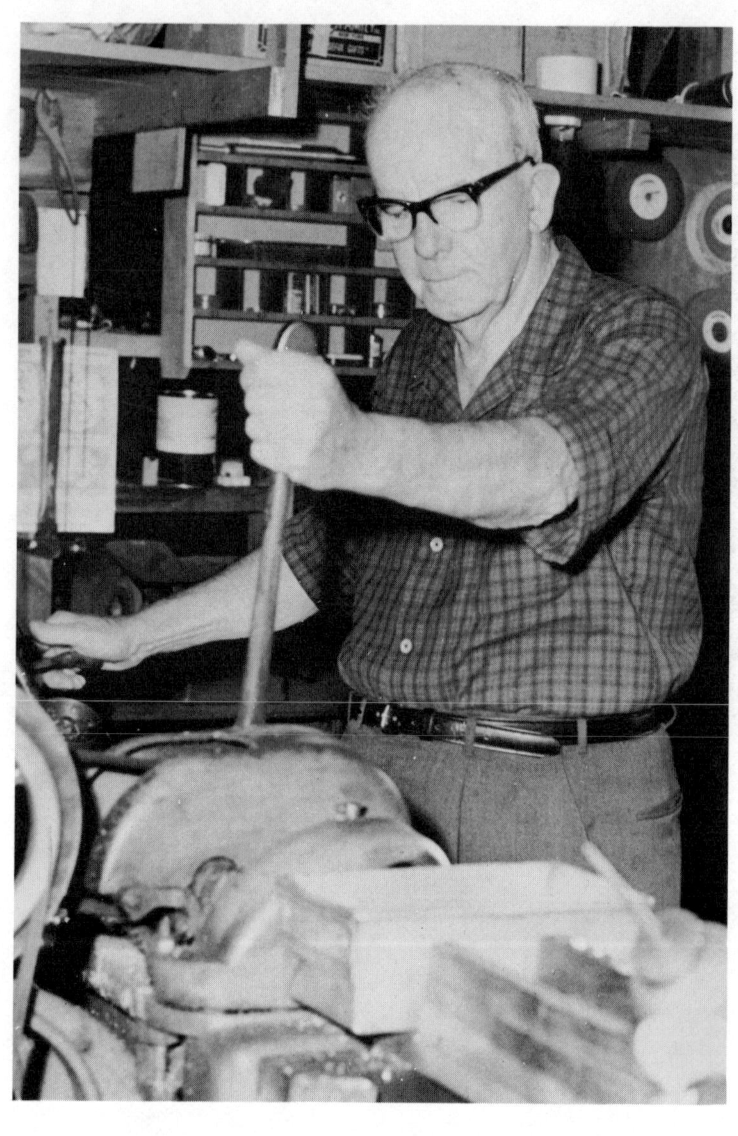

And still working on his 80th birthday. News photo by Hawthorne Press.

ORGANIZE!

CHAPTER ONE

MY PARENTS

I am writing the story of my life in response to the repeated prodding of my daughter Irma, and many others, who appear to think that somewhere back along my life's pathway there is an interesting story, and that others, particularly my grandchildren, Jery and Chip, would profit from reading an account of my experiences during the eighty-odd years I have been meandering around this good planet Earth. I hope they will read it. I hope that it will not only interest them, but that it will have some point for them. The lives of my two grandchildren are very different from what mine was at their ages, and in some respects the best thing I can say of my childhood is that it is past and gone.

My Father

My father was an Englishman. He was born in a small village called Creaton, Northamptonshire, England. The records of the village church reveal that he was born February 8, 1852, and was christened Thomas George Mortimer. His father, George Mortimer, was a brewer by occupation, although the church records give his occupation as a laborer. His mother's maiden name was Mary George.

My grandfather's earnings were not enough to feed his large family, and poverty decreed that the children had to earn their own way in the world. At the age of ten my father was hired by a cattle dealer, who took him and several other boys to Wales, where the dealer bought sheep and cattle for the English market. It was the task of the boys to drive the animals to London. After about three years of this unsettled life, his mother having died during his absence, my father lost all desire to return home. He found work in the coal mines in the town of Neath, South Wales. He was then about fourteen years of age.

When he was about seventeen he met my mother, who was fourteen and doing the work of a man, pitching hay in the fields. It is my impression, obtained from discussions with both my parents, that at first they were unable to converse, since she could not speak English and he could not speak Welsh.

My father continued to work as a coal miner and learned to speak, read, and write the Welsh language (Celtic). He thus became bilingual, since he had also learned to read and write English. This ability was an asset, and he was often called upon to read the letters of the many illiterate men and women of his time. To all intents and purposes he became a Welshman and was accepted as such by the Welsh people.

My parents were married in 1872 in the town of Neath. My father was twenty and my mother was seventeen. It was a period when many people from Britain were emigrating to America and the colonies. Exaggerated stories were told about the fabulous wealth to be had in America, and since a coal miner's life in Wales promised nothing but poverty and toil, my parents decided to come to America where gold was to be found in the streets. In 1881 my parents emigrated to America, arriving in Philadelphia on the day President Garfield died. The family consisted of my father, my mother, and three children, Mary, Margaret, and Benjamin. Benjamin, the youngest, died soon after the family's arrival. My father went to work in a coal mine at a place called Houtzdale, in Clearfield County, Pennsylvania. He was a devoutly religious man, but unlike many deeply religious people, he was not narrow. Race prejudice and bigotry were foreign to his nature as illustrated in the following incident:

My brother Tom and I came home from the mine one day

and, as was the practice of all miners, we bathed and changed clothes before entering the house. (A wash shed outside was built for this purpose.) Upon entering the kitchen we found our father, who had not worked that day because of a cold, seated at the table with a Negro. They were both eating plates of beef stew, which my mother had prepared for supper. Both Tom and I were startled because Negroes were seldom if ever encountered in that area. The Negro, upon finishing his meal, arose and thanked my parents for their kindness, and went on his way. Tom, somewhat amused by the sight of our father and a Negro eating together, made a remark that implied the Negro was of a lesser breed. My father said, "My boy, if God has seen merit in making people of all shades of color, and of all shapes and sizes, it does not fall to us to criticize his handiwork." I have never forgotten his words, and I know they have played a great part in shaping my own attitude toward people of other races and of other tongues.

My brother George and I, together with another boy, once raided an apple orchard belonging to a farmer named Mulholland. We were about eight years old. Boys of that period wore what were called "blouse waists," shirts with a string around the middle. We used these shirts to store things in lieu of pockets. We all filled our waists with apples and went home. My parents asked us where we had gotten the apples, and when we had revealed the source of our booty, my father wanted to know if Mr. Mulholland had told us we could have them. I said, "No. We just climbed the tree and took them." He then marched George and me all the way back up to the farm, about two miles, and we had to tell the farmer we were sorry. My father then asked Mulholland if there wasn't some work we could do to pay for the stolen apples.

Mulholland pointed to a huge field of potatoes and said, "Yes, those potatoes will soon have to have all the bugs picked off them, and I'll let you know, Tom, when they are ready." We were then taken back home with the impression that we would be forced to pick about ten acres of potato bugs. Mulholland never called, but the whole thing left a lasting impression on George and me.

Another time several of us boys noticed a barrel of molasses kept by a Jewish storekeeper on the front porch of his store. We decided it would be great fun if we could get an auger and bore a hole up through the floor and into the barrel. We did just that, and much of the molasses ran out onto the boardwalk before the storekeeper noticed it. He knew that I was one of the culprits and told my father. A paddle was applied to that part of my anatomy where it is supposed to do the most good. My father told the other boys' fathers about it, and among them they reimbursed the storekeeper.

My father was a hard-working, honest, and kindly man. He insisted upon all his children attending church and Sunday school, and never failed to go along with us. He held the same conviction that many do today—that somehow religion had something to do with, and was necessary to, good morals. It is true, of course, that the church and Sunday school do teach the Golden Rule, which is not a religious but rather a moral teaching, and to this extent he was right. He was not a learned man. Like millions more of his time and generation, he was too much absorbed in the struggle to live to have much time for reading or study, and such things as libraries did not exist in the coal camps. My father was an ardent union man, a trait he brought with him from Wales, and he soon became active in the Knights of Labor.

Coal mining in America was no different from what it had been in Wales. Twelve- and even fourteen-hour working days were standard. In fact my father began to wonder if he hadn't made a mistake in coming to America. He told me years afterward that the American coal operators were just as greedy and indifferent to human welfare as the Welsh mine owners had been.

My father died in April, 1919, at Lorain, Ohio. He is buried in the Elmwood Cemetery there.

My Mother

My mother, as I have said, was Welsh. She was born into a coal miner's family in a town called Ynys Meudwy in South Wales.

Her name was Rachel Jenkins. Her father was William Jenkins and her mother's name was Sarah. Like all coal miners of the time, her family was extremely poor. Her father died of silicosis (or what was then known as "miners' consumption") when my mother was six years old. His death left my grandmother with six children. Soon after, my mother was "bound out" to a local farmer who agreed to pay her one gold guinea a year for her labor. He agreed, too, to feed, clothe, and house her. What a six-year-old child could do in the way of labor will puzzle most of us today. My mother in later years revealed that she was put to making candles, caring for babies, washing dishes, and similar tasks. There was no time for play and she completely missed the carefree period of childhood.

Mother was born in the year 1855, and since, in the half-civilized Britain of that period, it was regarded as a waste of time to educate girls, she grew up illiterate. Free compulsory education was not yet the law in Britain. The only schools existing at that time were run by the Episcopal Church, and there was a charge of a few pennies a week to attend. Only those boys attended whose families were able to make this financial sacrifice. It was not until the Liberal government of William Gladstone in the 1890's that British capitalists decided there was a need for workers who could read and write.

Mother lived the hard life of a farm hand until she was seventeen. She was an unusually powerful person physically, I think because of the hard and rugged life she had lived. But she had also inherited an extraordinarily sturdy body. I have seen her lift a tub filled with water onto her head, and with a full bucket in each hand, a baby wrapped in a shawl on her back, and with my younger sister clinging to her skirts, carry this load several hundred yards from the spring to the house.

Fourteen children were born to her, but only seven survived. Large families were the rule and infant mortality was high. Epidemics of scarlet fever, diphtheria, and typhoid were frequent, and the toll among children was appalling. Competent doctors were scarce and such doctors as could be induced to live in the coal camps were not of the best. There were no hospitals, and

and to reach one would entail a day's journey by train and horse-and-buggy, so that was out of the question. The coal barons saw no profit in building hospitals.

Mother's life was a round of continuous hard work. Even when she sat down her fingers were busy knitting stockings, mittens, sweaters, or sewing and mending the numerous garments necessary for her large family. There were no bake shops, so she baked all our bread, cakes, and pies. She made all her own and my sisters' clothes. She made shirts for us boys, and cut down my father's old clothes, which were passed down from the older to the younger until they were threadbare. Nor was she lacking in courage. I was awakened one night by a gun going off close to my head. It was my mother shooting at a prowler. Thinking it was my father returning from the mine, mother took an oil lamp and went downstairs. Before opening the door, as was their custom, she called out in Welsh, asking who was there. She got no answer. She repeated the question, again in Welsh, and again got no answer. She returned upstairs and saw a man climbing the scaffolding that had been erected to weatherboard the house. He was making his way to an open window where my brother George and I slept. It was then that my mother shot him. The man fell or leaped from the scaffold and ran away. He was hit, because he was tracked for some distance by blood along the dirt road. The culprit was never caught, however.

The laundry, or the "washing" as we called it, was done on the old scrub board by hand, and this was almost a daily chore, with seven children, four of us boys, dirty ones at that, around a coal mine. It is small wonder that the lives of many women were short. They were literally worked to death. My mother survived because of her unusual physique. Only the strong survived such a life.

She knew many of the old traditional Welsh songs, and would softly sing that old Welsh lullaby, "Ar Hydd Y Nos" ("All Through the Night"), as she lulled a baby to sleep. She frequently sang "En Wlad Fo Naddau" ("Land of My Fathers") or would sing or hum "Mentra Gwen" ("Lovely Gwen") as she busied herself doing the many things her large family required.

Mother enjoyed and looked forward to the frequent gatherings of the many Welsh women of the community. They would gather at our home to drink tea and talk of the days gone by. Their conversations as they showed each other some needlework or discussed recipes, were always conducted in Welsh.

Her pleasures were simple. Her joy and satisfaction lay in seeing her family grow to manhood and womanhood. This sturdy little woman who gave me life, who taught me to talk and to walk, who nursed me through all my childhood ills, passed away in the summer of 1920 in her sixty-sixth year. She was buried beside my father.

CHAPTER TWO

THE PATH I TROD

I was born March 11, 1884, in a two-room log cabin beside the Susquehanna River, about two miles downstream from a small town called Karthaus, in Clearfield County, Pennsylvania. The scene of my birth, a tiny place of but two log cabins, was called Salt Lick. It was named from the salt deposits along the mountainside, to which deer and other wild creatures came for their needed salt. I have no memories of this place because my parents moved to Karthaus shortly after my birth. There I spent the first twelve years of my life.

It was a settlement of a few hundred people, largely of British origin at that time, with a small number of native-born Americans who were referred to as "Yankees." The principal industry was coal mining, with lumbering a close second. There was also a grist mill to which the farmers brought their grain, and a saw mill that provided the area with lumber.

The spring of the year was always an active time, for then the loggers came down the river on what was called the "Ark," a log cabin built on a huge raft made of logs, in which the men lived and did all their cooking, sleeping, and drinking. The task of the loggers was to break the huge log jams that had built up during low water. They spent the winter in cutting down trees, hauling the logs to the river, and rolling them into the water, where they started on their way to the large saw mills at

Williamsport and Lock Haven. The Ark would be the center of attraction, and we children were dismissed from school to participate in the holiday atmosphere that prevailed. To us small boys, the loggers were real heroes as they waded out into the cold rushing water to release logs or to break up a jam and start it on its way downstream.

Karthaus was not a "captive" town in the sense that many other mining towns were. No one employer was large enough to dominate. The three coal mining companies were small, independent operations whose financial resources were limited. The huge monopolies that grew up later had not yet arrived there. The miners were able to purchase their groceries and supplies in any one of several small general stores that handled a variety of merchandise and lived by trading with the miners and people from the surrounding country.

The chain store had not yet been born, although some of the coal operators had begun to operate the "pluck-me" or company-owned stores. They did all business on credit. Pay day was once a month, when we would pay all bills and begin all over again. All month my mother would send me to the store with the "store book," in which all items bought were written down together with their prices.

The village of Karthaus was surrounded by a dense forest, or the woods, as we called them around the year 1890. These woods teemed with wild life, deer, bear, squirrel, rabbit, pheasant, possum, and groundhog. There was also the bobcat, whose screams we could hear at night.

Mosquito Creek emptied into the Susquehanna River at Karthaus, and in the summertime we swam in the creek and river. Bathing suits were unheard-of, and we never dreamed that some people actually dressed to go in swimming. We skated and bob-sledded in the winter, hunted rabbit, groundhog, and squirrel, played ball, and climbed trees. We made our own balls and bats, and also our own sleds in the winter. We made whistles from the new growth of the birch tree, and bows and arrows out of hickory. We played a game called "Old Sow" with an empty tin can and broom sticks. It was a fast and furious game, and skinned shin bones were the rule. We went barefoot in summer, and stubbed toes were every boy's lot.

Such things as automobiles, telephones, television, radio, movies, and electric lights were not even dreamed of. The prevailing mode of travel was walking, or riding a wagon drawn by a horse or perhaps a team of oxen. A horse and buggy was tops, and a surrey with the fringe on top was downright luxury. Few could afford it.

Coal mining was, and still is, a hard, dangerous, and dirty occupation, which took the lives of many men whose families then faced a future of grinding poverty and want. The coal companies cared nothing for a dead miner. They were more concerned over their mules. Mules cost money. Little wonder Mother worried when my father was late coming home from work. Our lives were governed by the state of the coal industry. If work was steady, we ate regularly. If work was slow or hard to find, we lived accordingly. Things were not as stable as they are today.

There were times when the coal companies were unable to pay the miners at month's end, because of their inability to collect monies due them. Bank failures were frequent, and the money put into circulation by a defunct bank was worthless. The result was that the miners were sometimes paid in worthless money. This led to strikes, which to us youngsters were a lot of fun. We were too young to understand what such things meant to our parents.

A Strike

In the spring of 1893 (I was then nine years old), the miners could no longer tolerate the long hours (twelve and thirteen hours a day underground), the low wages, and at times no wages at all, and in desperation they went on strike. They had joined the Knights of Labor, and my father, as president of the local Assembly, was very active in leading the strike. This struggle lasted all through the summer and into the autumn. The miners, having very small resources to begin with, were hard pressed for food, clothes, and heat. In late summer the coal companies began to import foreigners as strikebreakers. Word reached the union that a trainload of about two hundred foreign workers had left Philadelphia on its way to Karthaus. My father and another Welshman, whose name was Prosser Thomas, walked twenty-five miles down river to a junction called Keating to intercept this train. They boarded the train and found one of the group who spoke English. Through this man they were able to explain the situation, and they promised the men that if they would refuse to work in the mine, the union would feed and house them and help them to find other employment. These immigrants were Hungarians. Their passage had been paid by the coal companies, who had told them they must pay back this money or go to jail. It was carefully explained to them that they were now in a country where one could not be sent to prison for debt, and that they had nothing to fear from this quarter. They were instructed that when the train reached Karthaus, they were to follow my father and his companion and pay no attention to anyone else.

In Karthaus, representatives of the coal companies, together with a large number of Coal and Iron Police, were on hand to herd the Hungarians toward the mine shacks prepared for them. But a much greater crowd of striking miners and their wives was also there. With much shouting of insults at the Coal and Iron Police, and with some pushing and shoving, the Hungarians were led up toward the miners' hall, where a hot beef stew awaited them. I recall my fear and excitement at the sight of these strange men with their fierce-looking mustaches and their huge bundles, all talking at once in their unfamiliar language.

There were now two hundred more mouths to feed! Finding food for these additional people was a task that staggered the small mining town. But all miners had gardens, and many were part-time farmers, and with some help from outside, the strikers were able to feed the additional men, who had proved their sympathy and good intentions by refusing to scab. After several weeks, work was found for them making grade for a railroad at a place called Snowshoe.

After several months of striking, when winter had come, it became obvious that the strike was lost. Hunger and want had won. For my family and for some others, hunger and misery were to continue. All the strike leaders, my father among them, were blacklisted and unable to find employment for over two years. Those years were lean beyond description. Such things as unemployment insurance, county relief, or any other provision for those unable to find a buyer for their labor, were unheard-of. For the unemployed there was no income, and thus no means of support. My family and several others were face-to-face with starvation.

Thus does capitalism hold the power of life and death over those who must live by selling their labor and skills. But through many long and bitter struggles, by organized labor over the years, this hard legal fact has been softened somewhat by legislation forcing monopoly capitalism to grant some relief through unemployment compensation, severance pay, pensions, and Social Security. The threat of starvation is not now as immediate as it was in 1893.

Without work, and without income, there was but one way to obtain life's necessities, and that was through credit. Fortunately, my parents' reputation for honesty was exceedingly good. The small merchants knew that sometime, somehow, the bills would be paid. We bought only the barest necessities—tea, sugar, and what was called blackstrap molasses. These items were supplemented by vegetables from the garden, a small flock of chickens, a Jersey cow, and bread which my mother baked from flour which Sam Briehl, owner of the grist mill, let us have on credit. In this manner we passed our last three years in Karthaus.

Bitumen

On March 11, 1896, I was twelve years old. I was very thin and underweight, but I was twelve and therefore old enough to work in the mine. On March 17 (St. Patrick's Day), my sister Margaret and I left Karthaus for a mining patch in Clinton County, where my father and older brother Tom had finally obtained jobs in the mine of the Kettle Creek Coal Mining Company, and where my father had been assigned a house. My oldest sister, Mary, now twenty-one years of age, had found employment in Williamsport, and Margaret was to keep house for us until mother arrived with the three younger children, George, Sue, and Sam.

The miners' patch called Bitumen was a double row of flimsily built two-story shacks lining both sides of a narrow dirt road. The road was dusty, icy, slushy, or muddy, according to the season of the year. All the shacks were exactly alike, and all were painted a barn red. The miner who had partaken of too much joy-juice often found himself in the wrong shack. The word "bitumen" means coal tar. Never was a place more appropriately named.

Upon seeing the kind of place we were to live in, my sister Margaret sobbed as though her heart would break. She was eighteen, and the thought of being buried alive in such an isolated and ugly place was more than she could endure. My father tried to console her, but it was several days until she settled down and decided to make the best of it. Mother soon arrived with the rest of the family, and life began to assume its normal course.

Bitumen's population did not exceed five hundred. About sixty percent were Polish. The other forty percent were Swedes, Finns, and Croatians, with only a few English-speaking families, including our own. The others who spoke English were all company bosses and their families.

The mine boss, of course, ran the mine and, except for the superintendent, his word was law. The store boss ran the company, or "pluck-me," store. He was also the paymaster and general snoop. The weigh boss weighed all the coal, and made sure the scales were rigged in favor of the Kettle Creek Coal Mining Company.

Life in Bitumen was the nearest thing to peonage to be found anywhere in America. It was a completely captive town. There was but one employer. We worked in his mine. We rented his shack at six dollars per month. We bought all our groceries and supplies in his "pluck-me" store and paid high prices for inferior goods. The name "pluck-me" was an invention of the miners that explained the nature of the company-owned store. To work in the mine, one was required to buy in the company store. To attempt an evasion of this rule by patronizing a certain famous mail-order house was an impossibility. The mine superintendent was also the postmaster, and such an evasion was met by discharge. To ensure the pluck-me store's monopoly of the retail business of the coal camp, the constable, who occupied the first house as one entered this God-forsaken village, was charged with the responsibility of stopping strangers who might have something to sell. (Or perhaps they might be United Mine Workers organizers?) I have seen this constable, whose name was Eisenhower, stop and threaten to jail the old-time pack peddlers, who had climbed up the long mountainside in the expectation that they might sell the miners' wives a few yards of dress goods. He would drive them back down that long road, without an opportunity to make a sale.

Mining camps were usually located in out-of-the-way places. The coal companies owned or leased the land for miles around. The so-called houses were unplastered, and built with the boards set perpendicularly, the cracks covered by narrow slats called bats. The snow blew in through the cracks, and it was not unusual to see one's footprints in the fine snow inside the house. Heating such a place was an impossibility, so we concentrated on keeping one room warm—the kitchen. I arose each day at five and would grab my clothes, which I had placed beside my bed, and make a mad dash for the kitchen, where I proceeded to dress.

The company doctor, referred to as the vet, lived in a village called Westport, three miles away, and could be reached only by walking or running down the winding road along the mountainside.

Trapper Boy

A few days after my arrival in Bitumen, I went to work in the mine as a trapper-boy for the fabulous sum of seven cents an hour. A thirteen-hour day earned me ninety-one cents. The term "trapper boy" was a misnomer, since it had nothing to do with traps. The job was to open and close a huge door as the mule teams came and went, hauling cars of coal. The function of the door was to keep the flow of air moving in the direction of the working areas. I was located about a mile from the entrance, and the long days seemed endless. The only light in the total darkness was a flickering oil lamp that hung from my miner's cap. The lamp was a primitive lighting device that burned lard oil and was widely used at the turn of the century. It gave off a black smoke that contributed considerably to the putrid atmosphere throughout the mine.

To pass the time between mule trips, I would read. At this age I read books of adventure. Since a public library did not exist in American coal camps, I would buy books from a book dealer in Philadelphia. I read a series of books by G. A. Henty, for example. Henty was an Englishman and a staunch supporter of the British Empire. His books were supposedly the experiences of British boys who had performed great feats of bravery in the service of their king and country. I read *Under Drake's Flag,* a story of Drake's piracies and his circumnavigation of the globe. Another of his books was *With Clive in India,* a story of Britain's subjugation of the Indian sub-continent. I also read the works of H. Rider Haggard, especially *King Solomon's Mines* and *She*. I read the *Life of Lincoln* by Colonel Morgan, and books about the Civil War by various authors whose names I do not now recall. When I tired of reading, I would trap the many rats that infest coal mines.

After about two years as a trapper-boy, I went to work as a miner's helper with my father. I now spent the long days digging and loading coal onto a car that held two tons of coal. I was no longer paid an hourly rate, instead I earned my wage on a tonnage basis. We were paid thirty cents a ton for digging and loading coal. A strong miner could dig and load about five tons a day. Between us, we were able to produce about seven tons, which earned us $2.10 for a twelve-hour day. We furnished our own tools, powder, and dynamite, also oil for our lamps. Fifty cents a month was deducted from our pay for the blacksmith who kept our picks sharp. Another fifty cents a month went for the company doctor who furnished our placebos. My brother Tom worked with another man, while George, my younger brother, took over my job as trapper-boy.

Single men and married men with two or three boys old

enough to work were able to keep out of debt, and did receive small amounts of cash at the month's end. My father, with three boys working, was able to keep his head above water and eventually pay off his debts in Karthaus. Our combined earnings went into the family purse, as my parents were anxious to repay those who had trusted them. On payday I usually got a quarter and thought I was a millionaire. Occasionally, after our daily baths, we would sit down to a hot supper of Irish stew, homemade bread, and homemade butter. We would light up the pot-bellied stove in the parlor and relax. During the winter we saw daylight only on Sunday, but as my parents were deeply religious, we spent a good part of Sunday at church.

The semi-starvation we had endured in Karthaus was having its effect on me. I was very thin and considerably underweight. The long hours underground deprived me of needed sunlight, and the air so far underground was foul beyond description, polluted by coal dust, powder, and dynamite smoke and fumes, lamp smoke, and the tobacco smoke of the miners, including my father's. This, together with the breathing of several hundred men and several dozen mules, contributed nothing to my general health. The oxygen content in the mine depths was often so low that my oil lamp would stop burning, and I would become drowsy and listless. On such occasions, the miners would stop working and go back toward the entrance where the air was better. I was now fourteen years old. There was no alternative for me at the moment, and I continued as a miner's helper.

Life was primitive, but it became more bearable with the passing of time, especially since it was shared with others who were in the same predicament. As one gets acquainted and makes friends, life improves even though it remains difficult. There were a number of boys my age working in the mine. Even though most of them, recent arrivals from Europe, could speak no English, we managed somehow to communicate, and they learned to speak our way in a remarkably short time. The learning was mutual though, and I learned a lot of Swedish, Polish, Finnish, and Slav. My sister Margaret, too, found girls and young men her age who made life more enjoyable. She eventually married a young Swedish man whose name was Gustav Anderson.

We lived in the first house at the top of the hill, right next door to the constable. One day a spring-wagon stopped in front of our house with a great large box on it. Two men came to our door and tried to interest my mother in buying the piano which they had on the wagon. Of course it was out of the question when they told her how much it would cost, and she finally convinced them it was way beyond our means. But she evidently gave them the idea she would like to have a piano if she were able to afford it. They went to every house in Bitumen and found no buyers. On their way back they cooked up a story and again stopped at our house. They said their wagon was breaking down and they were afraid they could not make it back down the mountain, and asked if they could leave the piano in our parlor for a few days until they could get a heavier wagon and better horses. My mother, of course, let them do it and they hauled the beautiful big Chickering piano into our parlor. At that time we had an old-fashioned foot-pump organ that reached to the ceiling with shelves and bric-a-brac.

That evening Mother kept the parlor all dark when we came home. While we were finishing supper she quietly sent Sue in the parlor to play a simple little waltz on the new piano. Of course the minute she started to play everything stopped and we all rushed into the parlor. There was no more supper that night.

When the salesmen came back a few days later, they still had the same wagon and the same horses, but they had made up their minds that they were going to leave that piano. My mother haggled and haggled and finally got it at her price and they took the organ in trade. It was the only piano that ever hit Bitumen. After I learned to play fairly well people often stood around out in front of our house on warm evenings listening.

We always had several instruments around the house. My brother Tom took cornet lessons from a Swedish man named Gustafson. George learned to play the drums. On Sunday afternoons we went with all of our friends to an old abandoned meeting hall which we called Miner's Hall. Mr. Gustafson came every Sunday afternoon and taught us how to play all of the assorted instruments we could gather together. He helped us organize a little band and we thought we were pretty good. Miner's Hall had seen better days. The windows were gone and the doors were off, but the floor was intact and we could make as much noise as we liked without bothering anyone. Many pleasant Sunday afternoons were spent there.

Bitumen was a place that mirrored all sides of the struggle between the miners and coal operators. Although the miners were unorganized, the union was in their thoughts and minds. They would show deep interest in any news of strikes and organizing efforts of the United Mine Workers elsewhere. The coal operators were interested too, and were determined to keep the union out if at all possible.

One time about a dozen miners came to my father and asked him to teach them to read and write English. He was glad to do so and took steps to obtain the necessary books from the school board. He was called into the mine superintendent's office and asked to explain the purpose of this group meeting in our home. My father said the purpose was clear; it was to teach these men the language of their adopted country. He was told the company did not approve of activities of this kind. Their real objection was that my father might teach unionism or at least discuss it with his pupils.

In addition to the company's fears that such a gathering would breed unionism, there was another reason. The coal, iron, and steel companies had a policy of hiring foreign labor with the idea in mind of creating a Tower of Babel atmosphere. Where so many languages were spoken it would be difficult to unite and organize the workers. They were not about to teach all these people to speak one language. Such schemes were stupid in the extreme, however, because the children of these immigrants went to school and soon learned to speak English, while we who spoke English learned enough Polish, Swedish, and other languages to be understood by them. The language barrier did not last long.

A Visitor

Four years after we came to Bitumen, we heard a rap at our door at two in the morning. My father went to the door, and there was a man named Jim Purcell, an organizer for the United Mine Workers. They talked until dawn about conditions and the possibility of organizing the mine. Purcell left shortly before daybreak to escape detection. My father told him that since the majority of the miners were Polish, and the next largest group was Swedish, it would be advisable to send in organizers who were able to speak these two languages. Purcell returned some time later with the speakers my father had suggested.

A meeting was held in an old abandoned barn on a neighboring farm, and over a hundred miners attended. Eisenhower, the constable, who was also a company snoop, tried to get into the meeting but was refused admittance on the grounds that it was a meeting for miners only. The company must have been panic-stricken. They knew the sentiment for unionism was very strong, but since they were unable to discover who was responsible for arranging the meeting, everyone was suspect.

The assembly elected an organizing committee, composed of two Poles and one Swede. The Poles were fired from the mine, but this did not stop activities or discussion. One of the Poles returned as an organizer for the United Mine Workers. My two brothers and I were as active as we could be, but since we were still in our teens, our efforts were not too spectacular. My father did not take an active part in the effort because he spoke English. Since the mine superintendent spoke English, as did the mine foreman, the weigh boss, the store boss, and the barn boss, there was a strong feeling among the Poles, Swedes, and Slavs that anyone who spoke English was not to be trusted. My father, therefore, played a passive role, but he was glad to see the foreign miners getting together and learning to act as one.

About this time my father arranged to buy a side of beef from a farmer who lived in the country outside the company's domain. It was arranged that the farmer was to deliver the beef at 2:00 A.M. so that Eisenhower the snoop would not know it.

Since there was a heavy snow on the ground and the beef would be delivered by sled, my father thought we would not be detected. In spite of the precautions the snoop found out. The following day revealed that the pluck-me store knew about it: the company butcher, on his rounds taking meat orders, passed us up.

When my father returned from work in the mine, Mother spoke to him in Welsh and told him that the butcher had not stopped for a meat order. My father, answering her in English, said, "Well, if that's how things stand, I had better find out from Schatz himself." My father went directly to the butcher and asked him why he hadn't stopped to get a meat order. Schatz replied, "Why, Tom, we figured you had enough meat for a while." My father said, "Yes, we do have, and I will let you know when to stop again." The following day, returning from the mine, we were stopped by the mine superintendent, G. L. Miller, who upbraided my father for buying meat from Farmer Smith.

My father said, "George, I left England and came to America because I was told America was a free country, and now you tell me this is not true." An acrimonious argument ensued, the upshot being that my father, my brothers, and I were fired. We returned to work the next morning to "square up," as the miners say. That means to load any coal already dug, and to bring home our tools. When we were passing the superintendent's office, he stopped us and told us to go back to work. This puzzled us for a time until we learned that Farmer Smith had threatened to sue the Kettle Creek Coal Mining Company for preventing him from selling the produce of his farm.

Another episode in this same drama involved our next door neighbors, a Hungarian couple by the name of Gmitro. Mary Gmitro had walked down the winding mountain road to a small town called Westport. Taking a small hand-wagon with her, she loaded it with supplies, among which was a bag of cow feed called chop. She laboriously pulled this small wagon back up the three-mile road and of course was observed by the constable.

The following morning she was visited by G. L. Miller, who

threatened her because of her purchases elsewhere. He said, "You know, Mary, we provide John with a job, and we expect that you shall trade in this store." When these words had sunk in, she became angry and said, "Oh, you go to hell! I buy which place I get cheap, you son-of-a-bitch!" Miller beat a hasty retreat, but John Gmitro was fired forthwith.

In the spring of 1900, I was taken out of the mine. I was just sixteen years of age and was seriously underweight. I was five feet, six inches tall and weighed sixty-eight pounds. My parents were sure I had contracted tuberculosis and was nearing the end of the road. Fortunately, there was nothing wrong that fresh air, sunshine, and rest would not cure. I was sent to live with my sister Mary, who was now Mrs. Frank Griggs, living in Williamsport, and to attend the Dickinson Seminary for one semester.

This seminary turned out Methodist ministers, and the discipline was everything one could expect from such an institution. I studied English and the three R's. One semester did not make much of an impression, or contribute greatly to my meager store of knowledge. It did allow me to get out in the open air and sunshine, where my lungs could begin to function normally without the incredible pollution of the coal mine. I never doubted that my poor physical condition at that time was caused by the two years of borderline starvation resulting from my father's blacklisting and the four years underground which followed. After one semester at the seminary, and three additional months just resting, I returned to Bitumen and the coal mine. I had gained weight and felt much better.

During my absence, the union had consolidated its position. It now had a charter and had elected officers. It had also elected a "pit" committee and a checkweighman, whose duty it was to prevent cheating on weight as the loaded cars rolled over the scale. There was a different atmosphere around the mine. The old fears were gone. There was now a relaxed feeling among the miners. They could speak out and express themselves without fear.

Having completed two years as a miner's helper, I was now regarded as a miner. I was given a "buddy" and a place to work.

My buddy was a Polish peasant, strong as a horse and just as illiterate. He was completely ignorant of the coal mining craft. He did not speak a word of English, but I knew enough Polish to make him understand. I taught him to mine coal. I taught him to speak, read, and write English, and he in turn taught me to speak Polish. He could not teach me to read and write the Polish language because he could not do so himself.

Around the 1890's a tremendous wave of immigration occurred. A burgeoning capitalism needed labor to build railroads, mine coal, make steel, and do all the tasks that arose out of the rapid industrialization of America. It was then that the basis of vast fortunes was laid by the Rockerfellers, Harrimans, Carnegies, and Schwabs. It was also a time that produced a Gene Debs, a Mother Jones, a Robert Ingersoll, and a Clarence Darrow. It was during this era that the Nebraska farmers decided to raise more hell and less corn.

Wages were low. Ten cents an hour, a dollar a day for ten hours' work, was the rate for common labor. The immigrants who came to the coal fields were entirely of peasant stock. They were illiterate, and had been told that in America everyone was rich. Steamship lines were subsidized and the immigrants came over to America in steerage for almost nothing. The Poles, Croatians, and Italians were extremely superstitious. They believed all sorts of fantastic stories about witches, devils, and evil spirits. One Pole uprooted the entire vegetable garden of his Hungarian neighbor because she had bewitched his cow so that it gave only sour milk.

A Croatian was killed by a rock fall. My father went to the dead man's home to do what he could to alleviate the grief of his family. The body still lay in its work clothes because there was a belief among his people that the first person to touch the corpse would assume all guilt for his sins. My father told them this was nonsense, and placed his hand on the dead man's face. They then began to wash and dress the dead man in preparation for burial. In Bitumen, undertaking establishments were unknown. The nearest was at a place called Renovo about ten miles away, so the dead were buried by their friends and loved ones as soon as the coroner had made a report.

While the Kettle Creek Coal Mining Company usually had things under control, there was an exception to this rule. An Englishman named Tom Guildford brought his wife and five children to Bitumen. Tom was condemned to years of hard work without hope of ever getting out of debt. His children could never become miners, being all girls, and in a place like Bitumen, there was little opportunity for them to earn their way.

Tom had worked for the Kettle Creek Coal Mining Company elsewhere before settling in Bitumen and in all his years as an employee had never drawn any pay. He was never able to get out of debt. He was shrewd, however, and carefully planned his revenge. Being an Englishman, he would not become a citizen. My father had many discussions with him about this but he would reply, "Tom, I think thee is a fool to become an American citizen." He would give no reason for his failure to forswear his allegiance to the Queen, but he did have one, and as it turned out, it was very shrewd.

As I recall the episode, Guildford knew there was a treaty in force between Great Britain and the United States which read something to the effect that "the citizens of each country, residing in the other, must be paid for labor performed in the coin of the realm." It was the custom of the coal companies to pay once a month. Each month Tom Guildford received a slip of paper called a "statement" which revealed his indebtedness to the coal company. He carefully preserved every one of these statements, and had a complete record of his years of toil without pay.

One day, at last, he got in touch with the British ambassador in Washington, and submitted to him all his statements, which showed the coal company to be in violation of this British–American treaty. The ambassador took the case to the State Department and the Kettle Creek Coal Mining Company was ordered to pay Guildford. There was much wailing and gnashing of teeth, but Guildford received fourteen years' back pay. And when the coal company tried to sue Guildford for indebtedness, he had already gone back to Britain.

Following this experience, no miner was permitted to work unless he could produce a citizenship paper. Wagonloads of miners were transported to Lock Haven, the county seat, where they took an oath of allegiance and received their first papers. It was a simple procedure at that time. The prolonged and intensive tests required now were not yet in use.

In spite of their backwardness and lack of education, these foreign miners were a generous and kind people. I am glad I lived for seven years in Bitumen. It taught me many things. I learned that the one and only reason for the existence of the coal operation was to squeeze as much profit as possible out of the flesh and bones of the miners. Anything that interfered with, or remotely threatened this lofty purpose, was anathema to the coal company and its snoops and stooges. I learned, too, that despite differences in language and culture, people were people. Once I got acquainted and mingled with them, I soon learned that their needs, hopes, and desires were no different from our own.

An observant working man once said, "I go to work to earn the coin, to buy some bread, to get the strength to go back to work!" That, in a capsule, was life in Bitumen.

Winburne

In the spring of 1903, after seven years in Bitumen, my family decided we had had enough of the place. Although Bitumen had been organized by the United Mine Workers during our stay there, and conditions were much better when we left than they were when we arrived, still it was a captive town and would never be anything else, because one coal company owned and dominated the land for miles around.

After some inquiries, we decided to move elsewhere. We located in another coal mining town called Winburne, in Clearfield County. Conditions were much better and life was more pleasant. It was a larger town with more activities. (In 1903–1905 Winburne was a town of about 2000 population.) To work for either of the two coal companies one had to get clearance from the United Mine Workers Union. It was a union shop, one hundred percent.

The United Mine Workers had a well-organized, nicely functioning local union which maintained decent working conditions. The work day was eight hours, and we were paid sixty-five cents per ton for coal. Several privately owned general stores made it possible to maintain normal prices.

There was a YMCA which conducted programs of various sorts. Basketball, volley ball, and handball were favorite games on summer evenings, while home talent entertainment was staged at certain periods. It was the sort of community center where the old and the young met, and I am sure it had a good influence in the whole area. The Sommerville Coal Company supported the YMCA financially.

Two coal companies operated in Winburne: Bloomington Coal and Sommerville Coal. Both maintained company stores, but the union saw to it that the miners could buy wherever they wished. The coal seam was low, about four feet thick, which meant the miner could not stand erect. We had to work on our knees, or lying down.

The miners' homes were individually built, and none was painted barn red. We lived in Winburne for over two years. My older brother, Tom, was now twenty-one years of age. I was nineteen, and my younger brother, George, was seventeen. We were getting restless, and talked of going elsewhere to find work in some industry that operated above ground and where the sun shone every day. We knew nothing about any other industry, but we boys felt that most anything would be an improvement over coal mining. It was a hard, dirty, and dangerous occupation and had little to offer us at that period in our lives.

We continued for a time to work in the mine, however. I became active in the local union, serving on committees and playing trumpet in the band. We boys continued to urge our parents to leave the coal mines. My parents, like fathers and mothers everywhere, wanted to keep the family together as long as possible. Father was now in his fifty-first year, but appeared much older and suffered from what was called miner's asthma, lung damage caused by long years of breathing the polluted air in the mines.

There was an abundance of good clean air in the hills of Pennsylvania, but to get this air to the miners' place of work, or "face," as it was called, cost money. It was much cheaper and more profitable to let the miner spend his last days in misery, oftentimes gasping for air. My father was a living example of what the future held for me and my brothers.

It was in Winburne that I met the most wonderful girl I had ever seen, a petite little person in her late teens. She was the daughter of a Scottish miner. Her name was Margaret Hunter, and she would become my wife a few years later. Her home was in a mining town called Ginter.

CHAPTER THREE

WE MOVE OUT OF THE COAL FIELDS

We decided at last to leave the coal fields and seek a new life elsewhere, where the family would be together for at least a while. We moved to Elyria, Ohio, where my father's sister had often urged us to settle. In the summer of 1905 we left Winburne and the coal mine, and began a different, but not much better, way of earning a living.

Elyria, the county seat of Lorain County, was a pleasant city of about 14,000 people. Its broad streets and wide lawns, with spacious homes set well back from the thoroughfares, were a wonderful change from the coal camps of Pennsylvania, with their stinking culm banks and shabby dwellings. But this part of Elyria was where the steel executives lived. They got as far away as possible from the dirt and filth of their huge operations in Lorain that stretched for miles along the Black River. The working class of Elyria lived like workers elsewhere. They were huddled around the factory district and in the less desirable areas of the city. Wages were low, and the hours long. The open shop prevailed everywhere, and labor was condemned to a cutthroat competition for jobs. Lorain was six miles north of Elyria along the shores of Lake Erie. The two towns were connected by streetcar.

I found work at the United States Steel plant in Lorain, where I was given a job running a machine called a rail-straightener. To get the job, I had to sign what was known as a "yellow dog" contract. I was interviewed by the personnel manager, and the interview dealt mainly with my background and sympathies toward labor unions. It goes without saying that I lied like hell when asked about labor unions. The interview over, I was sent to the doctor for a perfunctory physical examination. This examination was about the same as one would require were he buying a horse. There were papers to sign, and if you wanted to eat, you didn't quibble or read the fine print. So, like all the other workers, I signed the "yellow dog" contract, and a statement releasing U.S. Steel from all liability in the event of injury or death. The contract stated that I was not a member of a union. (This was not true. I still belonged to the United Mine Workers.) It also said that I would not join a union, and that I would report any union activity to my foreman. To my everlasting credit, I broke this pledge at the first opportunity.

I worked at this job for a year and then went back to visit the girl I couldn't get out of my mind. Margaret and I had been corresponding regularly since I met her in Winburne, and we both were looking forward to meeting again and spending a few days together. A brief visit of three days only confirmed what we both already knew. Life without each other was unthinkable. But marriage costs money, and in my straitened financial condition, I wondered if a wedding would be possible in the foreseeable future.

Returning to Ohio, I learned that my parents had bought a home in Lorain. I found work in the National Tube Company, a subsidiary of U.S. Steel, as a roll-setter helper, again at the starvation wage of eighteen cents an hour. The tube mill was, of course, open shop, and working conditions were terrible. The mill operated twenty-four hours a day, seven days a week. We worked days one week and nights the next, which meant that every two weeks we had to work a twenty-four–hour shift, with twenty-four hours off on alternating weeks. We worked twelve hours a day.

To those who marvel at the docility of a working force that could accept this kind of insanity, let me explain the conditions existing at that time. Unemployment was widespread. The hordes of idle men besieging the employment offices of U.S. Steel had their effect. Men were kept in a state of fear; workers were fired on the slightest pretext, or for no reason at all. Nor was the fear confined to the worker; it extended up through supervision and even to higher officials, such as plant managers. Pittsburgh issued orders to produce more "or else" which were sent down through a chain of command until they reached the foremen and the workers in the mill.

In the absence of a union, some workers became sycophants and stool pigeons. They bent over backwards to please the boss and ingratiate themselves with him. So great was the fear of losing the precious job that men would even work through their lunch periods. Only furnace men, whose jobs required the endurance of intense heat, were allowed rest periods.

The National Tube Company had two other pipe mills, one in Middletown, Pennsylvania, and the other in McKeesport. The gimmick was to pit these three mills against each other in an endless struggle to see which one could produce the most pipe in any twelve-hour shift. The superintendent would come through the mill with the story that both Middletown and McKeesport were producing more tubing than we were, and that, beginning in the morning, we would be in a competition with them to see which mill could turn out the most pipe in the ensuing twelve hours.

This gimmick of pitting the Lorain, Middletown, and McKeesport mills against each other created a madhouse effect. This was my undoing. One day I stopped for lunch. The foreman reminded me that we were in competition with McKeesport this day. I told him I didn't care a damn what sort of fools worked at McKeesport, that this was my lunch hour, I was hungry, and I was going to eat my lunch. The following morning my time card was not in the rack. I was fired!

It was now June, 1907. Again unemployed, and twenty-three years of age, I was anxious to fulfill my plans of marrying my "bonnie wee lassie." Margaret's family had moved to Latrobe, Pennsylvania, in the meantime, so I went back to Latrobe and spent the Fourth of July with her. We had a really enjoyable time at Idlewild Park near Ligonier. I tried to find work in Latrobe, without success.

I Become a Railroad Man

I hired out as a brakeman on the Pennsylvania Railroad, running between Pittsburgh and Altoona. The life of a railroad man, especially that of an extra man, who depended on work by "bucking the list" or who worked only when a regular man stayed home, was neither pleasant nor profitable. Its one redeeming feature was that I was able to visit Margaret frequently. We decided to get married. I had little money, yet if we kept on postponing our wedding until sufficient money was available, we would both die of old age. Wages being what they were, and jobs scarce, the task of saving money was well-nigh impossible. The old saying that "two can live as cheaply as one" is a monumental exaggeration, of course, but true or not, we were ready to try it.

We were married on Christmas Eve in 1907. The ceremony was performed by Reverend Hill in the United Presbyterian Church in Latrobe. For better or worse, for good or ill, we were now man and wife, facing a long, hard struggle to live in a world that was anything but hospitable.

For the next fifty-four years, until her death on April 8, 1961, Margaret was everything a wife and mother could be. Words are a weak and inadequate way of expressing our thoughts at times, and this is especially true when I try to write or tell what this little woman meant to me and to her two daughters. She was a loyal wife and mother, and a true daughter of the working class.

I took two weeks' leave of absence after we were married and returned to Lorain, Ohio. I planned to continue as a railroad man until I could find something better. At the expiration of the two weeks' leave, I returned to Pittsburgh and found there had been a cutback in train crews. I was seventy-two times out on the extra list. This was equivalent to being unemployed.

The years 1907–1908 were depression years. It was called a "Money Panic." There was a shortage of money. The moneylenders had gone on strike for higher interest rates, and employers had to print what was known as scrip or promises to pay, which merchants had to accept in lieu of money or go out of business.

Again out of a job, and with a newly acquired wife, I returned once again to Lorain on the urging of my father, who felt that the chances of finding work were as good there as anywhere. But there, too, idle men in the hundreds stood patiently in all kinds of weather outside the employment offices of every employer. Every morning I was one of those idle men just standing and waiting. Saloons attracted hordes of hungry men because one could get a bowl of bean soup and a glass of beer for a nickel.

After six months of idleness I found a job driving a team of horses hauling paving stone for the magnificent wage of twelve-and-a-half cents an hour. A dollar and a quarter for a ten-hour day. That summer I went out to an old Englishman who had a big farm, and asked if he would mind if I used part of his land to raise something to eat. He said, "Fine, fine, go right ahead," so I did. I spent that summer using his implements, his plows, and his horses. I plowed up about ten acres of ground and planted potatoes, cabbage, carrots, and other vegetables.

Finally, around September, after about two months of hauling paving stone, I was rehired on my old job of roll-setter helper in the tube mill at eighteen cents per hour. It was a hot, nerve-racking job because the pipe just kept coming at you, continually. The pipe would come out of the furnace and pass through rolls, and the rolls would make the pipe perfectly round. There was no let-up, just one right after another all day, and they were white-hot. I was back again working under the same bad conditions. They were still trying to beat McKeesport and Middletown, but I was earning two dollars and sixteen cents for a twelve-hour day.

Gene Debs

Nineteen hundred eight was an election year. Three candidates were running for the United States presidency, Bill Taft, the Republican, Bill Bryan, the Democrat, and Gene Debs, the Socialist.

As I left the mill one evening, I was attracted to a tall, sharp-nosed man standing in the back of a small delivery wagon. He was speaking to a crowd of mill workers that had gathered. He was saying, "You know, men, two 'bills' stopped on their way through here today, and they are both counterfeit!" (He was referring, of course, to Bill Taft and Bill Bryan, both having stopped on their way through town.) I joined the crowd and listened. It was Gene Debs, the only candidate who thought it worthwhile to stop and talk to the working people.

I listened to him with great interest when he said, "You know, men, the boss doesn't hire men, he hires 'hands,' and if you fellows would use your heads more, you would not have to use your hands so much!" There was much more that he said that struck home. Here was a man saying the things I had been thinking for a long time. It opend up a new world, the world of socialism.

That something was wrong was obvious. Why, for instance, should a hard-working, honest, and kindly man like my father, after a lifetime of hardship and toil, be unable to live in peace and comfort? Why was it that I, a young man, could look forward to nothing better than the fate of my father? Why was it that the many thousands of idle men who wanted nothing more than an opportunity to earn an honest living were compelled to go from one employment office to another and beg another individual for that thing which is the birthright of all? I had long since discovered that all the Horatio Alger stories I had read were pure bunk!

I was able, willing, and anxious to work at any occupation that offered a livelihood, yet up to then a large part of my life had been wasted because of unemployment and through no fault of my own. There was nothing that I, as an individual, could do about it, but I had seen what could be done if the millions of working people united and pooled their strength. I knew the power of organization in the coal fields. I had experienced, too, the lack of organization in the steel mills. If somehow, I thought, these unorganized men and women, each struggling as an individual to live (and in too many cases becoming sycophants and stool pigeons to hold a job) could only be shown a better way, be shown it was not really necessary to grovel and betray their friends and fellow workers.

In the autumn of 1908 I joined the Lorain local of the Socialist Party. I read and studied the works of Marx and Engels. I read the pamphlets of Kate Richards O'Hara. I studied *The Struggle for Existence* by Walter Thomas Mills, and other books by John Spargo, Ernest Unterman, and many others. I met Bill Haywood and heard him speak of the Industrial Workers of the World (IWW). Gene Debs, too, would always stop at Lorain when he was on a speaking tour. I never missed an opportunity to hear him. I decided to try to organize a local of the IWW in the tube mill. I was well aware of the dangers involved, but the intolerable drive for more and more production had turned the mill into a madhouse.

I approached two other workers who, I was sure, could be trusted. The three of us met in Oakwood Park on a Sunday morning and decided to contact a representative of the IWW in Cleveland. Returning to work on Monday morning, our cards were all missing from the time clock. We were fired, and the three of us stayed fired. How U.S. Steel learned of our meeting, or of our plans, I never found out, but a reasonable assumption is that one of the group made a chance remark to the wrong person. In any case, I was again fired by U.S. Steel, and was once again unemployed.

Back to the Railroad

On February 1, 1909, our first child, a daughter, arrived. We named her Alda Evelyn. I was unemployed and badly in need of a job, so I left Lorain in search of work. I tried the various industrial centers of Ohio such as Akron, Youngstown, and Warren, and finally wound up in Cleveland working as a brakeman on the New York Central Railroad.

I brought my small family to a section of Cleveland called Collinwood, the Cleveland terminal of the New York Central, which had a huge railroad yard. I started as an extra man, bucking the list. The extra list was short so I managed to work quite steadily.

Train crews were paid on a mileage basis. I averaged about

seventy dollars a month. The hours were very irregular, and our time was not our own. In effect, we were on duty twenty-four hours a day, seven days a week. We dared not leave the house for fear the call-boy would come. This was true especially for the extra men, who were liable to be called at any and all hours of the day or night.

One could be sure of being called if the weather was bad. Regular men got sick frequently during blizzards or extremely cold weather. There was little or no home life for the crews who handled the long freight trains. They spent more time on the caboose track than at home with their families. It was a job I detested, but the need to provide a livelihood for myself and my family kept me at it for over four years.

I immediately joined the Brotherhood of Railway Trainmen (BRT). The leadership of the railway brotherhoods was painfully conservative. They were advocates of the "identity of interest" jargon, and many of them were active participants in the National Civic Federation, the fountainhead of the notion that the "interests of capital and labor are identical." Brotherhood officials would attend meetings of the local lodges and make long speeches on this topic. We were told over and over to work toward a prosperous company. The reasoning was that if the carriers were prosperous they could afford to pay higher wages. I heard this silly argument so often, and argued against it so strongly, that I became notorious.

The climax came in the winter of 1913. A special meeting of all trainmen's lodges in the Cleveland area was called for a Saturday evening. The main speaker was to be no less a personage than William G. Lee, the Grand President of the Brotherhood. I reported in sick in order to attend the meeting. The hall was filled, and the Grand President was ushered onto the platform. I knew the purpose of the meeting. For some time the newspapers had carried stories about the carriers losing money, and there was a campaign on to increase freight rates. Lee's talk contained all the spurious arguments about the identity of interest. When he had finished, and after the resolution had been introduced, I arose, and the ensuing dialogue went something like this:

MORTIMER: Brother Chairman, I wonder if our Grand President would answer a question, since there are some points not clear to me?

PRESIDENT LEE: Yes, of course, but let us bear in mind that one fool can ask more questions than ten wise men can answer.

MORTIMER: Am I to assume that I am the fool, while you are the ten wise men?

PRESIDENT LEE: I am very sorry you took that meaning out of it, as I meant nothing of the sort.

MORTIMER: All right then, now for the question. You tell us the interests of the company and us workers are identical. What then is the reason for this union we call the BRT? Why don't we join the same organization as the carriers?

PRESIDENT LEE: I do not mean that our interests are identical in every way. I mean it is to our interest to work for, and advocate higher rates that will ensure a solvent and prosperous employer. If they are making money, they can pay us higher wages.

MORTIMER: Can you tell us when, if ever, the New York Central or any other carrier has ever raised wages regardless of their financial condition unless they were compelled to do so? Moreover, there is no doubt in my mind, nor in the mind of any railroad man that I know, that they are able to pay higher wages now, and they are not doing so.

PRESIDENT LEE: You are a Socialist!

MORTIMER: I am asking you why the New York Central does not raise wages now. My politics are not relevant.

PRESIDENT LEE: We just got through throwing twenty-seven men out of the BRT and it looks as if there will have to be twenty-eight.

MORTIMER: I am not surprised, but it does appear to me that since we are paying your salary, you should be advocating a raise for us instead of for the carriers. If you are going to continue spending our time and money advocating a raise in rates for the carriers, don't you think you should get on their payroll, if you are not already there?

The Chairman ordered me to sit down on the grounds that I was questioning the honesty and integrity of our Grand President. But the Grand President was much shaken up. The resolution was then put to a vote. A majority refrained from voting, but the Chairman ruled it had carried. I fully expected charges would be filed against me and that I would be expelled from the BRT, but nothing happened.

Margaret and I discussed the advisability of my leaving the railroad, and finding a job somewhere else. But jobs were very hard to find, and as Gene Debs once said, "For six months before, and six months after an election, it is always hard times." I reported in sick and looked for another job. I found work as a streetcar conductor and never returned to the railroad. We were now a family of four, Irma, our second child, was born on January 22, 1914, just when I started to work for the Cleveland Railway Company.

Streetcar Conductor

I went to work as a conductor on the Euclid Avenue line of the Cleveland Railway Company. It was the kind of a job that requires the hide of a rhinoceros and the patience of Job, and I had neither. The public knew nothing of the tensions under which the streetcar men worked. Many simple souls think streetcars and buses are operated to carry passengers from hither to yon. Nothing could be further from the truth. If the profits are not high enough the car or bus is taken off, and the public can damn well walk! The new man going to work for the Cleveland Railway Company was required to work ten days with an older man, without pay. At the end of the ten-day period, his name was placed on the bottom of the extra board, and for the first year or two the only work available was what was called "three swingers." In other words, we showed up at 4:30 A.M. If we were lucky, we would be assigned a run that left the barn sometime between 4:45 and 6:00 A.M. The first swing, which handled the morning rush hour traffic, was over at 8:00 A.M. We went back to the barn then and relieved the men with regular runs for lunch. The lunch period lasted from 11:00 A.M. until 1:00 P.M. The third swing went to work at 4:00 P.M. and lasted until midnight. You could then go home and sleep until 4:00 A.M. and start all over again. In the event you were assigned to work the "Owl" car, as I was for months, you worked from 8:00 P.M. until 6:00 A.M. It was impossible for an extra man to get a good night's rest.

Having completed my ten days of donated labor, I was placed on the extra board. I showed up at 4:30 A.M. and was assigned a run that began at 5:30 A.M. and ended at 11:30 P.M. As I was leaving the Public Square on my last trip of the day, a young man about my own age and size boarded the car. He made no effort to pay his fare. I said, "Fare, please." He glared at me and said, "Now who in hell ever told you that you were a streetcar conductor?" My first thought was that he had had one drink too many. I repeated my request that he put his fare in the fare box. He continued to use very vile language in describing me. The car was filled with people going home from shows, and his obscene language raised my temperature to the boiling point. I said, "Do you intend to pay your fare or not?" He replied, "Now, who in hell is going to make me pay a fare?" I told him either to pay his fare or I would put him off the car. He then became so insulting that I stopped the car and ordered him off. He refused, so I struck him on the chin. The blow stunned him momentarily, and I grabbed him by the collar and the seat of his pants and forced him toward the door. He clung to the door handles, so I rapped his knuckles with my transfer punch, put my foot in his back and out he went onto the tree lawn. I followed him out and really finished the job. I left him bleeding at the nose and mouth.

I reported the incident, according to company rules, thinking I would hear no more of it. I reported for work again at 4:00 A.M. and worked the first swing of another three-swing run. Returning to the car barn at 8:00 A.M. I found a notice on the bulletin board which said, "Conductor Mortimer, please report to Superintendent Stampfli's office." I felt sure this would be my last day as a conductor.

I went into the office and Superintendent Stampfli said, "I

see you had some trouble last night." I said that I had some trouble with a crackpot who refused to pay his fare and that I had to put him off the car. Stampfli asked, "Do you know who that fellow was?" I said "No, but no one could get away with the abuse and insults that fellow gave me." Stampfli then said, "Well, he is John Stanley, Junior!" (John Stanley, Senior, owned the Cleveland Railway Company.) Stampfli said, "I have been ordered to reprimand you, so consider yourself reprimanded, but between you and me I feel you did a long overdue job." This young playboy got a lot of fun out of harassing and tormenting streetcar men. Most car men knew him, and were afraid to clash with him for fear of losing their jobs, so he had been getting away with this kind of cruelty for a long time. Episodes of this kind, in addition to all the drunks, religious crackpots, and the like, helped to make life quite miserable. I was involved in more knock-down, drag-out battles in my three years as a streetcar conductor than in all the rest of my life put together.

One of the worst features of the streetcar job was the tight schedules. The street railway company employed what were called "checkers." Their job was to stand at busy intersections and count or estimate the number of passengers carried at any given time of the day. It was upon their reports that the schedules were made. These schedules were so timed as to ensure the greatest number of passengers possible during the various hours of the day. Schedules were so tight there was no room for lost time, and woe be unto the car crew that got a half-minute behind schedule. The car was then picking up the passengers of the car following. The more people you picked up the later you got, and in no time at all the car would put a sardine can to shame.

Then there was the "spotter," or stool pigeon, who got on the car and pleaded poverty. He says he is flat broke, and if you will only let him ride across town where his sister lives, he will be forever grateful. If you fall for this, rest assured it will be your last trip. Another all-too-frequent annoyance is the sweet little old lady who sits in her seat until the car stops. She then toddles up and wants off. She opens her handbag, takes out a purse, closes the handbag, and opens the purse. She takes out a quarter and wants change. You change her quarter and she opens her purse, deposits the change, opens her handbag, and puts in the purse. She then puts her fare in the box and gets off. So, between the crackpots who are forever trying to save your soul, the drunks, the many people who regard the conductor as their personal servant, and the sweet little old ladies, I had a hectic three years with the Cleveland Railway Company.

The two saving features about the job were that I saw my family every day, even though I seldom got a good night's rest, and that the streetcar men were organized. The union did give us protection. Grievances were mainly against stool pigeons. The company would penalize a man on the basis of a stool pigeon's report. The union would refuse to accept any penalty unless the accused were allowed to face his accuser. If the pigeon failed to appear, then the union would not acquiesce in a penalty of any kind. If he did appear (which seldom happened) his career as a stoolie was at an end at least as far as the Cleveland Railway was concerned. This job became unbearable, so I quit the street railway company and went to work for the White Motor Company.

CHAPTER FOUR

I BECOME AN AUTO WORKER

In September of 1917, just after we had entered the war against the Kaiser to "make the world safe for democracy," I made the change. The starting wage at White's was thirty-seven cents an hour.

The White Motor Company, one of the original companies in the automotive field, was founded by Thomas White. He began by manufacturing roller skates. He then invented and produced the White sewing machine, and when the automobile appeared on the scene around 1904, Tom White became interested. Around 1910 he built the famous White Steamer, a steam-powered automobile. In 1917, when I went to work at White's they were one of the best known manufacturers of trucks and buses in America. When America became involved in World War I, their entire production was Army trucks, and equipment for the armed forces.

I was put to work running a drill press in the transmission machining department. My first job was to drill a number of holes of various sizes into the transmission housings. I operated what was known as a radial drill. The work was simple, since it was all jig and fixture work requiring no layout of any kind. In other words, the precision was built into the jig or the fixture. This was, in a sense, the beginning of mass production.

Tom White was dead when I began working at White's, but his son, Walter, had taken over the business and carried on his father's policies. Both Tom White and his son Walter were what was known as "benevolent" employers. Hourly rates were a dime an hour more than in comparable shops in the Cleveland area. Working conditions were good. There was an absence of tension, and one felt relaxed. It was, of course, an open shop, as were all factories at that time. For those of you who were born much later, a few extra words should be said about the "open shop."

Safe topics of conversation in an open shop were sports, women, dirty stories, and the weather. When these subjects were exhausted, conversation ceased or one talked to oneself. Under such circumstances it was every man for himself. Some workers would keep the bosses' lawns mowed in summer, the snow shoveled in winter, while others would kick back five dollars on payday.

The Ford Motor Company had its own private method of spying on its workers. Every tenth worker was a monitor who received five cents an hour more than the others. For this additional nickel and a promise of promotion, the monitor spied on his fellows and made daily reports to the office of Harry Bennett (Ford's right-hand man). To join or speak in favor of a union meant instant discharge and your name on a blacklist, which was used when you appeared at an employment office looking for another job. Union membership was considered worse than a prison record as far as the open shop employers were concerned. In fact, Henry Ford employed hundreds of men out of the Jackson, Michigan, prison and used them as a "Service Department" (goons). These unfortunate men were paroled to the Ford Motor Company and did not dare to disobey Henry Ford or Harry Bennett on penalty of being sent back to prison. By contrast, no union man was ever knowingly hired by Ford until the union smashed the open shop in its Dearborn plants.

There were no Federal employment offices during the open shop days. The jobless worker went to the personnel department of an employer, or he went to a private agency, or to an agency run by the Chamber of Commerce. It was not uncommon for the private agency to be in cahoots with the personnel director of the plant where you found a job. Your first pay went to the private employment agency. This was its fee, and sometimes the fee was split with the personnel director as a reward for his cooperation in fleecing you.

The White Motor Company was unusually liberal in its views, and the men felt a sense of security in their jobs. Only Walter White could exercise the power of discharge. Superintendents and foremen could only recommend such action.

Strangely, and in contrast to any other job I ever had, it was really a good place to work. For the first time in my life I was enjoying my work. I had regular hours. I was home with my family in the evenings. I was able to get a full night's rest.

There was a company union, or shop committee as it was called. It held monthly meetings, when the elected representatives from the various departments listened as the management sold company policy. A monthly slick sheet magazine was published and mailed to the homes of all employees. It was called "The White Book," and its editor was a newspaperwoman named Edna K. Wooley. The magazine's appeal was mostly to the women of the family, and was filled with dress patterns, recipes, and chit-chat about the "one big happy family" at White's.

Because I was working at White's, Margaret and I felt secure enough to build a five-room cottage on Renwood Avenue in a working-class area in a suburb called Euclid. One of the troubles we ran into in trying to finance our cottage was in getting a loan from the banks and building and loan associations. The banks I contacted (and I contacted quite a few) were all the same. They would issue a one-year mortgage for forty percent of the appraisal. They would appraise it very low, at six percent. However, if I went back to renew the mortgage at the end of the year, they charged two percent for renewal, which in effect meant I was paying eight percent. It was virtually impossible for a working man in my circumstances to get a loan. I finally went to the Prudential Insurance Company, with whom I carried my life insurance. They granted the loan and bought the mortgage from the Jensen brothers, who had built the house for us. They gave me a fifteen-year mortgage loan at six percent interest.

We moved into our new cottage in the spring of 1923. Alda was now fourteen years of age, and Irma was nine and both girls were going to school. We had to settle for the bare essentials. We moved into our new home with none of the interior finishing done, no bathroom, no furnace, etc. We were so pleased to be buying our own home that we did not mind the inconveniences and the hard work ahead.

Although I had worked steadily and my income was above average for the kind of work I did, life was still a real struggle. Mortgage payments, taxes, and insurance put a strain on my income. There was little money for anything except the essentials. Like other wage-earners with families, I was a do-it-yourself man. If the house needed repairs or paint, I did it myself. If my shoes needed half-soles, I did it myself. We had gotten rid of the landlord, but were now in the clutches of the mortgage-holder. Fortunately, Margaret knew the real value of a dollar. To her goes the credit for making my income meet our obligations, and finally paying off the mortgage, but only after years of scrimping and cutting corners.

The shop committee, or company union, met on the last Friday of each month in the factory dining room. A company official would give a talk on some phase of the company's business, and at the conclusion of his talk would make a request for comment or questions. The real purpose behind these monthly meetings, and of the shop committee itself, was to find out what was on the workers' minds. Every opportunity was actually given for questions or comment during this period. If there was dissatisfaction among the workers the company wanted to learn of it before it became unmanageable.

I was the representative from the transmission machining department, and since great stress was laid on the fact that we had nothing to fear, I decided to ask some questions and perhaps get some benefits for the hourly worker out of this company union. Accordingly, at a meeting addressed by Tom White (Vice-President and son of Walter White), the following occurred.

MORTIMER: Mr. White, there is a matter that has been on my mind for some time, and I know the same question is on the mind of every hourly paid man in the shop. It is this: Why does the company give the office force a vacation with pay every year while we who are also White employees must work through the year without a vacation of any kind? If we take a vacation it must be on our own time, and at our own expense.

Mr. White was obviously taken aback at this question. He was having difficulty formulating an answer. After a whispered conversation with his personnel director, Art Rietz, he answered as follows:

MR. WHITE: Mr. Mortimer, we think there is a difference between the office force and the hourly paid worker. The office force is paid on a monthly salaried basis and there are times when they must work overtime without the added earnings the hourly paid workers receive when they work overtime. The vacation with pay is the company's way of compensating them for the overtime they have worked.

MORTIMER: It has always been my understanding that a vacation is for the purpose of rest and relaxation and the need for a change so that one can return rested and refreshed.

MR. WHITE: We would be glad to give all our employees vacations with pay, but for us to do so when our competitors do not would be to put us at a disadvantage, and this we cannot do.

This question and short discussion between Mr. White and me went through the plant like a forest fire. Many workers expected me to be fired. The average worker believed the management's request for questions and comment was for the purpose of finding out who the "agitators" were, and were therefore silent. I did not share this view. I was sure it was for the purpose of uncovering any areas of potential trouble. They wanted to know what the workers were saying and thinking, and this was their way of finding out. Other employers had stool pigeons who reported every chance remark or trivial activity to the office, but as far as I was able to determine, the White Motor Company did not stoop to this practice. Moreover, there were no "agitators" at White Motor at this time. Wages were above average. Working conditions were very good, and employment was steady. To advocate organization during this period would have gotten one nowhere.

About this time, Miss Wooley had written an asinine editorial in the "White Book" called "The Cost of High Living" in which she said, "There are too many people trying to get rich by their wits, and not enough by hard work." Since the "White Book" invited letters and comment, I wrote Miss Wooley the following:

Miss Wooley, Editor
The White Book

Dear Miss Wooley:

I really must take issue with your recent editorial "The Cost of High Living." I am, I believe, an average working man, and when you speak of the cost of high living I am sure the average worker here at White Motor would not know what you mean. Certainly our standard of living is not "high."

When you speak of people trying to get rich by their wits instead of by hard work, I am sure such people realize the utter impossibility of ever getting rich by work. The simple fact is that hard work does not pay. There is no money in it. I know, because I have been working hard for the past twenty-four years, and I have yet to entertain any hopes whatever of getting rich by working.

Respectfully,

Wyndham Mortimer
Department 312
Transmission Machining

Two days later the office boy came and said "Miss Wooley wants to see you." I went into her office and asked if she had sent for me. She replied, "Yes, I got a letter from you." She appeared nervous and unwilling to discuss the contents of the letter, but arose and said, "Mr. Hewlett would like to see you." She took me into Mr. Hewlett's office, where I was given a seat.

Mr. E. W. Hewlett was known as an unusually liberal-minded person. He was Production Manager of the White Motor Company and also an inventor of note. On one occasion, May Day of 1919, when the "Bolshevik" hysteria had seized large segments of the population, and when rioting had occurred in Cleveland, two super-patriots refused to work with another worker because he had participated in the May Day celebration. The Superintendent sent them to see Mr. Hewlett. After hearing their story, he turned to his secretary and said, "Mary, have the checks ready for these two men by 3:30." This of course was not what they wanted nor expected. They demurred at this turn of events. Hewlett then gave them a very pointed talk about the rights of others to think as they pleased. He told them to return to work and respect the rights of others.

When I had taken a seat at Mr. Hewlett's side, he produced the letter I had written. He read it over again, and then proceeded to discuss its contents with me. Miss Wooley, obviously relieved at Mr. Hewlett's taking up the discussion, sat in silence. His basic argument was that if the worker would save his money and put his savings in a bank at interest, he could eventually become financially independent. To emphasize his point, he referred me to a large chart hanging on the wall. This chart showed the amount of money being spent on such things as movies, candy, cosmetics, automobiles. Automobiles were still a luxury in 1920.

I attacked his theory from three angles. I said that for one to put his savings in a bank at interest was not work. It was a form of exploitation, since money does not beget money. The interest paid on savings came from somewhere. Where did it originate? It was a form of getting something for nothing since no service had been performed for it.

The second angle of my argument was that it was the money people spent that made the wheels of industry turn. I said that the money spent on such things as candy, movies, and cosmetics furnished employment to thousands of people. If they were thrown out of work, they would have no income and therefore no buying power. They would cease to become consumers and would become recipients of charity.

I then took apart his theory about savings. I said, "Mr. Hewlett, suppose every gainfully employed person in America saved fifty cents a day. There are thirty million men and women working at the present time (1920). This fifty cents per day saved means fifteen million dollars' worth of goods that remains unsold every day. Two days means thirty million, six days means ninety million, and don't you see what this means in terms of prosperity? At this rate how long will it be until the merchant begins to lay off his help, and they in turn become recipients of charity?" I finally said, "Mr. Hewlett, what would become of your job and mine if people stopped buying automobiles?"

This obviously hit home, and he was at a loss for an answer. He finally said, "Are you a Socialist?" I assured him that I was. He then asked if I would regard him as a Socialist. I said, "No, definitely not." He inquired about the kind of work I was doing and I told him I ran a boring lathe. He said, "My God! A man with your ideas running a lathe?" I said I thought that running a lathe required considerable skill, but if he had something different in mind I was quite receptive. We exchanged a good laugh. The factory had by this time stopped for the day and the workers had gone home. We shook hands and I, too, went home.

The following day I had difficulty doing my work because so many workers wanted to know what had taken place in Hewlett's office. It was episodes of this kind that caused me to be well-known throughout the plant, and contributed greatly to the confidence so many of the workers had in me later, in the days when the union finally came to White's. At this point in my story it will be difficult if not impossible to separate my own life from the struggle to build a union in the auto industry, since for the next several years the union was to be a way of life for me.

Things began to change at White Motor. The economic

facts of capitalism were beginning to squeeze smaller independent auto companies like White's. They would have to change or die. It had been the policy of Tom White, and this policy was continued by his son Walter, that every component that went into the White truck or bus was manufactured by the White Motor Company at its own plant, located at East 79th Street and St. Clair Avenue. But time marched on, and if White Motor was to live as an independent entity it would have to forsake old methods and ideas that had endured so many years.

About this time Walter White was killed in an auto accident, and soon afterwards the financial pages of *The Cleveland Plain Dealer* revealed that the Morgan interests had bought control of the White Motor Company. The new owners were out to increase efficiency, which is just another way of saying that there must be more production with fewer men.

Strange men appeared in the plant. They said nothing. They just observed and studied methods of production. This new administration introduced a bonus system known as the Parkhurst plan. Every operation was timed, and the worker's earnings were determined by his production based on the stopwatch. The time study man with his stopwatch appeared at your machine. His object was to synchronize the operator's time with the machine's time. In other words, neither the machine nor the man was to remain idle at any time.

Before making the test, he would check your tools, and if the cutter was not a perfectly new and sharp one, he ordered another. He saw to it that the work or material you were working on was close at hand without your having to take a step to reach it, as well as a container in which to place the finished work. In other words, he created a situation in which the job timing would be done under conditions as "perfect" as possible.

He timed the operator by breaking down the operation into several movements, timing each movement in terms of tenths of a second. He would check the spindle speed, and increase the speed if in his judgment it was not fast enough. He timed the operator's picking up the material, and then timed his securing it in the machine. He then timed the machine to see how long it took to make the necessary cut. If the machine was slow enough, and the operator must wait until the machine had finished the cut, another machine was placed alongside so the operator could load this second machine while the first one was cutting and removing the required material. Production rose over one hundred percent, while earnings increased about twelve percent. All of this had its effect on the workers.

Management was extremely nervous, and it was obvious that new people were in command. The working force was getting old. Many of them had been hired by Tom White, the company's founder. For many of them, it was their first and only job. They had grown old in the service of White's, and could not visualize such a thing as being fired, yet that was exactly what was about to happen. The long years these aging men devoted to building White Motor to an enviable position in the motor world meant nothing whatsoever to the new owners. They too were caught in this jungle called "free enterprise," where every human instinct is suppressed in the mad chase after the dollar.

A new president appeared at White Motor. His name was Ashton J. Bean. He was the exact opposite of Walter White. He was a large, pompous individual who believed the only way to handle working people was through fear and intimidation. One of his first acts was to abolish the company union as a waste of time and money. Time revealed this to be a fortunate move, since its death removed the only obstacle to a real union later on. Ashton Bean believed in the philosophy of the mailed fist; such subterfuges as a company union were considered worthless, and were not a factor in his reckoning. His roughshod methods did much to re-educate the workers to the facts of life. All the old ideas absorbed over the years of White family control were now vanishing and men came closer together as workers.

During this difficult period I never lost the opportunity to point out the need for and advantages of a union. None would disagree, but the old fear of losing the precious job was still strong. Moreover, there were some who indulged in dreaming. They expressed the thought that somehow, sometime, the White family would again gain control. I argued that yesterdays never return just as chicks do not return to the egg. The vast majority were willing to let someone else build the union.

One man in particular on whom I had some influence and who in turn had some influence on me was Bill Dieter. We ate lunch together every day. Bill was a hard worker and very interested in building a union. He was a dependable, steady sort of person on whom you could always rely. Even to this day I regard him as one of my finest friends.

I gathered around me a group of men whom I could trust. In this group, besides Bill and myself, were Frank Kliskey, Adam Bucklad, Chester Zecchini, Harry Frowen, and a few others whose names escape me. We planned on asking the Cleveland Central Labor Council (AFL) for assistance in organizing the plant. Conditions for bringing a union to the White Motor workers were now more favorable than at any time. The old illusions of a benevolent employer had all but disappeared. The hour of truth had arrived, and the vast majority now realized the need for unity and unionism.

The transmission machining department employed approximately sixty men. We machined and assembled all the transmissions used in the trucks and busses. Carloads of new transmissions began arriving from the Spicer Company in Toledo, Ohio, and the number of men in the department was reduced to about thirty. The others, all old white-haired men, were laid off. These men were simply left to starve or become a burden on their children, since there were no provisions or plans whereby they might live. It was during the administration of Herbert Hoover and the period of rugged individualism. Such things as pensions or unemployment compensation were unheard of, and no one but a Socialist or a Communist advocated old-age pensions. The aged or worn-out worker was left to get along as best he could.

The Communists were the first to raise the matter of unemployment insurance. They did this while Bill Green, President of the American Federation of Labor (AFL), was touring the nation speaking against any kind of compensation for the unemployed. Green denounced the idea as "Moscow propaganda" and as being against our American way of life. He sneeringly referred to it as a "dole," saying that our "free American workers" would never accept such a humiliating thing! He was expressing the policy of the AFL Executive Council while untold millions of American workers did not know when or where they would eat again.

The Great Depression

In 1929 the great stock market crash occurred, but work continued steady at White Motor for another year. Then 1930 saw great changes at White's. The workers were sent home and told to wait until they were called. They were not laid off, and were still therefore technically employed, and on that account were automatically excluded from county relief. All hourly wage rates were abolished. Straight piece-work replaced the hourly rate, and piece-work rates were very low. We worked only when called. From June, 1931, to June, 1932, I earned $53.65.

The year 1931 was an especially hard and bitter year for me and my family. There was little work, and on Thanksgiving Day our oldest daughter, Alda, twenty-two years of age, passed away from pneumonia. She had been married a brief six weeks when she fell victim to this once-dreaded illness, and in three days was dead. It was a heartbreaking experience, and only those who have endured it can fully understand the shock and heartache that attends the death of one so close.

The years 1931–1935 were years of indescribable poverty and misery for millions. Everybody I knew was working part-time or not at all. I don't know if there has ever been an accurate computation of the number of people who were unemployed during that period. With no work to be had, thousands of working people could not make the mortgage payments on the homes they had bought during better times. This meant mass foreclosures and the loss of homes, furniture, and possessions. An organization called the Small Home and Landowners League, organized with the assistance of the Communist Party, mobilized the little people and fought back, providing legal aid as well as physical help. The leader was a man named E. C. Greenfield. I attended their meetings and joined their association and became very well acquainted with Greenfield. I was not so much interested in the labels the newspapers attached to the organization as in the work they were doing: saving people's homes.

Near me there lived an old man, a widower, who had built himself a home. He was a brickmason. He had paid the mortgage except for the last $500, but he was out of work and could not meet his payments, so the bank was foreclosing on him. The sheriff came with deputies to remove him from the house. In the meantime the Small Home and Landowners League spread the word and mobilized a crowd. When the deputies arrived there were thousands of people around the house. They filled the neighborhood and flowed into the side streets. The deputies looked at the crowd and did not even stop. Several days later, they came back at two o'clock in the morning and evicted the old man. They put his furniture out on the street, boarded up the windows, and sealed the door with the sheriff's seal, then went away. Word about the eviction spread fast, and the people came in the morning to take the boards off the windows, tear the seal from the door, put the furniture back in the house, and turn on the utilities.

This action posed a new problem for the bank. Under Ohio law the man could not be evicted without another court order. Even if they did evict him, they knew that the people would come back and put him in again, and obviously this could go on and on indefinitely. They could have had the man arrested for trespassing, but it was only a misdemeanor. He still occupied the house and he could not be ousted except by another court order.

Foreclosures and evictions became a costly procedure, in some cases more than the property was worth. A moratorium on mortgage payments was eventually established, and thousands of little people's homes were saved, largely through the leadership of the Communist Party and organizations it influenced. I became very active in this movement, and worked with the Communists in organizing picket lines, demonstrations, and other activities. In fact the only effective struggles against unemployment and evictions were those organized by the

Communist Party. I joined the Small Home and Landowners League because I was in sympathy with it and because my own condition was rather precarious. I was able to meet the monthly payments by borrowing on my life insurance, and also because my daughter Irma had a job in the school library. By very stringent economies we were able to meet our payments, but many months we could pay only the interest on our mortgage.

We did not know what tomorrow had in store. I did not know that I would even be working "tomorrow," and therefore my sympathies were all with the Small Home and Landowners League, Communist or not!

Thousands of desperate men and women demonstrated before relief offices and demonstrations of 10,000 people were not unusual in the Cleveland Public Square. I recall an instance when a farmer drove to town with a wagonload of strawberries which he was trying to sell to the unemployed for four cents a box. Among the thousands demonstrating for work in the Public Square not one could buy his strawberries. I spoke to him and explained why he could not sell his berries. It was because these desperate people did not have four cents. The farmer finally told the huge crowd to come and eat the berries. He said, "But, for God's sake, put the boxes back. They cost me a penny and a half apiece." The hungry crowd soon ate the berries and the farmer went his way, shaking his head.

To recount all the misery and hunger of that period would take many volumes. Suffice it to say, the Communists helped people while others wrung their hands and denounced Moscow. And I found out quite early that any time any organization or any individual spoke up in favor of the working people, they were immediately labeled Communist—even though they might not have known the difference between Communism and rheumatism![1]

CHAPTER FIVE

WE BEGIN TO ORGANIZE AT WHITE'S

In the summer of 1932 it was clear that the time had come to organize White Motor. The Depression had forced living standards down so low there was but one way we could go, and that was up. Every mass industry was open shop except coal, and the United Mine Workers Union (UMW) was fighting for its life.

Union sentiment was strong throughout the plant. I decided at last to contact the Cleveland Federation of Labor to seek help. Bill Dieter, Frank Kliskey, and I went to call on Harry McLaughlin, Executive Secretary of that body. I presented our request for assistance and said, "Brother McLaughlin, the White plant is ripe for organization and the Federation could be of much help by providing leaflets, speakers, and meeting halls." To our amazement the labor leader sat back in his chair and laughed. "Why, no one can organize that bunch of hunkies out there," he shouted. After some argument and hot words we left in disgust. I was puzzled by McLaughlin's attitude. What did he mean when he said that the White Motor workers could not be organized? They were ordinary working people, and had all the problems of working people everywhere! Moreover, I knew from daily contact with them that they were more than ready to join and support the union. Because a man or his parents came from

Hungary, Poland, Italy, or wherever did not mean that he was ready to work for starvation wages under intolerable conditions. I concluded that Harry McLaughlin was a stupid ass.

I was convinced later that in his discussion with us he was carrying out the policy that had been laid down by the Executive Council of the AFL. A further explanation of this strange behavior was given to me later by a newspaperman named Moran. He insisted that a "gentlemen's agreement" existed between the AFL and the National Association of Manufacturers (NAM) to the effect that the former would make no effort to organize the open-shop, mass-production industries, and would do whatever it could to maintain the open shop there. In return, the NAM agreed that the craft unions were to remain unmolested in the building trades. It is impossible, of course, to document such an agreement. Subsequent experience with the AFL Executive Council convinced me beyond a shadow of a doubt, however, that such a pact did in fact exist. During our campaign to organize the auto industry, at no time were we free from interference by the Executive Council, right up to the moment the first agreement was signed between the UAW and the General Motors Corporation in February, 1937.

Upon our return to the plant from the meeting with McLaughlin, I called our group together. We met at my home. Dieter and I related our experience with McLaughlin, going into detail about his arrogance and general stupidity.[2] I expressed the opinion that since the AFL refused to help, we must find a way to organize ourselves. Out of this meeting there came the beginnings of the union at White Motor. This small gathering at my home occurred three years prior to the formation of the CIO.

While I was determined to make every effort possible to build the union, the actual job of organizing still remained. We lacked the tools, such things as application cards and an accounting system to handle finances properly. And there was no money to buy them. A Slovenian friend, a printer by trade, printed the application cards and forms for an accounting system for us on a sixty-day credit basis. We raffled off suits of clothes to raise money to pay the bill. Tickets cost a quarter, and we made about thirty dollars on each suit. We used this money for organizational purposes.

Our group filled our lunch boxes with packets of application cards, in order to distribute them around the plant. They were given especially to workers whose duties gave them the run of the plant (truckers, expediters, inspectors, sweepers) with instructions to get them signed as quickly as possible and return them. By noon of the following day, 430 signed cards had been returned.

As was inevitable, someone blabbed to the company. My foreman came to me and said, "Bill (my nickname at White's), I hear a union is being formed in the plant." There was no point in pretending ignorance or denying the obvious, so I said, "Yes, we have a thousand cards signed as of now and more are being signed very fast." The foreman then said, "Jesus Christ!" and turned on his heel and went straight to the head office. I was sure of being fired, but as it turned out they were more afraid of me than I was of them.

The following day Art Rietz, the personnel director, came to me and said, "Mr. Mortimer (I was now Mr. Mortimer), we are thinking of restoring the old shop committee and wondered if you would cooperate with us." I said, "Art, I will have nothing to do with a company union. The only kind of an organization that meets our needs is one that reflects the wishes of the workers." He replied, "Very well, just forget that I raised the question with you."

We began to hold meetings in the Slovenian Hall on St. Clair Avenue. There was no formal election of officers. That was to wait until the membership was much larger. I chaired the meetings by common consent.

In the winter of 1933 the daily papers ran stories about a series of strikes in the Detroit auto plants, conducted by an organization called the Auto Workers Union. This union was led by the Trade Union Unity League (TUUL), a left-wing group dedicated to the principle of industrial unionism in the mass industries. They had originally belonged to the AFL, and they had hoped to be able to work within the framework of the

AFL and eventually persuade the Executive Council to see its error and adopt the only practical method of organizing the mass industries.

The Auto Workers Union had organized Briggs Body and Hayes Body, and was making good progress in organizing the auto workers of Michigan into an industrial union. It gave the auto workers an honest and militant leadership and had become a threat to the open shop. I wanted to contact them. I had sincerely tried to get help from the AFL's Central Labor Council and had been laughed at. I went to call on John Williamson, the Ohio District Organizer of the Communist Party, hoping that he could put me in touch with the Auto Workers Union. Williamson gave me the address of Phil Raymond, the leader of the union in Detroit.

Phil Raymond was a Communist, or so it was said. But I have never been afraid of words or labels. I had seen what the Communists had done in the Small Home and Landowners, and calling a man or an organization "Red" did not scare me at all. I wrote to Phil Raymond and invited him to address a meeting we had arranged in Cleveland. He accepted and came out and spoke to us. He assured us that we were not alone and that the time was ripe to organize.

In the minds of the moribund, craft-dominated Executive Council industrial unionism was a plot laid by the Kremlin. Although the TUUL was a left-wing group led by Communists and other forward-looking people, the leadership of the AFL was living in the eighteenth century and regarded any movement forward as the work of evil men.

The signing of union application cards was proceeding satisfactorily. We had about fifty percent of the workers signed up and it appeared we would succeed in our efforts to organize White Motor. We had not counted on AFL collusion with management, however. Leaving the plant at quitting time a few days later, I found two organizers from the AFL Metal Trades Council at each of the five gates to the plant. They were distributing a very nice slick leaflet, printed with a beautiful American flag on one side and a Red-baiting tirade on the other. Beneath the flag were these words:

> Join the only bonafide AMERICAN labor union. Join the American Federation of Labor, the only union endorsed by our great President Franklin Delano Roosevelt.

The reverse side had a vicious attack on our independent union and the TUUL. The following day, several workers who had refused to sign our application cards began distributing application cards for the AFL. Another leaflet distribution by the Metal Trades Council offered us a federal union charter. It read, in part, "All White Motors production workers under one charter now. CHOOSE BETWEEN FRANKLIN DELANO ROOSEVELT AND JOE STALIN."

A more dishonest statement, or bigger lie, would be hard to imagine, but it had its effect in that it contributed to the confusion and disruption of the first honest effort to organize workers at our plant, who were so badly in need of a union.

At first glance the federal charter gave the impression that White's was being given an industrial organization. There was much confusion on this point. In reality, according to the AFL plan, the federal union was a corral into which all the mass-production workers were to be herded for branding by the various craft unions claiming jurisdiction in the industry.

I was certain that the Executive Council had been asked to intervene and keep White's shop wide open. The success of the TUUL in Michigan had caused cold chills to run up the spines of the auto moguls. Here was an entirely new organization, led by the left wing, threatening to breach the open shop "gentlemen's agreement," and the Executive Council of the AFL was being called upon to stop it. There was no denying, however, that this move by the Metal Trades Council (a subordinate body to the Cleveland Federation of Labor) had done much damage at our plant. It had confused the workers to the point where many of them could see little difference between the federal union and the industrial-type organization. The injection of the "Red" issue confused them even more. New applications in our independent union dropped off entirely, though very few were being signed up by the AFL.

It was clear that something had to be done to restore unity. I had several serious conversations with such men as Richard

Reisinger, Fred Price, and others. These men were anxious to build a union, but felt that a union affiliated with the AFL was preferable to an independent union. They felt it would be more acceptable, and therefore more permanent. I could not disagree with this, but I pointed out that it was the TUUL independent union that had forced the Executive Council to get off their easy chairs and show some faint signs of life.

Reisinger had already signed an application card to join the AFL. The same went for Price and others. It was obvious then that we had to do something in order to achieve unity among ourselves. I called a meeting of our group. We went into the situation thoroughly and decided to call a mass meeting of all production workers for the purpose of clarifying the problem and charting our future course. Every effort was made to ensure a large attendance. The meeting was held on schedule in a packed hall. I had prepared a statement as a means of getting discussion started. I called the meeting to order, and, quoting from memory since verbatim minutes were not kept, I made the following remarks:

> Fellow workers, I am sure you all know the purpose of this meeting. It is for the purpose of deciding our future course. Up to this moment, the employer has won, I am sorry to say. They have won in the sense that they have succeeded in dividing us over the question of union affiliation. We must find a way to restore unity among ourselves. I have no quarrel with those who prefer the federal union. I do not doubt that they are just as sincere in their thinking as we are in ours.
>
> I am personally interested in one thing. I want to see a united and strong union at White Motor, and a union that is run by the membership. It will matter little what we call such an organization as long as it is ours, and as long as WE, the membership, determine its policy.
>
> I, therefore propose the following, and I want a thorough discussion of this proposal. I propose that we dissolve the independent union and that we all join and become members of the federal union of the AFL. I am

> fully aware that the federal union is not the complete answer to our needs. It is not an industrial union, but under it we can organize our plant. And if we fight for and retain real democracy in our ranks, we can, I am sure, use the federal union as a base to build the kind of union we need and must have. Whichever road we choose, LET US ALL STAY TOGETHER.

This statement precipitated a heated discussion which became extremely critical of the AFL bureaucracy and the reactionary policies it espoused. The discussion lasted until 2:00 A.M.

When everyone who wanted to say something had spoken, the proposal was put to a vote. It carried overwhelmingly. I drove home tired but satisfied that the White Motor Company and the AFL Executive Council had lost, and that we, the workers, had taken the first step toward eventual victory.

At this point I should mention an incident involving one Joe Zack, whom John Williamson had introduced to me as the trade union organizer of the Communist Party in Ohio. When I told Zack that our TUUL union was joining the AFL and the Metal Trades Council, he argued vociferously against it. Finally I got tired and told him that we were joining the AFL and there was no point in arguing the matter further. Seeing that I was determined, he quickly changed. "All right," he told me, "go ahead and do as you say. But don't forget, you are joining the AFL only to smash it!" I told him flatly that was not my intention and that I did not contemplate smashing anything. I wanted to build, not destroy.

After this conversation I again went to see Williamson and questioned him about Zack. In particular I repeated Zack's admonition about smashing the AFL. Williamson was enraged. Zack was expelled from the Communist Party about a year later. It was eventually revealed that he was an informer and stool pigeon for the FBI. His testimony before various government agencies during these past few years has resulted in many workers losing their jobs and some of them were even deported.

Zack's real name, it turned out, was Joseph Kornfeder. He

was an Austrian. He wrote me during the General Motors sit-down strikes in Flint, threatening to expose me as a "Red." I did not think his putrid threats worth an answer.

We Join the AFL

That the White Motor Company and the Metal Trades Council were disappointed by the new unity in the plant was obvious. George McKinnon, the representative of the Metal Trades Council, was heard to say, "I don't know who is advising this guy Mortimer, but he hasn't made a mistake yet."

Another incident revealed the fears of the AFL leaders. One night around midnight my phone rang. A voice said, "Mortimer, under no circumstances must you go to the Central Labor Council or the Metal Trades alone. They are out to get you." Needless to say, I took this unknown friend's advice.

A few days after the mass meeting, several carloads of workers, all leaders in the TUUL union, drove down to the Metal Trades Council and we all signed applications to join the federal union. A charter had been applied for.

There was now the beginning of real unity in the plant. A deep and healthy distrust of the AFL existed among the workers, but they were convinced of the correctness of our course. I knew the time would soon come when the craft-minded Central Labor Council and the Metal Trades Council would attempt to raid the federal union, so the minds of the workers were prepared. They were instructed on a course of action. They were told, and it was strongly stressed, that should they receive a letter of any kind from the Central Trades or the Metal Trades, they must bring the letter either to me or to Bill Dieter or Dick Reisinger.[4]

The signing of federal union applications was resumed. Organizational meetings were held in the Metal Trades Hall on Walnut Avenue. Application for a federal charter was sent to the Executive Council of the AFL. The charter was granted, and federal union 18463 came into existence.

As I had predicted, a number of workers, especially those in the more skilled categories, began to receive letters from the various craft unions claiming jurisdiction in the industry. Among them were Blacksmiths, Plumbers and Pipefitters, Carpenters, and others. The workers brought the letters to us and we paid a visit to the Metal Trades Council.

We left no doubt in their minds that this maneuver on the part of the craft unions would not succeed. We had no intention whatever of permitting our federal union to be weakened or broken up. I pointed out to Bill McWheeny, another AFL leader, that the craft unions now claiming jurisdiction had made no moves to exercise their so-called rights since the auto industry was born. But now they put forward a phony claim to the right to collect dues from the workers they had neglected and shunned for the past thirty years. We were not bothered again and we continued to build the federal union.

The Metal Trades Council of the AFL was under the national leadership of John P. Frey, a typical bureaucrat who had learned nothing and forgotten nothing in the past fifty years of his life. To hide his all-too-apparent ignorance he would quote Shakespeare. He boasted of his close relationship with J. Edgar Hoover, and never failed to remind us that the real enemy of the laboring man was Communism. He represented monopoly capitalism inside the labor movement. He repeatedly told us that labor and capital were "partners" and that the interests of labor and capital were identical.

The two local representatives of the Metal Trades Council were James McWheeny and George McKinnon. Neither of them had the slightest knowledge or understanding of how mass production operated, nor could they be made to understand the futility of talking craft unionism to us. They were accustomed to presiding at meetings where not more than a dozen men were in attendance. The great gatherings of mass production workers (many of them boisterous and highly vocal) which they were soon to experience actually horrified them.

It quickly became clear to me that these were not the men who could be trusted to build an industrial union in the auto industry. Their background, traditions, and sympathies were craft-oriented, and they believed that the idea of building a mass movement of skilled, semi-skilled, and unskilled workers was

"Communistic." Their sole weapon in fighting such a union was Red-baiting.[3]

Our federal charter was presented to us by George McKinnon. He announced that it was the policy and custom of the Metal Trades Council to appoint temporary officers. I arose and asked what had happened to the vaunted AFL democracy? McKinnon was taken aback. "But, Brother Mortimer," he said, "this is a traditional and temporary arrangement for a brief period." "What is a brief period?" I asked. McKinnon replied, "Not over three months." I did not press the matter further.

McKinnon appointed the President, Vice-President, Recording Secretary, Financial Secretary, and a twelve-man Executive Board. All came from the most conservative elements of the plant. Some of the workers challenged this procedure. They wanted an election. I cautioned patience because I did not want to widen the split that was to some extent still evident among us.

The constant hysterical tirades of John P. Frey, and the parrot-like repetitions of McWheeny and McKinnon, served to confuse some of the members. I felt we had succeeded so far in preventing the AFL and the employer from irreparably dividing us, and to have to wait a little while longer for an election was not worth muddying the waters.

I was firmly of the opinion that the company was in league with the AFL and its subordinate body, the Metal Trades Council. If by some maneuver they could still split our ranks and prevent unity among us they would certainly do so, and I did not want to give them the slightest opportunity. I was satisfied we could elect an entirely different slate of officers at any time we chose.

In the meantime we continued to build and strengthen local 18463. Although I was not an officer of the local, I became chairman of the grievance committee. With me on the grievance commitee were Richard Reisinger, Ted Rieff, and Ed Stubbe. I decided to go to work on several pressing grievances. There was also the matter of working out a collective bargaining agreement with the company.

Like all employers, the company had formulated a set of

rules known grandiosely as "company policy." They insisted on enforcing this policy as though it were something holy. I said the union must also have a "union policy" and must insist upon that policy's being carried out. If union policy conflicted with company policy, then it became a matter for negotiation.

One grievance that had reached the critical stage was the matter of working Saturday and Sunday for straight time. Company policy was opposed to paying more than straight time. Union policy was that time-and-a-half must be paid for all hours worked over eight hours a day, and for work done on Saturday and Sunday.[5]

Every union member was instructed to tell his foreman about this union policy. He must not refuse to work if he were paid time-and-a-half, but he was instructed to tell his foreman that the union would not permit him to work unless he received compensation in accordance with the union's decision.

This worked very well for a while; the company paid time-and-a-half. After a few weeks, about five hundred men were told to report for work on Saturday. They fully expected to be paid time-and-a-half. However, that Saturday morning a notice was posted on the time clock reading:

> AS OF THIS DATE, STRAIGHT TIME ONLY WILL BE PAID FOR SATURDAY AND SUNDAY WORK.
>
> Cavanaugh, Production Manager

Needless to say, there was much excitement among the five hundred men. I arrived about fifteen minutes before starting time and was immediately surrounded by men asking what to do. Since none of the local union officers had been asked to work this day, I realized that the decision rested more or less with me, so I mounted a table and called everyone to come close. I came to the point at once.

"Fellows, you are all acquainted with what our union policy is regarding working Saturday for straight time. I want every one of you to follow me out that door and return to work

Monday morning." I got down and started for the door, followed by every last man in the place. I stood at the door to be sure that no one remained inside. Cavanaugh, the production manager, appeared at that moment and rushed over to me. "Mortimer," he shouted, "you cannot do this to us. We have forty thousand dollars worth of gears in heat treat, and unless they are taken care of they will be burned up."

I asked, "How many men do you need, Mr. Cavanaugh?" He replied, "Two." "How much will time-and-a-half for two men cost?" I demanded. He became angry and shouted, "But time-and-a-half is against company policy."

"Well, it is against union policy to work for straight time on Saturday and Sunday!" I said as I walked away with the others. Supervision had to work on the gears that day. But the company paid time-and-a-half for Saturday and Sunday work thereafter.

We Meet Management

President George Lehman of our local sent a letter to the White Motor Company, requesting a meeting for the purpose of negotiating a contract covering wages, hours, and working conditions. As chairman of the grievance and bargaining committee, I was spokesman for the union. We met at the appointed time and presented to the company's representative (Vice-President George Smith) a copy of a proposed contract. To our amazement, we found James McWheeny of the Metal Trades Council already sitting in Mr. Smith's office. We had not asked him to be present, nor had we even told him of the meeting. However, he did not make us wait long before showing us why he was there.

"Mr. Smith," he started off, "the Communists are trying to take over the American labor movement, and my advice to you is, do not sign any contract or agreement of any kind with this local 18463. If you sign a contract it must be with the Metal Trades Council and the American Federation of Labor." Mr. Smith surprised us. "We are capable of handling our own affairs," he replied curtly. Then turning to me and the committee he added, "We will study your proposals and you will hear from us."

The entire committee was furious at the position taken by McWheeny. Reisinger said to me, "Mort, I didn't think the AFL was as bad as you claimed, but now I am ready to believe anything you say."

The following week we received a letter from Mr. Smith requesting a meeting. At this second meeting a stenographer was present and a verbatim report was typed. Each member of the committee received a copy, called a Memorandum of Agreement. Now, a memorandum of agreement is not a contract. It is merely a record of oral discussion. To understand why the White Motor Company would not, and in fact could not, sign a contract with us, we must understand something about an organization called the Automobile Manufacturers' Association.

This Association was the auto manufacturers' "industrial union." It was dominated by the big three, General Motors, Ford, and Chrysler, and by the National Association of Manufacturers. Woe be unto any employer who failed to comply with the rules and regulations of this association. Members could, within certain limitations, "deal" with a union "for such of its employees as are members of the union." But it could not recognize a union as the sole bargaining agent, nor could it sign a written contract with the union, as this would constitute "recognition" and the penalties were such that smaller companies could not afford to risk incurring them. The result was that the smaller companies resorted to verbal understandings with union committees in settling grievances, just as our company wanted to do with us. (One well-known employer once said to me, "Mortimer, we will give you everything you ask for, but don't ask me to sign anything. If I sign that contract you presented to me, we will be out of business tomorrow.")

Under such circumstances we decided that as long as our grievances were settled and the union was growing strong, the matter of a contract was not an immediate issue. In fact, I personally felt a contract could very well prove a hindrance at this point. A formal contract can be a two-edged sword. It would bind us to observe rules that could very well slow us down.

What I wanted was for us to be footloose and free to act at any time we desired, to take whatever measures seemed advisable to advance the union to a position of strength. We could not be charged with violation of a contract that did not exist.

Our organization was very well set up. We had a shop steward for every foreman, and a chief steward for every superintendent. The shop stewards collected dues, and kept their departments and groups one hundred percent in the union. If a worker had a grievance, he took it up with his steward, who wrote the grievance up in triplicate. One copy went to the foreman, and one copy to the worker; the steward kept the third. If the grievance was not settled at the foreman level, it was taken up at the chief steward and superintendent level. Failure here meant it was handled by the grievance committee and management. Not all grievances were settled favorably, but a great many were. All grievances were handled, however, and the worker did get an answer to his complaints.

We were a functioning local union at long last. The Depression and the anti-labor Ashton Bean had been of great assistance in bringing about a victory that would have taken many years to accomplish otherwise. We all got much pleasure out of his saying that "NO UNION WILL EVER TELL ME HOW TO RUN THIS FACTORY," and then having finally to meet and bargain with our union.

In the autumn of 1933 we demanded a raise in pay. The answer was, of course, that the company was losing money and that raising wages was out of the question. This issue dragged along until the spring of 1934, when *The Cleveland Plain Dealer* and all the other papers printed a story to the effect that the White Motor Company had paid a handsome bonus to its top officials. Ashton Bean's bonus was $125,000. We demanded another bargaining session. At this meeting, Ashton Bean was not present. We were met by Mr. George Smith. I told him we felt that our demands were timely, that unless they were granted, we were planning on a strike vote, and that I was sure that neither the company nor the union desired a work stoppage. Smith introduced a lot of figures to show us the company was losing money every day it operated. I took the *Plain Dealer* out of my pocket and put it on the table, showing the headlines about the huge bonuses being paid by the company.

I said, "George, we might have believed those figures two days ago, but not today." He had little to say after that, but still stood pat on refusing an increase. We had ballots printed, and took a strike vote. The vote was ninety-two percent for the strike.

We again went into session with Vice-President Smith, and after three days of fruitless argument, we fixed a deadline for a strike at 10:00 A.M. the following day. We met with Smith at 8:00 A.M. Ashton Bean either would not or could not be present. At ten minutes before 10:00 A.M. the atmosphere was tense. Workers in every department were putting their tools in their tool boxes, ready to take them home. Mr. Smith said, "Mr. Mortimer, the company is prepared to grant the increase asked by the union, although our financial condition does not warrant it." The shop stewards, who were all waiting outside the conference room, were told the news, and they immediately ran to their departments and informed the men.

Our demands were a minimum of fifty cents an hour in place of the forty-three cents fixed by the National Recovery Act (NRA), and an increase of five cents an hour for everyone whose rate was above fifty cents.[6]

During the last hour of negotiations Dick Reisinger nudged me, and said, "Look who is just outside the door." I looked and saw McWheeny and McKinnon of the Metal Trades Council. I excused myself, and Dick and I went out to see what they wanted.

McKinnon said, "We understand you are going on strike, and we came out to get this thing settled." I said, "George, we feel quite able to handle things ourselves." He replied, "Well, all right, but when you get yourselves into trouble, don't come to us for help." I said, "If we need help we know the Executive Council is the last place to look for it." It was our opinion that they had been called by the company to intervene.

CHAPTER SIX

OUR MOVEMENT TAKES ON A NATIONAL SCOPE

In June, 1934, our local was summoned to a conference scheduled by the AFL at the Fort Wayne Hotel in Detroit. We were entitled to three delegates. George Lehman, Dick Reisinger, and I were elected to represent the local union. Upon our arrival at the conference, we were each given the usual pad of paper, a pencil, and a copy of a "resolution," evidently prepared by the AFL Executive Council. The purpose of the conference was to act on the resolution, thereby giving the whole matter some semblance of democratic procedure. In reality, the whole conference was rigged, a cut-and-dried affair, out of which nothing of consequence was to emerge, as far as the auto worker was concerned. Delegates from nearly every auto plant in the nation attended, and on the basis of per capita tax paid, represented 350,000 organized auto workers in the various federal unions. So it was claimed.

The Executive Council's resolution fell far short of what we needed or desired. It called upon the conference to approve what was called a National Council of eleven members to be elected by the conference. This eleven-man council was powerless, however. It could meet only upon call of the representative of the Executive Council, and it could act only in an advisory capacity.

The conference was chaired by Bill Collins, the AFL

representative. Collins was also supposed to be in charge of the drive to organize the auto industry. Since the conference was just a weekend affair (Saturday afternoon and Sunday afternoon), and since the delegates were very much strangers to each other, the necessary organization to oppose the resolution was not possible in so short a time.

Saturday afternoon was devoted to long speeches by Collins, Bill Green, and others. The entire session was a mutual admiration orgy, in which Bill Green and the Executive Council were depicted as being only slightly lower than the Deity Himself. It was necessary to sell the Executive Council to the delegates, and to convince us that our only salvation rested with this self-perpetuating, craft-minded group of bureaucrats, who were planning to steer us up a long blind alley. They were now offering us the shadow but not the substance of an international union.

At the Saturday afternoon session a man from Kansas City exhausted all superlatives in the English language in his extravagant praise of Bill Green and the Executive Council. This man was later chosen as one of the eleven-man National Council. His name was Homer Martin, about whom we shall hear a good deal more.

The conference reconvened at 1:00 P.M. on Sunday. It was liberally sprinkled with AFL organizers. They would monopolize the discussion, and with Collins in the chair, no real debate was possible. It was clear that the resolution would pass without any real discussion. I tried desperately to get the floor, but getting recognition from the chair was impossible. Adjournment time was getting close and debate would soon be closed, so I decided to take the bull by the horns. Leaving my seat, I walked down the aisle toward the chair. When I drew near the platform, in as loud a voice as I could command, I shouted, "Brother Chairman! I want to speak in opposition to this resolution. It does not meet the needs or desires of the auto workers. What we need and must have is an international industrial union of all automobile and parts workers!"

There was a hush in the hall. Then Chairman Collins brought down his gavel hard and shouted, "Sit down! I know who you are speaking for. Every time I hear the words 'international industrial union' I know where it comes from. It comes straight from Moscow!"

One of the AFL organizers then quickly moved the previous question. All discussion ceased. The vote was taken, and Collins ruled that the resolution had carried. I was immediately surrounded by delegates wanting to know my name, and what local I represented. They were in agreement with me, they said, but it was now too late. The eleven-man advisory council was elected. The AFL organizers (pie-cards) participated in the voting and made sure that only "loyal" elements were chosen. Thus, George Lehman was chosen from Cleveland.

The conference did serve one good purpose: I was able to talk to and get the names and addresses of many of the delegates present. We used these to good advantage in the period ahead.

The Auto Labor Board

Following the June conference, I was asked by Richard Byrd, cousin of his famous namesake, to visit the Automobile Labor Board. The Board was appointed by President Roosevelt in the spring of 1934. Its headquarters were in Detroit. Composed of three men, it was charged with the responsibility of formulating a code of fair practice that would ensure peace in the auto industry. It was also empowered to conduct elections to determine the workers' choice of a bargaining agent in the various plants. A certain number of such elections were held, notably at Dodge, Plymouth, and other plants. The independent union known as the Automotive Industrial Workers of America (AIWA) came into being as the result of such an election. The three men composing the Board were Leo Wolman, a master sophist who beclouded every issue with a multitude of words; Richard Byrd (as far as I could determine, he was appointed to represent labor because he had never done a day's work in his life); and a man named Kelley (whose first name I cannot recall), a Chrysler Corporation attorney who represented the Automobile Manufacturers' Association.

This Board finally formulated a code of ethics based strictly upon the policy of the open-shop employers. The Executive

Council of the AFL and the daily press tried to sell this code to the auto workers, but without success. For instance, part of the code of fair practice was a seniority clause. This clause was nothing more than a statement of policy taken from the code of the National Association of Manufacturers. It said: "Seniority shall be based upon length of service, ability, skill, merit, and dependency." Obviously that meant nothing but what the employer designated it to mean.

When I appeared before the Board I made the remark that this clause was not worth the paper it was written on. Wolman, in a hurt tone, asked, "What is wrong with it?" I replied that seniority involved but one factor, and that was length of service. To clutter up seniority with such abstract things as merit, skill, ability, and the like, negated the whole matter.

The Auto Labor Board played only a minor role in the struggle then shaping up between the auto workers and their employers, and was soon forgotten by all concerned.

Strikes

During the spring of 1934, a wave of strikes occurred: Auto Lite in Toledo, Fisher Body in Cleveland, Seaman Body in Milwaukee, and others. The auto workers wanted a showdown. The most effective argument of the AFL to enroll the auto workers into the federal unions was the promise of support, financial and otherwise, that it would give in the inevitable struggle with the General Motors Corporation. The federal locals in the GM plants, early in 1934, constituted an organization of considerable size and power. The workers were convinced that the time had come to redress grievances and settle old wrongs. They believed that these promises of support by the AFL were sincere. But the powerful movement of early 1934 in the GM plants came to nothing. Delegates were sent to Washington and given a lot of talk, but in the end the AFL called off the strike, and the workers left the union by the thousands.

The AFL called a mass meeting in Pontiac during this crisis. Delegates from all over Michigan, Ohio, and elsewhere were in attendance. These were all General Motors workers, and strike sentiment among those present was strong. Bill Collins,

Frank Dillon, and a large number of AFL organizers were present and were, of course, bent on preventing a strike.[7]

Collins and Dillon painted a very gloomy picture for the delegates. Collins said, "A strike means hunger for your families." Dillon stressed the point that pay checks would stop and that no one knew when they would be resumed. These so-called leaders, who a short time before were making lavish promises of support, now told the auto workers that the Executive Council would not authorize a strike, nor would it help financially or in any other way if they went on strike. Such arguments were meaningless to these workers whose pay checks were already far too small for their needs.

When he realized that he could not convince these determined and militant workers, Collins pulled an old ruse out of the bag. He left the hall, then suddenly returned, rushing down the aisle to the platform waving a telegram. Going to the microphone, he read this telegram to the meeting:

"STRONGLY URGE AGAINST STRIKE SITUATION DEMANDS PEACEFUL NEGOTIATIONS. [Signed] FRANKLIN DELANO ROOSEVELT." The telegram was a fake, but the name of Franklin Delano Roosevelt was magic in 1934. The men were seduced by fair words and foul deeds to stay on the job.

A committee was elected to go to Washington and lay their case before the President. They did talk to General Hugh S. ("Iron Pants") Johnson, and to Frances Perkins, Secretary of Labor. Some were won over to the side of the AFL Executive Council. The committee returned and urged patience and reliance on the AFL.[8]

After the disappointments of this period, masses of members tore up their union books in disgust. The names of Frank Dillon and Bill Collins were dirty words among many auto workers, and the influence of the AFL had touched bottom.

I recall a visit Bill Collins made to my local union. He made a Red-baiting tirade, after which he turned to me and said privately, "Mortimer, if you think the AFL is so lousy, why don't you get the hell out?" I snapped back, "I am not opposed to the AFL, Brother Collins, but I *am* opposed to some of the people in the leadership and the way things are being done.

However, I intend to remain in the AFL and do my best to make it function the way a real union should!" Collins said nothing more and left the platform.

The Executive Council used this period of frustration and disgust to decapitate the real leadership of the federal unions. Many an honest and militant leader was fingered as a "Red" and fired from his job. They were refused the protection of the union on the grounds that they were agents of Moscow. Without charges, without a hearing or a trial, against all the history and tradition of America and its Anglo-Saxon forebears, hundreds of honest men and women were blacklisted, discharged, and driven from the industry. The list of good union people who met this sort of punishment is long.

The red herring had become the most potent weapon in the employer's arsenal. The craft-minded bureaucrats of the Executive Council, fearful of the drive for industrial unionism in the mass industries, flooded the auto areas with so-called organizers from the building trades, all of whom were as craft-minded as their employers. They were willing and anxious to go to any lengths to protect their outmoded racket in the building trades.

The federal unions in the auto big three became leaderless and disintegrated. Some were taken over by stool pigeons; others just folded up from fear or impotence.

In this connection, I might mention that William F. Knudsen, President of General Motors, testifying later before the Senate Committee headed by Robert M. LaFollette investigating industrial spying, admitted that his company spent $839,764 for spies over a two-and-a-half-year period. Now this was the amount spent by GM alone. How much Ford and Chrysler spent was never revealed. I submit that this amount of money would buy a lot of informers, and this alone would, to a great extent, account for the sad state of affairs that developed during the years 1934–1935.

Father Charles E. Coughlin

I might also mention at this point another force that succeeded in spreading confusion among the auto workers. This was

Father Charles E. Coughlin, a Roman Catholic priest from Royal Oak, Michigan. Coughlin was an excellent example of how a fascist demagogue is able to influence and sway millions of hungry and desperate men and women. His unctuous and soothing voice poured forth a river of dubious stories, half-truths, and just plain lies. His weekly radio talks over station WJR at 2:00 P.M. every Sunday had a huge audience, exceeded only by the "Fireside Chats" of Franklin Roosevelt.

The millions of unemployed, hungry, and desperate men and women wanted an end to their misery, and they were ready to follow any Pied Piper who promised them a better future than the present they were currently enduring. To those who think "it can't happen here," I would suggest they do some research on Father Coughlin, the anti-Semitic fascist priest from Royal Oak.

In August of 1935, Henry Kraus and I attended a meeting on Belle Isle Park in the Detroit River. This meeting was organized and conducted by the AIWA, the independent union organized by Father Coughlin, which attracted thousands of workers from the Chrysler Corporation. Coughlin was the main speaker, and thousands were in attendance. Henry and I were watched, and every move we made was trailed. The great man arrived amid much cheering and shouting. But what did he have to say to these confused workers of the Chrysler Corporation? What was the message he had for them?

He first denounced the UAW, then in session at its first convention. (That was the reason for our presence in Detroit.) He then denounced the "International Bankers" and mentioned specifically Kuhn, Loeb, and Company. The main enemy of the auto workers, he maintained, was not capitalism, but Moscow. He urged these working people to look eight thousand miles away for the source of their troubles, rather than to examine the main enemy at home.

Like most demagogues, this one finally overreached himself. As I was driving from Detroit to Flint on a Sunday afternoon in 1936, I turned on my car radio to hear what Coughlin had to say. He was in good form, and was denouncing President Roosevelt and the measures being taken to restore employment and business. In one of his flights of oratory he said, "I tell you, ladies and gentlemen, that Franklin Delano Roosevelt is a liar!"

I immediately said to myself, "Charlie, you're through!" And through he was, for no one could call President Roosevelt a liar in 1936 and expect to retain the respect of the American people. Coughlin had become a victim of his own propaganda to such an extent that he believed Roosevelt could be defeated in 1936. He persuaded a former Congressman named William Lemke to oppose Roosevelt for the Presidency. I doubt if a more miserable failure ever occurred in American politics. Coughlin was finally silenced by his bishop, but not until he had been exposed, together with his secretary, for having gambled in the silver market with the money thousands had donated to him.[9]

Another leather-lunged demagogue who had come to prey on the auto workers was a Negro-hating, anti-Semitic, flag-waving, Ku Klux Klansman from Fort Worth, Texas. His name was J. Frank Norris. It was the accepted opinion among union people that this character was imported to Michigan by the General Motors Corporation. If this was true, they made a poor investment, since some of the strongest and most militant among the automobile workers were from the southern states. Norris did not enjoy the nationwide radio broadcast that was Coughlin's medium, but his vitriolic tongue did cover the state of Michigan. His Alice-in-Wonderland stories about the CIO and the Reds could also be heard all over Ohio, Indiana, Illinois, and the Province of Ontario.

The Cleveland District Auto Council

I returned from the June, 1934, conference more determined than ever to do everything possible to build an international industrial union in the auto and parts industry.

Election of officers was soon to be held in our local. George Lehman, the incumbent President, declined to run for re-election, but a man from the office force announced his candidacy for the job. His name was Klavon. I also was nominated, and accepted the nomination. I was elected overwhelmingly.

As the president of local 18463, I soon arranged a meeting, a sort of social gathering, of all the officers of the federal unions in the Cleveland area. I ran into immediate opposition from the Metal Trades Council. McWheeny called me and said it was against policy for me to communicate in any way with other federal unions except through his office. I reminded him that there was an extremely hot place where he could go.

The purpose of the meeting was to decide what our next step must be. I proposed the formation of an "Auto Council" which we could use as a base of operations to carry on our struggle. The Cleveland District Auto Council which was eventually formed was composed of the federal unions in the Cleveland area: Fisher Body, Hupmobile, National Carbon, Baker Rau Lang, Bender Body, Willard Storage Battery, and White Motor. Since the White Motor local was the largest and most stable, and since we were the only local able to support the Council financially, our local union hall was used as the Council headquarters. Local 18463 voted a two cent per capita levy to finance the Council.

The Cleveland Auto Council was immediately denounced and ordered to disband by the Executive Council, the Central Labor Council, and the Metal Trades Council, on the grounds that it was against AFL policy and that a charter would not be issued for such a body. I wrote a letter to AFL President Green, to the Central Labor Council, and to the Metal Trades Council, in which I said:

> As President of the Cleveland District Auto Council, and speaking for the Council, please be informed that your protest and order to disband is hereby rejected. It is our opinion that since the Executive Council has deemed it necessary and good to form and charter Building Trades Councils, Metal Trades Councils, and so forth, we can see neither reason nor logic in your demand. We cannot see why the auto workers should be denied the same rights and privileges accorded other segments of the American Federation of Labor.
>
> (signed) Wyndham Mortimer, President,
> Cleveland District Auto Council

Since we were refused a charter, we operated without one. The Metal Trades Council referred to us as the "Kremlin."

We decided to publish a paper, called *The United Auto Worker*. A young journalist named Henry Kraus, a graduate of Western Reserve University, a mathematician and a writer, volunteered to edit the paper. There were no paid officials in the Council. All activity was on a voluntary basis, and this included Henry Kraus, who, although not an auto worker, worked assiduously and contributed his considerable knowledge and talent, many times far into the night, so that the paper would appear on time. Henry Kraus is one of those rare individuals who placed principle above any personal gain. The automobile workers owe him a debt of gratitude that will be hard to pay.

The United Auto Worker was distributed in bundles to all the names and addresses I had obtained at the June conference. The editorial policy was to advocate and fight for an international industrial union in the auto and parts industry, chartered by the AFL.

The Cleveland Auto Council decided to take the offensive and called a national conference of all federal unions in the auto industry. Printed invitations were sent out. The conference was held in a hall known as *Slovenski Dom* (Slovenian Home) near Fisher Body on St. Clair Avenue in Cleveland. There were about thirty-six federal unions that sent official delegations, some from as far away as Kansas City.

A delegation led by Arthur Greer, representing the Associated Automotive Workers of America (AAWA), an independent union in the Hudson plant, appeared and requested that they be seated. The conference refused to seat these delegates, since all delegates were required to be members of the AFL. George Lehman, the former president of local 18463, appeared at the conference as an observer for the Metal Trades. His role was to see if there were grounds for our expulsion from the AFL. His eyes goggled when we took the action against seating the Hudson delegation.

No AFL paid representatives or politicians came to waste our precious time. The entire period was given over to discussion and reports of delegates. There was unanimity of opinion on the deplorable situation in which the auto workers found themselves. We were unanimous also that we needed an international industrial union embracing all automobile and parts workers, a union that would be responsible to the men and women who paid their dues.

A resolution was passed demanding that a constituent convention be convened by the AFL Executive Council. The proposed convention would adopt a constitution, elect officers, and assume jurisdiction over all workers in and around the automobile industry.

Our exploratory conference had a considerable impact on the auto workers, and even though the AFL Executive Council and the Metal Trades Council denounced us as an outlaw group, our District Auto Council gained widespread prestige and support. We became the center of activities striving to build the kind of organization we so badly needed.

Three months later, in November, 1934, our Auto Council called another conference in Flint. This conference too was highly successful, and a number of federal unions were represented, though most of the delegates had to pay their own expenses, since their local unions had been destroyed by the AFL.

A resolution exactly like the first one was sent to the AFL. We received no reply. But the Executive Council sent letters to all federal unions in the industry, advising them that these conferences were Moscow-inspired and forbidding participation in them upon threat of penalties.

The United Auto Worker was doing an excellent job of educating the union membership and spread widely over the nation, mobilizing sentiment for the industrial union and exposing the leadership of the AFL. Federal unions in Toledo, South Bend, St. Louis, Cincinnati, and elsewhere made monthly contributions to the cost of printing. I became widely known and was invited to speak at union meetings throughout Ohio, Indiana, and Illinois.

In March, 1935, a third highly successful conference was held in Detroit. The AFL had now decided the time had come to smash this center of agitation for the industrial union. It was well-versed in negative tactics. So successful had the AFL been in destroying the federal unions in the big three that not a single one of the federal unions in GM, Ford, or Chrysler had enough members to hold meetings in the state of Michigan!

The Chrysler Corporation (Dodge, Plymouth, and Chrysler) had come under the influence and leadership of Father Coughlin. He operated through a protégé, Dick Frankensteen, who had fallen for the fascist priest's wiles. Independent unions were formed at Chrysler and at the Hudson Motor Car Company, under the leadership of Arthur Greer, who, it was claimed, was an officer in the Black Legion (a Ku Klux Klan-type outfit). The GM workers had become helpless. Their federal unions had been destroyed, and by and large were in the hands of spies and stool pigeons. The only union organization left in the industry was in plants of secondary importance, located in outlying centers at Toledo, South Bend, Milwaukee, Kenosha, and Cleveland.

A major obstacle to a return of the open shop was undoubtedly the Cleveland District Auto Council and the White Motor Local. We had already learned that the AFL realized this fact. When the third conference to promote the industrial union was scheduled for Detroit in March, 1935, the call for it was read at the regular meeting of our local. After some opposition by the few pro-AFL members, it was endorsed by a large majority and we elected four delegates: Dick Reisinger, Ed Stubbe, Ted Rieff, and me. But this was not the end of the matter.

Every member of our local received a card from the office of Bill Collins in Detroit, which read as follows:

> Dear Sir and Brother:
>
> You are strongly urged to attend the meeting of your local union 18463 this coming Friday evening. Decisions must be made as to whether or not there will be a local union at White Motor.
>
> Signed, Bill Collins.

I inquired at the Metal Trades Council as to the meaning of this postcard and was told to wait until Friday evening to find out. Friday evening arrived, and the hall was filled to capacity. I called the meeting to order promptly at 7:00 P.M. The secretary was reading the minutes of the previous meeting when the following AFL representatives strode into the hall and headed for the platform: Bill Collins, Representative of the AFL Executive Council; Tom N. Taylor ("TNT"), President, Indiana Federation of Labor; James Flaherty, Representative of the AFL Executive Council; Harry McLaughlin, Cleveland Federation of Labor; James McWheeny, Metal Trades Council; George McKinnon, Metal Trades Council. As the president of the local, I arose and welcomed them to our meeting, and found them seats on the platform. These six representatives had scarcely been seated when a member named Ed Gockel, a staunch AFL supporter, asked for the floor and said he wanted to make a motion. I ruled him out of order. "Just as soon as we are through with the present order of business, Brother Gockel," I said, "I will entertain your motion. I, too, want to know what this is all about and where we are going."

After the minutes were read, I recognized Brother Gockel. His hands trembling, Gockel read from a slip of paper, "I move that local 18463 rescind its action of two weeks ago, and refrain from sending delegates to the proposed conference in Detroit." The motion was seconded by Charles Walsh, another pro-AFL stalwart.

The motion having been made, I asked for comment. Beginning with Bill Collins, every one of those six "pie-cards" took the floor in one of the fanciest Red-baiting tirades I have ever heard, and I have heard plenty! One after another, they alternated in hurling epithets at me and threatening to revoke our charter. Their wild arm-swinging ravings differed only in intensity. Boiled down, they said we were a bunch of Communists, and that I was getting my orders direct from Moscow, and that our charter would be taken away. George McKinnon pointed to me directly, "And you, Mortimer, are a ComMUNE-ist and I will lift your charter!" After this flood of invective had subsided and the six had sat down, I asked if there was further comment. The meeting became as silent as a cemetery. I turned the chair over to the Vice-President, as I said, "Well, *I* have some comments to make."

Reporting from memory, as verbatim minutes were not kept, I took my stand.

"I will not dignify the wild charges made against me and our local union by either denying or admitting them. Red-baiting is, and has always been, the employers' most potent weapon against those of us who believe in and fight for industrial unionism." I answered each of the speakers in turn, recounting our experiences with these very men, and how they had, without exception, done everything they could to prevent our building an international industrial union in our industry.

Turning to Harry McLaughlin, I asked, "What did you tell Bill Dieter and me when we asked you for help in organizing White Motor? Didn't you say it was impossible to organize those 'hunkies' out there?" A deep growl went through the crowd. Practically all the workers at White Motor were either foreign-born or the sons and daughters of foreign-born, and the word "hunkie" was unpopular, to say the least.

"If you representatives of the Executive Council would get off your fat bottoms, and do the job that needs doing, I would be the happiest man in this hall. But it is just because you have failed to do the job, and in fact have done your best to prevent the job from being done so as to keep the open shop in the mass industries, that we must do what you have failed to do." I added, "If you will start even now to help us build an industrial union in auto, I will be the first to grasp your hand. But I am sure that the people who sign your pay checks would sign them no more, should you decide to do so."

To George McKinnon, the overweight loudmouth who pointed his finger at me and called me a ComMUNE-ist, I said, "George, you say I am a Communist and that you are going to lift our charter. Well, so what? Is being a Communist a crime? As for your lifting our charter, there it is. We keep it in your office, and we pick it up every meeting night to lean there against the rostrum. But if you want it, I am sure you can have it. We learn fast. We found out some time ago that a union without a charter is a damned sight more important than a charter without a union! Now, if you want that piece of paper, take it with you!"

The crowd cheered and stomped, and it was several minutes before order was restored. I put the motion to a vote, but before doing so I called the members' attention to a very clever trick. This was in the way that Gockel and the AFL representatives had worded the motion. I said, "Remember, if you vote Yes, it means No. If you vote No it means Yes. If you vote Yes on this motion, it means we will not send delegates to the Detroit conference and if you vote No on the motion, it means we will attend the Detroit conference. In other words if you want our delegates to attend the Detroit conference, you must vote No on this motion."

Turning to Tom N. Taylor, who supposedly was an expert on Roberts' Rules of Order, I asked, "Am I stating this motion correctly, Brother Taylor?" He nodded his head solemnly. I put the motion to a vote, saying, "All those in favor of this motion will signify by saying Aye." The silence was deafening. "All those opposed will signify by saying No." A tremendous roar of Noes swept the hall. The motion was defeated almost unanimously.

The six "pie-cards" left the hall amid cat-calls and boos. Tom N. Taylor turned to me and said, "President Mortimer, I intend to memorialize President Green of your actions and statements here tonight." I replied, "Thank you, Brother Taylor." I called for the next order of business, but further business was impossible. The entire membership, as if by previous arrangement, stood up and cheered. A motion to adjourn was made, and the workers showed their pleasure by adjourning to the bar in the basement.

CHAPTER SEVEN

HOW WE FINALLY WON OUR INTERNATIONAL UNION

The Detroit conference called by the Cleveland Auto Council once more revealed the deep and widespread determination of the auto workers to build their own international union, one that would not be controlled by the backward-looking, craft-minded, middle-class mentality of the AFL Executive Council. Again a resolution was sent to the Executive Council, to Bill Collins, and to the Central Labor Councils of Detroit, Cleveland, and other important auto centers. We had by this time about sixty federal unions in the auto industry that had officially declared for our own industrial union, and we were planning another nationwide conference to be held in St. Louis.

However in June, 1935, the AFL Executive Council finally sent out calls to all federal unions in the auto industry instructing them to send delegates to a convention to be held in August in the Fort Shelby Hotel in Detroit. The call stated that President William Green would attend and would present a charter establishing an international union. It did not mention an industrial-type union, and it specified important restrictions on jurisdiction. But we were pleased, nevertheless, feeling that at last we were making progress.

The convention was held on schedule. The chairman was

Francis (Frank) J. Dillon, who had replaced Bill Collins as chief representative of the AFL in the auto industry. Dillon was a man past middle age whose background was entirely craft-union oriented. He was a portly man, and a typical AFL bureaucrat. He could be counted on to run the convention in the traditional drum-major AFL style.

Approximately 250 delegates were in attendance, mostly from Ohio, Indiana, and Wisconsin. Michigan, the center of the automobile industry, had a smaller delegation present than they had had at the June, 1934, conference in the Fort Wayne Hotel. The federal unions in the big three—GM, Ford, and Chrysler—had been destroyed by the concerted attacks of the AFL and the automobile employers.

President Green appeared, made a flowery speech, and presented the charter. Our paper *The United Auto Worker* was visible all through the convention hall. President Green and Dillon were anxious to learn how the forces lined up. The test vote came on the second day, upon the presentation of a resolution calling upon President Green to appoint temporary officers. The resolution was defeated by a stunning vote of 164 to 112.

The leaders of the AFL looked as though they had been hit by a pile-driver. The convention was recessed for two days, during which time a large number of AFL organizers attempted to change the picture by playing on the supposed inexperience of the auto workers. Two days later, Thursday, August 28, the convention reconvened and the check had evidently revealed that no change had resulted. There was some more stalling. There was little business transacted at this convention altogether. However, a significant discussion on jurisdiction did take place, which showed near-unanimity of the delegates in favor of the industrial union. The AFL leaders could no longer put off settling the question of the officers. It was clear that the delegates, if allowed a free choice, would pick officers who would not be controlled by the AFL. Accordingly, a democratic election of officers must be prevented at all costs. At last, President Green strode to the rostrum and solemnly announced: "By virtue of the authority vested in me, and upon orders of the Executive

Council, I will now appoint the officers of this international union." He then named Francis J. Dillon, President; Homer Martin, Vice-President; and Ed Hall, Secretary–Treasurer. The completely discredited eleven-man National Council was reappointed, to a man, as the Executive Board.

Pandemonium broke loose! A large number of delegates from Toledo started to walk out in revolt against such high-handed action. Bob Travis, Henry Kraus, and I rushed to the door. We stopped them. We told them to go back to their seats. I said, "You damned fools, don't you see this is exactly what they want us to do?" Travis and Kraus also urged them to remain in the convention, as the fight had just begun. After much confusion and argument the Toledo delegation returned to their seats.

I have often been asked why the convention did not assert itself and elect a chairman to preside over them instead of permitting President Green to appoint Frank Dillon. We could have done so, as we could have decided to fight the AFL on a dozen other issues. However, in view of the overall situation in the auto industry, we decided to fight out our major differences with the AFL leaders inside the framework of the American Federation of Labor, even though this course might be long and difficult, and not to incur probable disciplinary action on issues that were, after all, only subsidiary.

It is well to recall at this point, besides, that there were at least three independent unions already striving for the loyalty of the automobile workers. There was the Automotive Industrial Workers of America (AIWA) sponsored by Father Charles Coughlin, the fascist priest; the Mechanics Educational Society of America (MESA), a craft union of skilled tool and die workers; and the Associated Automotive Workers of America (AAWA) led by Arthur Greer, whom we have already described.

While the shortcomings of the AFL were many, and very irritating, we recognized that it remained the center of union organization in the country. It was clear to us, besides, that the automobile industry was going to be organized. The time had come. It could not be prevented, and the only question was, by whom? The AFL Executive Council had decided that, since this was a fact, and that all indications pointed to the AFL as the organization that would eventually succeed, they would saddle this new international union with a leadership that was "safe." Had we, the delegates, acquiesced, the organization of the auto industry would have been set back for years. Certainly the present powerful union would not exist as it is today. Instead, we accepted our temporary setback, but felt greatly strengthened and encouraged to continue the fight.

The large Toledo delegation having returned to their seats, and order having been restored, Tom Johnson, a Ford delegate, asked for the floor. "Brother Chairman," he read from his notes, "I move that this convention elect a committee of five who will go to Atlantic City and protest the outrageous action of President Green in denying this international union the democratic right to elect its own officers." Green was forced to accept the motion, which was seconded and carried unanimously. Those elected were Carl Shipley, Bendix, South Bend, Indiana; John North, Hayes Body, Grand Rapids, Michigan; George F. Addes, Willys-Overland, Toledo, Ohio; Tom Johnson, Ford, Dearborn, Michigan; Wyndham Mortimer, White Motor, Cleveland, Ohio.

The reader will notice that not one of the committee was employed by either General Motors or Chrysler. Tom Johnson had been a Ford worker, but was fired for union activity, and so was unemployed. (Actually the AFL was nonexistent in the huge River Rouge factory.) We can judge from the makeup of the committee just how completely the federal unions were destroyed in these huge corporations.

I was elected chairman of the protest committee. Upon the adjournment of the convention, we proceeded to Atlantic City, where the Executive Council was in session preparing for the coming annual convention of the AFL.

We obtained an appointment with the Executive Council. Though we arrived at the specified time, the Council had not yet convened, and the various members present were in informal discussion. What was the subject of their talk? For the most part they were discussing stocks and bonds, personal investments, and the like. John North turned to me and said, "Christ, Mort! Are we in the right place?" I assured him that we were.

Bill Hutcheson of the Carpenters was telling Ed Wharton of the Machinists, "Why, I just bought fifty thousand dollars of Consolidated Edison last week. I think it is a good buy." Wharton demurred, and said he thought AT&T was better.

At that time, September, 1935, there were still millions of unemployed, miserable, and hungry men and women who wondered where their next meal was coming from; many thousands of teenage boys and girls were bumming their way across the land looking for some way to earn a livelihood. Yet the supposed "spokesmen" for these desperate millions could find nothing to talk about except buying stocks and bonds.

Meanwhile men such as ourselves, who were striving to do something for these millions of unemployed and desperate people, were forced to waste our time and precious money to travel many miles, in order to convince these old men that something had to be done for the working men whom they represented.

President Green arrived and took his chair. Bill Hutcheson, a huge man who gave every impression of speaking for the Council, asked the purpose of our visit. I said, "We are here to register a protest against the undemocratic actions of President Green in arbitrarily appointing the officers of our newly chartered international union. We maintain that we are as capable of electing our own officers as are the members of any other affiliate of the American Federation of Labor."

Hutcheson replied, "Maybe what we should do is recall the charter, and when you have organized the industry we can then discuss the question of a charter!"

"We are not here to discuss a charter," I told him. "The charter has been issued. We are here to demand our democratic right to elect our own officers; that is the only question at issue."

At this point, David Dubinsky of the International Ladies' Garment Workers turned to me and asked, "How many of your committee are Communists?" I said, "I don't know and I don't care a damn. Every member of this committee is a member of our international union in good standing and duly elected by the convention to appear here before you. Such a question is irrelevant and out of order!"[10]

We were told that our protest had been received by the Executive Council and that it would be given consideration. We would be informed of its decision in due time. Leaving the Executive Council, walking down the boardwalk, we discussed our reactions to the meeting and the question of why the Executive Council was so reactionary and out of touch with the working people. A member of the committee (Tom Johnson) said, "I think the explanation of the Executive Council's attitude can be found in the twenty-first verse of the sixth chapter of Matthew, where Jesus said, 'For wheresoever your treasure is, there will your heart be also.' " We all had a good laugh over this and agreed it was a very apt quote. Our brief visit with the Executive Council had demonstrated that many of its members had indeed laid up much treasure.

Remembering Tom Johnson makes me want to digress a moment to say a word about him and about the damage that is often done to working people who become heavy drinkers. Tom Johnson was a brilliant person and a very effective labor organizer, who could have gone very far in the labor movement. During the 1935 AFL convention he disappeared, although we were counting on him to be heard during the convention. He never showed up, and the story was circulated around that he had been murdered and thrown into the ocean because the AFL was afraid of his effectiveness.

A day or two later the landlady at the rooming house where I was staying during the convention said to me, "A man came here today and wanted to see you. He said his name is Johnson." She described him very accurately. "He just wants you to know that he is all right." The fact was that he had gone on a binge. We had to write him off, because we could not expect any further help from him.

I have often thought sadly about this talented man, who was lost to the labor movement and to himself by his addiction to alcohol. And how often in the past had I reasoned with fellow workers who had the same weakness, sometimes coming to work drunk and exposing themselves to grave accidents and loss of their jobs.

I recall one fellow in particular, who arrived intoxicated and went to work on his machine, a multiple drill press. He reached in while the drills were turning around and they twisted around his jacket and began to pull him into the machine. He would have been killed if I had not leaped over and pulled the switch, turning off the power. We had great difficulty in pulling him out of there, and he smelled like a distillery when we got him out. The company, of course, fired him.

I never indulged in liquor of any kind, because in my own family I had seen its effect. My youngest brother became an alcoholic. My grandfather on my father's side had also been an alcoholic and as a result was unable to support his family. It became an obsession with me. I wanted no part of it, and I stayed away from it. I used to say there were two places I would never be found—one was a saloon, and the other was in church.

The AFL's Historic 1935 Convention

The convention of the American Federation of Labor, held in October, 1935, in Atlantic City was its most historic in this century. It marked the founding of the Committee for Industrial Organization (CIO), and it placed the meaningful question of craft versus industrial unionism in the mass production industries on the agenda. Conventions of the AFL were traditionally given over to jurisdictional arguments, long-winded speeches, by politicians, and the adoption of high-sounding resolutions that were promptly forgotten. This one was destined to be different.

There were present at the convention quite a considerable number of delegates from federal unions in auto, rubber, electrical, aluminum, and other industries. These delegates were, to be sure, all for industrial unionism in the mass industries. While our combined vote was very small in comparison to the huge bloc votes of the Carpenters, Miners, and other great international unions, we were nevertheless able to make our presence felt. I was there as a delegate from my local 18463 and I carried eight votes.

The question of industrial versus craft unionism was brought to the floor through a minority report of the Resolutions Committee, which was signed by five members of that committee. This report said, in part,

> The time has arrived when common sense demands that the organizational policies of the American Federation of Labor be molded to meet present needs. In the fifty-five years of its existence, the AFL has enrolled only three and one-half million members out of a potential thirty-nine million organizable workers. We refuse to accept existing conditions as evidence that the organization policies of the AFL have been successful.

Matthew Wohl, Vice-President of the AFL, and one of the most reactionary officials of that body, violently attacked the minority report, accusing John L. Lewis, President of the United Mine Workers, of masterminding it. Following Wohl's attack, Lewis rose and slowly walked toward the platform. He began speaking in his deliberate manner and his words were among the most famous ever spoken by a union leader. "At the San Francisco convention [the year before], I was seduced by fair words. Now, having learned I was seduced, I am enraged, and I am ready to rend my seducers limb from limb!" He made an impassioned and extremely well-documented plea for industrial unionism and a real drive to organize the unorganized workers in the mass industries.

During the debate on the minority report I tried repeatedly to get the floor, but the chair would not recognize me.[11] John Brophy came to me and said, "John wants to see you." I went to the Miners' delegation where President Lewis was of course seated. He said, "Wyndham, I notice you have been unable to get the floor. Now, let me tell you how to do it. Just go up to the platform and stand behind Bill Green, and when the present speaker is through talking, step quickly to the microphone and begin talking. Green does not have enough courage to stop you. I know Bill Green."

I did as Lewis suggested. President Green was surprised, but he announced, "The chair recognizes delegate Mortimer." I said, in part:

> Brother Chairman. Other delegates have told you a great deal about conditions in the auto industry, and I will not consume any more of your time than is necessary. Since the inception of the auto industry in 1904, heaven knows there has been time enough for the craft unions to organize us if they ever intended to do so. Since they have not done so, and cannot possibly do so, I do not see where we would be taking anything from them by going ahead and organizing this great basic industry. It has been said, and with good reason, that the American Federation of Labor has no intention of ever organizing the mass industries. We believe this because we base our opinions on what you do, and not on what you say. I have sat here and heard a number of older trade unionists say, "In all my forty years in the labor movement . . ." trying to impress us working delegates with their long experience. Well, in my opinion, too many of you can remember *too* far back. The world has moved while you have stood still, and it appears to me that the least the Executive Council can do is to permit us to organize our mass industries in the only way it can be done.

All the oratory and logic were wasted on these old men who had lived too long and who had forgotten their mission, if indeed they ever felt they had one.

Following me as a speaker was delegate Hugh Thompson of the rubber workers. Thompson made a sincere effort to tell the convention of the rubber workers' determination to build an industrial union. But before he had gotten very far, Bill Hutcheson of the Carpenters' Union arose to a point of order. It was a transparent effort to harass the speaker. At this point Lewis rose and immediately he and Hutcheson began walking toward each other, finally facing each other in the aisle. I was quite close to them and could hear clearly their famous exchange.

Hutcheson having protested the chair's permitting Thompson to speak, Lewis observed to him, "I think it is pretty small potatoes when the President of a great international union takes advantage of parliamentary rules to prevent a working delegate from telling us of the problems confronting his people. This delegate has been sitting patiently for days, listening to empty jurisdictional arguments, and now when he tries to convey a meaningful message to this convention, he is prevented from doing so."

Hutcheson replied sarcastically, "I eat small potatoes, that is why I am so big."

Lewis stood glaring at him. "I would think you would be ashamed to do this sort of thing."

Hutcheson then called Lewis a "dirty bastard." These words were scarcely uttered when Lewis struck Hutcheson on the jaw, knocking him over a table. The Carpenters' chief landed on the side of his face, which was badly skinned.

The convention was in pandemonium. Sitting across the table from me was Wharton, President of the Machinists. Picking up his folding chair, he shouted, "Kill the bastard!" (meaning Lewis). I grabbed him by the shoulder and said, "Now just what in hell do you think you are going to do?" He glared at me and sat down. Our entire federal union delegation moved over to the side of the Miners, prepared to do battle, if necessary. President Green kept calling for order and urging everyone to take their seats. Finally calm was restored, and the convention was brought back to order.

A number of speakers had supported the minority report. Nevertheless, it lost by a vote of 18,024 to 10,993.

It was now evident that the AFL Executive Council, dominated by the craft unions in the building trades, was determined to prevent the unionization of the mass industries. With their substantial majority vote, it was clear to Lewis, as it was to all who desired the unionization of steel, auto, rubber, and the other industries, that organization could be accomplished only by defying the majority on the Executive Council. Why the Executive Council was so set against organizing the mass industries puzzled many delegates. For myself, I was satisfied they were still carrying out their "gentlemen's agreement" to keep the open shop wide open.

Another interesting episode occurred during the nomination of officers. I nominated Emil Costello, from Nash Motors of Kenosha, Wisconsin, and for the first time in his life, Matthew Wohl was challenged for the Vice-Presidency by a working delegate. We all knew Costello could not be elected but we wanted to express the contempt we felt for Wohl. We wanted to demonstrate our feelings about this man whose reactionary policies knew no bounds. The roll-call went halfway through when Costello withdrew and conceded election to Wohl.

At one point during the convention, John L. Lewis arose and asked permission to introduce a resolution. Now this was an irregular act for a delegate to present a resolution from the floor. After some argument from the craft unionists, permission was granted, and Lewis read briefly from his notes. "RESOLVED, that no officer of the American Federation of Labor shall be permitted to hold office of any kind in the National Civic Federation."

This resolution was aimed directly at Wohl, who was Secretary of the National Civic Federation at a salary of $25,000 per year. The resolution passed and Wohl was forced to resign from this ultra-reactionary organization. It was the fountainhead of that poisonous doctrine known as "identity of interest," and it financed a feverish campaign to convince working people that their interests and those of their bosses were the same. Many labor leaders echoed this sentiment. It was an anesthetic designed to induce a state of trance and thus abate the struggle that is inherent in an economy that regards workers as a commodity. Its effect is still apparent in the top leadership of the AFL–CIO, who are advocates of the racket known as free enterprise.

After two weeks of jurisdictional arguments, listening to politicians, and witnessing the mighty blow struck by John L. Lewis for industrial unionism, the convention adjourned. Lewis asked me to come to his office before returning to Cleveland, and we had a very fruitful talk. He questioned me at length on the level of organization in the auto industry. I, in turn, wanted to know what we could expect in the way of furthering the organization of the auto industry. He assured me of his willingness to help in every way. He congratulated me on the work we auto workers were doing and urged that we continue.

CIO

The most important result of the 1935 convention was the formation of the Committee for Industrial Organization (CIO). The full name was later changed to Congress of Industrial Organizations, but the identifying initials remained the same. Formed by John L. Lewis, Sidney Hillman of the Amalgamated Clothing Workers, Charles P. Howard of the International Typographical Union, and five others, its purpose was to bring industrial unionism to the mass industries. It was a bitter struggle, during which such words as "harmony" and "unity" were to be found only in the dictionary—the only place, as a matter of fact, where they could have been found for a long time back. Once the CIO was established, however, there was a home for industrial unions, one to which our own union was soon to gravitate.

There was, incidentally, a very specific reason why Lewis was anxious to organize the mass production industries, especially steel. The UMW was the only industrial-type organization in the AFL. It found little if any cooperation from the craft unions and was in constant conflict with them, an experience our young organization had already had on a smaller scale. Although the UMW was powerful and well organized, it was suffering badly from the AFL's determination to perpetuate the open shop in the mass production industries.

A rapidly growing tendency in the coal industry was the establishment of what were known as "captive mines." Huge corporations like U.S. Steel, Ford, and the railroads had acquired great coal fields by purchase or lease. These coal mining communities were being operated on the kind of peonage basis with which I was all too familiar. The towns, or coal camps, as they were called, were never incorporated. There were no elected officials. They were ruled by the mine superintendent, from whom there was no appeal. Union organizers came into town at the risk of their lives.

The development of captive mines had reached the point where a large proportion of all the coal mined in this country was dug in these non-union towns. If a proper living and wage standard for the miners was to be established, then the union had to be brought to the captive mines. President Lewis's plan was to organize the vast open shop in steel, and, through this organization, to develop the fight to smash the captive mines and unionize the entire coal industry.

I returned to Cleveland and to local 18463 more determined than ever to do everything within my power to build an international industrial union in the auto industry, and to do what I could to destroy the image of the AFL Executive Council as spokesmen for the American working class. I returned to my job at White Motor, and devoted all my spare time to the union and to the Cleveland District Auto Council, the center of our activity.

The District Auto Council decided to send me to Miami, where the Executive Council had once more gone into session, in order to demand that they tell us what they planned to do about the committee's protest against President Green's action in Detroit. I was preparing to leave for Miami when I received a phone call from Ed Hall and Homer Martin, the recently appointed Secretary–Treasurer and Vice-President of the new international union. They were in Cleveland, and asked me to meet with them in the Auditorium Hotel at East 6th Street and St. Clair Avenue. The urgency with which they requested the meeting gave me the impression that something of importance was happening.

I went immediately to the hotel. These two men had long been my opponents in the fight with President Green and the AFL pie-cards, but now they greeted me like a long lost brother. Ed Hall was a sincere and honest man. He really believed all the nonsense and anti-Communist hogwash put out by the AFL and by the press and radio. Ed was to learn differently, and was actually learning now in the school of experience. Homer Martin, on the other hand, was a dishonest and venal opportunist who would not hesitate to grow garlic on his mother's grave, if by doing so he could climb one rung higher toward the leadership of the international union.

The story they had to tell did not surprise me. Upon being appointed to their respective offices, they had gone to Detroit prepared to assume their duties. They were met by Dillon, who wanted to know, "Who in hell sent for you guys?" He told them, "Get the hell back where you came from, I don't need your help in running the affairs of the international union."

Ed Hall was not the type of person who could be intimidated, and he took over his appointed office by force. Their purpose in contacting me was for support. They were looking for allies and they knew that I was the recognized leader of one of the largest segments of the newly chartered union. They were on their way to Miami, but they were flying; I had reservations by train, so we decided to meet there.

By the time I arrived in Miami they had already met with President Green and had been given full authority to assume their appointed duties. Our committee was unable to get an audience with the Executive Council, but we did meet with Green. He urged us to be patient, as the matter had not yet been decided. I told him that time was not unlimited, and that my special trip from Cleveland to see the Council showed that we considered the question of the utmost importance. Moreover, I added, we planned to elect our own officers either with or without the Executive Council's approval. I left for a meeting with Hall and Martin.

Ed Hall spoke very seriously to me. "Mort, I have said a lot of nasty things about you and your group. But I have learned a lot in a short time. I know you represent the real union forces in auto and I want you to know that from here on in I am in your camp." Martin smiled and said not a word.

John L. Lewis Comes to Cleveland

Arriving home from Miami, I reported the results of my meeting with Green to the District Auto Council. I also proposed that the Auto Council sponsor a mass meeting in the Cleveland Public Auditorium, the principal speaker to be John L. Lewis. The Council approved unanimously.

Henry Kraus and I drove to Washington, D.C., to consult with Lewis, and to arrange a time most convenient to him, to discuss publicity, and other matters. President Lewis enthusiastically agreed to come to Cleveland and address a meeting under the auspices of the District Auto Council. His one concern was that such a meeting be a success, as it was to be his first attempt to speak directly to the workers in the mass industries. To have such a meeting poorly attended would not be a good start for the CIO.

We contacted the rubber workers in Akron and asked them to organize a mass meeting for the following day, also to be addressed by Lewis. Since these meetings were being held in midwinter, February 8 and 9, there was some concern about the weather.

The District Auto Council elected a publicity committee, and this committee, headed by Henry Kraus, publicized the meeting with professional skill. A large edition of *The United Auto Worker* was printed. The papers were distributed at the plant gates of every industrial plant in Cleveland. We arranged with the auto workers from Toledo, Detroit, and Cincinnati to charter buses which brought hundreds of out-of-town workers to the meeting.

I met with the officers of the AFL Central Labor Council and personally invited them to attend and occupy seats on the platform. The Administrative Secretary of the Council, a man named Finnigan, denounced Lewis and everything he stood for with bitter invective. One officer of the Central Labor Council did attend, Recording Secretary Max Hayes, a Socialist.[12] He delivered an address of welcome to President Lewis.

The great day arrived. It was a bitter cold day, snowy and windy, with a temperature of ten degrees below zero. Accompanied by a group of auto workers, I met President Lewis at the old union depot down on the lake front. It was clear he was not optimistic over the prospects of a large meeting. I assured him we would have a good crowd, but I was keeping my fingers crossed.

The meeting was scheduled to begin at 8:00 P.M. By 7:30

P.M. the hall, whose seating capacity was 3500, was already half-filled. At 8:00 P.M. the hall was filled to capacity, with many standing in the aisles and at least a thousand turned away. I chaired the meeting and introduced President Lewis. Following the meeting, Lewis held an impromptu get-together in his rooms. He was overjoyed at the enthusiastic reception, and also the favorable publicity the Cleveland newspapers had given the gathering.

The following day, a caravan of twenty cars accompanied Lewis to Akron, where he addressed another overflow meeting of rubber workers. This meeting, in fact, so enthused the rubber workers, that soon afterward the workers at Goodyear started their historic sit-down strike—the first of a famous series.[13]

These two huge mass meetings, the first in the country held in behalf of the new CIO, demonstrated beyond question the eagerness of the workers in the mass industries for organization. While I am confident that we would, by our own efforts, eventually have organized the auto industry into an industrial union, the arrival of President Lewis and the CIO on the scene helped enormously. Without him, the road would have been longer and much more difficult. We were now no longer fighting alone against the auto manufacturers and the AFL Executive Council.

In late February, 1936, and largely because of the influence of Lewis and the CIO, the Executive Council announced a new convention for the auto workers. It was to be held in South Bend, Indiana, in April, and we were at long last going to be allowed to elect our own officers. As I have said, we would have called a convention in the near future, with or without their consent, but this move greatly simplified matters for us.

On April 7, 1936, Francis J. Dillon called the convention to order. He introduced President Green, who spoke briefly and then read the decision of the Executive Council. A delegate from local 5 (Studebaker) immediately moved that the convention elect a temporary chairman. The purpose was, of course, to get Dillon out of the chair and out of our hair. This motion was seconded and carried unanimously. Homer Martin was elected as temporary chairman of the convention. President Green and Francis J. Dillon left the hall immediately.

The convention proceeded in an orderly way to conduct the business of the international union. A constitution was adopted and international officers elected. The four hundred delegates represented a dues-paying membership of approximately 20,000. We had a treasury of $25,000, a pitifully small arsenal to wage war against the auto barons. The five officers chosen were Homer Martin, President; Wyndham Mortimer, First Vice-President; Ed Hall, Second Vice-President; Walter Wells, Third Vice-President; George F. Addes, Secretary–Treasurer.

The selection of Homer Martin as President was the one action of the convention that caused me apprehension. We knew too little about him, except that he was a former Baptist minister with a good platform presence. He had no experience in the auto industry to speak of, and had been chosen by President Green to serve as Vice-President because of his oratorical ability and his readiness in the past to do what he was told. He was the perfect example of an ambitious opportunist with a glib tongue.

George F. Addes, a fine person and an honest man, was an excellent choice for Secretary–Treasurer. Ed Hall, with a good union background, was also a good choice. Walter Wells, a highly skilled master mechanic with a good union background, was the only officer selected from Michigan, the center of the industry.

An eleven-man Executive Board was chosen by regions. They were to serve without salary but would be paid for time lost and travel expenses. It was the thinking of the delegates that this Board, meeting twice a year and coming directly from the shops, would ensure an organization that represented the thinking of the membership. The policy of an Executive Board serving without salary was soon abandoned, however. Within a year, they voted themselves a salary.

The convention adjourned, the delegates went home, and the officers went to Detroit to assume their duties. We were at last masters of our own future. Mistakes and blunders would be our own and the sense of responsibility rested heavily on our shoulders.

Our first blunder had been the election of Homer Martin as president. I was apprehensive at the time of his election. But I had no idea how disastrous a choice it would prove to be. As the first President of the United Automobile Workers of America, he turned out to be a colossal liability to this young union that was destined to make labor history. He was a former Baptist minister from Leeds, Missouri, but he had been unfrocked for conduct unbecoming a man of God. We had only his own version of what it was that aroused his congregation, and whether or not his story was true we never found out, nor were we interested enough to check.

Following his expulsion from the ministry he took a job in a Fisher Body plant in Kansas City. My information is that he spent about two weeks as a worker there, and was fired. This occurred during the Depression years of 1932–1933. Martin had a good platform appearance, and was a trained speaker. These surface aspects, however, concealed an ambitious, unprincipled, and unscrupulous demagogue. Realizing his lack of experience and familiarity with the labor movement, and knowing nothing whatever of the problems confronting the membership, he sought counsel and advice from David Dubinsky of the International Ladies' Garment Workers Union (ILGWU). Dubinsky was as ignorant of the auto workers' problems as Martin himself. It appears, however, that Martin was not interested in the auto workers' problems so much as he was in his own problem, which was to remain in the Presidency of the international union without any knowledge whatsoever of the industry, or of the men and women he was supposed to represent.

Martin did not confide in the other officers of the UAW, all of whom had years of experience in the various automobile plants. George Addes, Ed Hall, Walter Wells, and I had all spent a good part of our lives as auto workers. We knew their problems and talked their language. But it appears that that was precisely why Martin mistrusted and feared us.

Dubinsky introduced Martin to Jay Lovestone, a former Communist leader who had been thrown out of the Party as a factionalist and a disruptive influence. From then on, for all practical purposes, Lovestone directed the affairs of the UAW through the office of President Martin. Henry Kraus, the editor and creator of *The United Automobile Worker,* the official publication of the international union, was fired and replaced by Bill Munger, a follower of Lovestone, who also served as Research Director.

Through the Lovestone apparatus, disruptive questions would be raised in the meetings of the Executive Board and meetings of the officers, thus preventing discussion of issues vital to the union.

CHAPTER EIGHT

WE GO INTO ACTION

fter taking in the independent unions soon after the convention, we had a total membership of 25,000 out of a potential one million auto workers. Many of these had become disillusioned and mistrustful of any organization that claimed affiliation with the AFL. Now that we had disaffiliated, to use President Lewis's term, they were willing to join up.[14]

Our first and most important task was to bring organization to the unorganized auto workers. The only money we had was the $25,000 treasury that Dillon had turned over to us. We had, however, something that money could not buy. We had confidence and a spirit of sacrifice that eventually enabled us to accomplish what many had thought was impossible.

We spent the first month after the convention in surveying the situation in the industry. After thoroughly discussing all angles of the problem, we decided that our main effort must be to strike General Motors after the Christmas holidays. We set January 1, 1937, as the deadline. The time to prepare for this strike was very short, and to think of organizing the vast GM empire in six months was almost unrealistic. Obviously, some unusual strategies and tactics would have to be devised.

Through John Anderson, President of local 155 (Tool and Die), we learned that the General Motors Corporation had made but two sets of dies. One set was installed on the huge presses in Fisher Body plant #1 in Flint. This set stamped the body components for Buicks, Pontiacs, and Oldsmobiles. The second set was installed on the presses in Fisher Body, Cleveland. It made all the stampings for Chevrolet.[15] It seemed logical then for us to concentrate our major efforts on organizing these two Fisher Body plants, since if we could strike them effectively, we could paralyze all GM operations. The Fisher Body plant in Cleveland was already fairly well organized, since that was my home town, but I was a total stranger to Flint.

Early in June, 1936, I went to Flint, the center of General Motors operations and power. I registered at a cheap hotel (The Dresden) obtaining a room costing twelve dollars a week. I had barely time to remove my coat when the phone rang. A voice said, "You had better get the hell back where you came from if you don't want to be carried out in a wooden box!"

"How would you like to go to hell?" I shot back, but the person had hung up. I was fifty-two years old and nobody had taken me out in a box yet; I'd be damned if this was going to be the first time! I ignored the phone call, which I attributed to the Black Legion, and proceeded to plan my work.

I began by making a survey of the problem facing me. I spent a week asking questions and gathering information. To organize this town that was so completely under the control of General Motors would not be easy, to put it mildly. A cloud of fear hung over the city, and it was next to impossible to find anyone who would even discuss the question of unionsm.[16]

Every GM employee was compelled, as a condition of employment, to join the International Motors Association, a company union. The dues in the company union were thirty-five cents a month, which was checked off, and with this thirty-five cents, the corporation published a slick-sheet magazine, designed to sell company policy to its workers, who were forced to pay for the poison given to them regularly. From these funds the corporation also built the IMA building, the only auditorium in town, and sponsored tremendous sports programs and various other activities. All this was insurance against unions, by creating the "one big happy family" atmosphere in which such nasty things as labor unions were not supposed to take root and flourish.

A city ordinance forbade the distribution of leaflets or literature of any kind. Another ordinance forbade the use of sound equipment. Legislation had been passed that made illegal any and all of the customary methods of reaching masses of people. It was clear that the job of organizing Flint would have to be done quietly with no publicity, and mostly at night, at least in the early stages. If we held open meetings, two kinds of people would come; one would be the very ardent union people who were willing to stick their necks out; the other would be company spies who would promptly report the good people, who would then be fired.

I went to the Pengelly Building on Beach Street, where the remnants of five auto locals still occupied offices. These five locals, which had been chartered by Francis Dillon, now had a combined membership of 122, out of a potential of 45,000. This was all that was left of the thousands of members that the AFL had once had in Buick, Chevrolet, Fisher #1, Fisher #2, and AC Spark Plug. Every member who had shown aggressive leadership qualities had been fingered as a Red and fired from his job, with the representatives of the AFL refusing to protect him. In this manner the leadership had been destroyed.

I soon learned that the vast majority of the GM workers regarded these 122 men as paid agents of General Motors and would have nothing to do with them. I did not have then, nor do I have now, any information that would prove that all of them were informers. Some of them surely were, as we learned later through the activities of the La Follette Committee.

I recommended to the international Executive Board that the five charters be revoked and that one charter be issued, covering all the GM plants in Flint. This new charter was issued. It became local 156. Having revoked all five charters, I seized all membership and financial records. The recommendation that one charter be issued was for organizational reasons only. I knew that separate charters would be required later. The vast majority of Flint workers were suspicious of the 122 union members, and since I had come to organize the workers of Flint,

I could not ignore this fact. It was clear I would somehow have to bypass these 122 men.

I recommended that an election of officers for the newly chartered local union be postponed until such time as there were at least a thousand dues-paying members in the new local union. Homer Martin, supported by Adolph Germer, convinced the other officers that an election must be held at once. Germer was not an official, nor even a member of the UAW. He was the representative of John L. Lewis, who had assigned him to assist the UAW. I was very much opposed to an election, since the only people eligible to vote were the 122 mistrusted members of the five defunct locals. I argued with Martin, Germer, and the other officers because "I cannot see where the democratic process is being served by allowing 122 men to elect officers of a local union whose potential membership is 45,000," I told them. "Moreover, for these 122 men to be in charge of this new local union means that I will have to bypass them if the campaign to organize Flint is to succeed."

President Martin was very insistent that an election be held. "We just cannot begin to build our international union by denying the local unions the right to elect their own officers," he argued and cited the case of President Green's denial of the right of the auto workers to elect their own officers. I could not, and do not now, see that there was any parallel. I was very much opposed to placing this new local union in the hands of men so mistrusted by the workers. I did not know then, but learned, later, that these 122 men were already in touch with Martin. Steps had been taken to sabotage all my efforts to organize Flint.

I met with George Addes, our Secretary-Treasurer, and arranged to have all applications for membership, initiation fees, and dues handled through his office. No application cards would be revealed to anyone except George Addes and myself.

This was a cumbersome arrangement, so it was later decided, with the approval of the international officers, that I open an account in my name in a Flint bank, and that all money received would be deposited in it. I did not like this idea at all, but Martin argued that the money must be handled in this way to circumvent the possibility of its being seized by court order. I refused to comply with this plan except upon written order of President Martin. This written order was furnished. The account then became known as the "Mortimer account." Later on it became known as the "Mortimer–Travis account."

I bought a copy of the Flint Directory which contained the names, addresses, and occupations of all residents in Flint. From the directory, and also from the membership lists of the five defunct locals, I compiled a mailing list of about five thousand names. I composed a letter each week and mailed it to the homes of these five thousand workers. These letters were short, but to the point. Each letter dealt with a specific issue, and each letter hammered home the fact that the answer to this problem was the union. Here is an example of such a letter:

> Fellow Worker:
>
> What does the future hold for you as a worker in the automobile industry? Does it offer you security?
>
> Do you face the future unafraid? When your children come out of school, what are their prospects for the future? Do you think GM will be kinder to them than to you?
>
> What will become of your aged parents? Are they thrown aside to live as best as they can after a lifetime of hard labor?
>
> Is the wife you promised to love, honor, and cherish able to enjoy the goods things of life she's entitled to? And is she not as precious to you as the employer's wife is to him? And are your children not as sweet and lovable as his?
>
> Why, as an American, do you permit this intolerable discrimination against you and yours?
>
> You know that you and your family are being deprived of much that belongs to you, and the remedy is in your hands.
>
> Sign the enclosed card for membership in the United Automobile Workers, CIO, and join with many of your fellow workers who have decided that in unity there will be found the strength needed to right many wrongs.

If you wish to speak to me personally, indicate this in the square provided for that purpose.

Fraternally,
Wyndham Mortimer

I composed the letters and then they were mimeographed in Detroit and mailed directly to the homes of the Flint workers. Another letter read:

Dear Fellow Worker:

It is fear of losing the job that keeps you from signing an application for membership in the union. I do not blame anyone for protecting his job, because a job is as necessary to the working man or woman as land is to the farmer, or a ship to a sailor. It means food on the table, clothing for the family, and a roof over their heads.

But the hard cold fact is that you will lose that job sooner or later. If you do not lose it as a result of joining the union, you will lose it because a new machine will replace you, or the boss's son, just out of school, will need it, or because gray hairs will appear around your brow.

You will then be too old to find another worthwhile job, and there will be no union to protect you. You will lose the job for any number of reasons beyond your control, because the job does not belong to you. It belongs to General Motors, and your chances of keeping that job will be infinitely better when you join with your fellows in a union, and fight for job security through seniority.

Sign the enclosed application card. Put it in the mailbox in a sealed envelope, and let me know if you desire to talk to me confidentially.

Fraternally,
Wyndham Mortimer

Many of these letters found their way into the plant and were read along the assembly lines. They had a powerful impact. Applications were returned by some of the workers, who requested me to call on them. I did so and would ask the applicant and his wife to invite trusted friends to a house party. Only those they invited would be present. I would arrange with the wife to serve any refreshments she desired, and the union would take care of the expenses. Such parties became very frequent, and many applications were obtained in this way.

A Buick worker, Ed Geiger, one of the 122 members still paying dues, offered to go with me and meet former active union members. I accepted his offer and he introduced me to a number of men and women who had been very active in the former federal unions, but who since had left the union. These people would invariably tell the same story. They would say, "Oh, we don't need a union. Everything is fine." After a week of this I decided to visit these same people myself and see if their attitude was the same.

There was a remarkable difference in the way I was received. I was told not to bring Geiger or anyone else from local 156. I do not mean to cast any doubts on Ed Geiger as a union man. All I want to show is that the auto workers of Flint were thoroughly disillusioned with the AFL in 1936, and since Geiger was a member of the Executive Board of local 156 they were suspicious of him. My own personal opinion is that Ed Geiger was an honest man, but fear and suspicion were strong against these men, and since I had a job to do, I was compelled to take this into account. From then on I was careful not to be seen in the company of any of these 122 men.

One person I visited along with Geiger was a Belgian woman. She really went all out in telling me how wonderful things were and what a wonderful employer GM was. I returned and talked to her by myself. Her husband had just arrived home from the forge shop. They invited me in and insisted that I stay and have supper with them. She wanted to know why I traveled around with a stool pigeon. I explained that I was a total stranger in Flint and that Geiger had offered to introduce me to former union people. I said, "Stool pigeon or not, if it were not for Geiger, I would not have met such good union people as you and your husband." Both were active in a Belgian lodge or fraternal order and through her husband I was asked to speak to its membership, practically all of whom were working in the forge shop. I was assured that the workers wanted and needed a union very badly, but their experience with the federal unions under the Collins–Dillon AFL leadership had made them extremely cautious.

The most capable local leaders from the federal unions were now walking the street unemployed. They had been fingered as Communists by Collins and Dillon. They were fired and blacklisted by General Motors. The federal unions they had helped to build were not permitted to help them in any way. Any move to protect them was denounced on the ground that the union could not defend or protect Communists.

I inquired of Geiger whom I should contact among the Negro people. He was obviously anti-Negro. He refused to go with me and said he wanted "nothing to do with the black bastards." He did tell me, however, that the most influential man among the Negro people was "Old Jim." He turned out to be about sixty, with snow-white hair. He was intelligent and well-informed. We sat on the porch, and he told me of the many shabby and mean things his people had to endure while they were members of the federal union. Negroes were refused admittance to dances, picnics, or any other social activities sponsored by the federal unions. Nor would these unions do anything to help the Negro people break down GM's unfair hiring practices. They were limited to janitorial and foundry work, where the labor was hot, hard, and heavy. And, I should add, extremely dirty. Buick employed about 4,000 Negroes.[17]

This man told me to contact his son-in-law, a young man whose name was Henry Clark. I visited Mr. Clark in the early evening when he and his wife were sitting down to supper. They asked me to eat with them. We talked as we ate. I spent the evening in their home and our conversation revealed that they were much more aware of the problems confronting the working people than were the white victims of GM's exploitation.

Henry Clark agreed to do what he could to help organize Flint. I gave him a number of application cards and instructed him to get them signed, and to collect a one-dollar initiation fee. I told him, further, not to take a chance with his job. I said, "Henry, I hope no one loses his job in building the union, but if anyone is to be fired, let it be a white man!" We would be challenging double jeopardy in trying to restore the job of a black man.

A short time later, I found a note under my hotel room door. It was hard to read because so many grimy hands had handled it. It said, "Tonight at midnight," followed by a number on Industrial Avenue. It was signed, "Henry." Promptly at midnight, I was at the number he had given. It was a small church and was totally dark. I rapped on the door and waited. Soon the door was opened and I went inside. The place was lighted by a small candle, carefully shaded to prevent light showing. Inside there were eighteen men, all of them Negroes and all of them from the Buick foundry. I told them why I was in Flint, what I hoped to do in the way of improving conditions and raising their living standards. A question period followed. The questions were interesting in that they dealt with the union's attitude toward discrimination and with what the union's policy was toward bettering the very bad conditions of the Negro people. One of them said, "You see, we have all the problems and worries of the white folks, and then we have one more: we are Negroes."

I pointed out that the old AFL leadership was gone. The CIO had a new program with a new leadership that realized that none of us was free unless we were all free. Part of our program was to fight Jim Crow. Our program would have a much better chance of success if the Negro worker joined with us and added his voice and presence on the union floor. Another man arose and asked, "Will we have a local union of our own?" I replied, "We are not a Jim Crow union, nor do we have any second-class citizens in our membership!"

The meeting ended with eighteen application cards signed and eighteen dollars in initiation fees collected. I cautioned them not to stick their necks out, but quietly to get their fellow workers to sign application cards and arrange other meetings under the leadership of Henry Clark.

The Black Legion

In our campaign to organize the GM workers we had to contend with one of the most sinister, evil, and cowardly organizations that ever appeared on the American scene—the Black Legion.

Fisher #1 employed about eight thousand workers in 1936. The Black Legion boasted a membership of three thousand in the plant at that time. Its membership was composed exclusively of *white, protestant, gentile, native-born individuals*. This fascist outfit was another powerful obstacle put in the path of the union. But the courage of those who defied it, and the fact that the front man of this sick organization was exposed shortly before our big organizational drive got under way, were very helpful in preventing their doing us real damage.

This group did not stop at murder if it served their ends. A number of union organizers had, in past years, been found shot. A bullet would be left on their chests and applications for membership in the union were found scattered about.

An abandoned Baptist church at Ledyard Street and Second Boulevard in Detroit was the headquarters of this murderous outfit. In the basement of the church was a laboratory they planned to use for making cultures of typhoid fever germs, which were to be placed in the milk left at the homes of Jewish, Negro, and Catholic families. This horrible scheme was never implemented because the law was on their trail.

Their trigger-man was named Dayton Dean, a mentally retarded individual who was arrested for the murder of a young man, Charles Poole. Poole was a Catholic who had committed the horrible crime of marrying a Protestant girl. Dean boastfully admitted to the murder of several other people.

It was generally believed that Henry Ford and the Ford Motor Company were behind this criminal organization. There were some investigations along this line by a journalist named John Spivak. His findings were inconclusive but the general impression was that Henry Ford was not blameless. The older Ford's outspoken anti-Semitism was notorious.[18]

The startling fact, however, was that such an organization could take deep root among the working people of America. It is frightening when thousands of ordinary working men and women can be convinced that the cause of their misery and poverty is the Jewish people, the Negro people, the Catholic people, and the Communists. But such was the case. The coming of the CIO industrial unions revealed who the real enemy was. It demonstrated, too, that once the American working class recognizes their real enemy, their courage in combating that enemy knows no bounds.

Although as I previously stated, the city of Flint had enacted ordinances prohibiting the distribution of leaflets, I felt the time had come to challenge these laws. I decided to make regular distribution of *The United Auto Worker* at the gates of the five major GM plants. This job required a number of people who would be willing to pass out the papers and take the chance of being arrested, or even of getting beaten up by the police.

I met with the Executive Board of local 156 and requested that they assume this responsibility. They agreed, and a schedule of distribution was made. I went to Fisher #1 gates at shift change but there were no distributors or any sign of them. I returned to the Pengelly Building and the papers were gone. I later found them at the bottom of an abandoned elevator shaft in the building, where they had been thrown. The following week they were thrown under a culvert on Dort Highway.

I decided to make other arrangements and contacted a former Buick worker whose name was Charles Killinger. He was one of the former active unionists who had been fingered by Collins as a Communist. Killinger had a wife and seven or eight children and was still unemployed. He agreed to make the distribution. With the help of his wife and children the papers were distributed every week. His wife was arrested one day; she had chained herself to a railing while she passed out papers. She had a chain and a padlock, so the authorities couldn't get her away from the railing, and she kept passing out the papers all the while they were trying to get her loose. She got a lot of newspaper publicity doing this. From then on the paper was handed out regularly in spite of police harassment.

Bypassing local 156 and refusing to reveal the number of applications or the names of those who had joined the union aroused the animosity of the local Executive Board. I knew they were in almost daily contact with President Martin and that Martin was encouraging them in their opposition to me. He had expressed the hope to them that I would run into a stone wall in Flint.

The Executive Board of local 156 used the old and discredited Red smear. They reported to President Martin that "Mortimer is building a Red empire in Flint." What a "Red empire" was I never found out. I was supposed to be in the pay of Moscow. However, since the influence of these men with the Flint auto workers was nil, I ignored their opposition and continued to work my plan.

Typical of their disruptive methods was the creation of an investigating committee. They summoned me to appear before them. When I complied, I was informed that the local union had established this committee, whose function was to investigate all new applicants for membership. The following dialogue took place:

MORTIMER: What is the purpose of such an investigation?

MINZEY: It has always been the practice here in Flint to investigate all new applicants.

MORTIMER: Investigate for what? What are you looking for?

MINZEY: We want to be sure there are no stool pigeons joining the union.

MORTIMER: Just how do you tell who is, or is not, a stool pigeon? Do stool pigeons have some identifying feature? I am aware of the role that has been played by stool pigeons in the past, and there is no doubt in my mind that GM employs plenty of them now, but, as far as this union is concerned, there is but one qualification for membership. Does the applicant work for General Motors? If he is in the employ of General Motors, then he belongs in the union. There will be no investigation, no revealing of names on applications as long as I am in charge here in Flint, nor as far as our international union is concerned.

Besides, this union is not interested, nor can it be

properly interested in any worker's view on politics, economics, religion, or anything else. I am not looking for ways to keep people *out* of the union. I am looking for ways to get them in.

I arose and left the meeting.

This maneuver was clearly not meant to uncover stool pigeons. It was an effort to obtain the names and addresses of new applicants as well as to keep out the union people who might become rivals for leadership. If successful, such a maneuver would certainly have prevented any sort of mass organization from ever being built in Flint.

House meetings were increasing in number. New applications were being signed at an increasing rate. I was getting many letters from workers urging me to keep up the campaign. Many letters contained information and advice from which I was able to write some very effective letters that were now going into Flint homes every week.

During this period I met a cleaning woman whose job it was to clean up the offices of Chevrolet in Flint. I asked her what she did with the papers she found in wastepaper baskets. She said, "I burn them." I asked her to give them to me as I wanted to find out something. She would put the contents of the wastepaper baskets in a sack and drop them off at the union office for me. Looking over this material I was amazed. Numerous slips of paper would read something like this, "Today at lunch, Badge Number so-and-so said that if he was going to buy a car it was not going to be a blankety-blank Chevy. Signed, K7." Each spy had a number and a letter.

Or another one, "I saw Badge Number so-and-so hide a copy of the union paper in his tool box this morning. Signed, G8," or whatever his symbol was. These short reports were apparently read by personnel, and the information was passed on to the plant manager. The reports were then discarded. Many auto workers lost their jobs without knowing why. The answers were to be found in those reports.

Organization was gathering speed, and as more workers joined the union, the Executive Board of local 156 became desperate and began making daily phone calls to President Martin. Martin, in turn, was urging the board to put as many obstacles in my path as they possibly could.

It was a strange situation for the President of the international union to ally himself with this group of a dozen men in an effort to prevent his own Vice-President from continuing a successful organizing campaign. Looking back now, after a quarter of a century, it is hard to believe that such conniving was possible. But such was the case.

President Martin wanted badly to remove me from Flint. He was at a loss, however, to find a reason or excuse to do so. He would call me and speak of urgent matters that needed attention in New York, Indiana, and elsewhere. I reminded him that the most urgent problem confronting the international union was the Flint campaign. All our plans depended on the success of my efforts in Flint. How could we hope to storm the fortress of General Motors without Flint?

The organizing went on, meetings became more frequent. I couldn't possibly take care of all of them, so I had other organizers come in. I brought in Roy Reuther, the younger brother of Walter Reuther. Bob Travis and Henry Kraus came up; a fellow named Ralph Dale from Wisconsin and a fellow from the rubber workers came and gave us some help. With these four working with me we bypassed all of the roadblocks that had been set up.

President Martin was still determined to replace me in Flint. He indicated that he was thinking of replacing me with Fred Pieper, the Executive Board member from Atlanta, Georgia. Pieper had been elected to the Executive Board on the expectation that he would devote his time doing some badly needed work in the South, which had but one auto local in the entire region. Pieper was anti-Negro and a Klan type, who boasted of his close connections with the FBI. He seldom went down to his own area. He preferred to stay in Detroit and help Martin sabotage the union. I told Martin that under no circumstances would I leave Flint in Pieper's charge.

One day in September, 1936, Fred Pieper appeared in Flint, accompanied by Bob Travis from Toledo. Travis was a worker

I knew well and trusted. The first chance he got, he called me aside and explained that Martin had sent him and Pieper to Flint to check on my work and activities. I knew Travis to be a dedicated and honest man. I had every confidence in him. But the exact opposite was true of Pieper. I never found out what Pieper's report to Martin was. I did see Travis' report and it was favorable to my handling of the campaign in Flint. Why President Martin had sent these two men to "investigate" me, I leave to the reader's judgment.

A short time later, Travis called me and asked why I was not at the meeting in the international office. I asked, "What meeting?" He told me that Martin had called a special meeting to discuss the situation in Flint. I immediately drove to Detroit and arrived while the meeting was still under way.

Present were the entire Executive Board of local 156, also Martin, Vice-President Ed Hall, Secretary–Treasurer George F. Addes, and Fred Pieper. I demanded to know why I was not notified of this meeting, since it was called especially to discuss the Flint campaign. Martin nervously turned to his secretary, Miss Loewe. "Why did you not notify Vice-President Mortimer of this meeting?" She replied, "I did not send him a notice because you told me not to." Complete silence fell over the meeting.

At this point, Ed Hall, who was famous for his colorful vocabulary, burst out with some very descriptive language, and wanted to know, "What in the hell is going on here?" George Addes, a soft-spoken, gentlemanly sort of person asked whose idea this meeting was, adding that he knew definitely that I was doing a good job in Flint, that I was really organizing GM there. Turning to the members of the local 156 Executive Board, Ed Hall asked, "How many applications have you fellows written up in the past three months?" The answer was none. He said, "Don't you fellows think you have a lot of guts coming to Detroit and complaining about Mort when the whole lot of you have failed to sign up one new member?"

The meeting broke up with the Flint Executive Board group licking their wounds on the way home. They were unable to get any applications for membership signed because their own people in Flint, the people who knew them best, would have nothing to do with them. They had failed in their mission, which was to replace me with Fred Pieper.

Anger was not the word to describe my thoughts and feelings. The meeting having ended, President Martin turned to me and said, "Brother Mortimer, you must think I am a heel." I answered, "What in the hell would you think?" and walked out. I returned to Flint with Henry Kraus and his wife, Dorothy. Henry, of course, was editor of *The United Auto Worker,* and we began to print a Flint edition of the paper called *The Flint Auto Worker*. Dorothy became active among the women and did wonderful work. I had already formed a committee of the most active and militant workers. On this committee were Bud Simons, Jay Green, Joe Devitt, Doc Maddock, Vic Van Etten, and Walter Moore, all from Fisher #1.

At a meeting of the organizing committee in Fisher #1, I revealed that I was planning to return to Detroit but that I would not do so until I was sure that a dedicated and dependable person would take my place. I told them there was one man I would agree should take my place—Robert Travis. If Travis should take over, I added, I wanted them to give him every cooperation possible. Just when this would happen depended upon President Martin, I said.

I arranged a meeting with Martin, Ed Hall, and George Addes. I told Martin that I would leave Flint and return to Detroit on one condition. That condition was that Bob Travis be assigned to take over the Flint organizing campaign. Martin readily agreed to this, so eager was he to get me out of Flint, and I returned to my office in Detroit. I did, however, remain in Flint for a time and then made frequent trips back there to help Travis get acquainted with the situation. Travis continued the policy I had inaugurated.

A few words of explanation are necessary in regard to the bank account mentioned earlier, which was known as the "Mortimer–Travis account." This account was used later by the Homer Martin–Jay Lovestone cabal to discredit Travis and me. Approximately $200,000 passed through this account, although it was never very large at any particular time, because the demands made upon it were constant. Both Travis and I, all through the great sit-down, wrote checks to cover such things as coal, food, clothes, rent, and the hundreds of things the families of the strikers needed. Not one penny of this money found its way anywhere else. Yet President Martin, during the bitter factionalism that followed the strike settlement, appeared in Flint and, at a mass meeting in the Pengelly Building, claimed that Travis and I had looted the account. He said, "Almost two hundred thousand dollars passed through this account and the account is now depleted. I ask you, where did that money go?"

I entered the hall just as he was finishing his tirade. As soon as Martin got through talking, I grabbed the mike and began to talk.

"President Martin has asked you where the money went," I began. "I will tell you where it went." And I talked about how we had organized and how the strike had come. For forty-three days there was no work in Flint, and our members' problems had become more and more serious. I turned to one woman and said, "Mrs. Perkins, you came to me, did you not, several times for money? Didn't you come to me and tell me that you couldn't pay your rent? Did I pay it for you? And didn't you tell me you needed coal in the house, and that your children needed shoes? Were you ever refused any help?"

I went around the audience to about a dozen others, and by this time the meeting was getting quite excited. Many volunteered to tell about the help they had received. One woman told how one of her children was sick and the union had taken him to the hospital and paid the hospital bills. And others brought up other matters of the same nature.

Of course, the whole discussion was actually academic and was of importance merely because Martin tried to make political capital out of it. For without Martin's knowledge, George Addes, Ed Hall, and I had long ago sent a certified public accountant to Flint to audit this account. And in spite of the fact that the money had been handled by girls who had volunteered to do the office work, the CPA found that instead of a shortage, there was actually $52.20 over. I ended by reading the CPA's report. "So the union cost you about $200,000," I said. "Was it worth it?" There was a tremendous roar of approval. I turned to Martin, but he had ducked out while I was talking.

The Midland Steel Strike

Almost simultaneously with the events in Flint a new development took place, one which further illustrated the power of large trade associations, dominated by the huge companies, over the smaller producers.

In November, 1936, there occurred a strike of the Midland Steel Company workers. This company operated two plants at that time. One was located in Cleveland, and the one I refer to was in Detroit. The Detroit plant produced automobile frames for Ford, Plymouth, and others. It was an important feeder plant, and in the highly synchronized automobile industry, the strike's effect was immediate.

Extremely strong pressures were brought against the international union to bring the work stoppage to an end. John Anderson, the international representative, Dick Frankensteen, and I represented the UAW, while a local union bargaining committee represented the local union. The two thousand workers were on a sit-down strike and would not leave the plant. It was the second time the workers had sat down at their place of work. The first instance was at Bendix in South Bend.

From the strike's beginning, we were unable to reach anyone in authority, someone who could give a yes-or-no answer, who had power to make decisions. The Ford Motor Company demanded possession of their dies, and threatened to take its business elsewhere. Ford sent a gang of his "Service" department to remove the dies by force, but the striking workers prevented them by blocking all entrances to the plant with huge piles of crates and debris. They were prepared to do battle if necessary.

During this time, while we were trying to conduct negotiations through personnel and other powerless individuals, Adolph Germer came over hurriedly from the international offices and urged that Frankensteen and I return to the Executive Board at once. He said that board member Pieper was up to no good. Returning to the Executive Board, then in session, we found that Pieper had introduced a resolution that called for a strike of all General Motors plants. At least half of the Board were in agreement. I took issue with this resolution, because it was in direct conflict with the international plans to postpone strike action until after the Christmas holidays, and for other reasons. Moreover, such a fantastic idea was like trying to kill a dog by cutting off its tail one inch at a time. I said that such a resolution smacked of stool pigeon activity.

Pieper, enraged at this remark, strode over toward me, and said, "Don't you call me a stool pigeon." I replied, "Fred, if you don't want to be regarded as a stool pigeon, then for Christ's sake stop acting like one." White with rage, he took his seat and subsided. The resolution was put to a vote and defeated.

We returned to the strike at Midland Steel. Failing to make any progress toward a settlement, and realizing the futility of continued talks with men who lacked authority to make decisions, the Federal mediator who had entered the case suggested that negotiations be moved to the Book–Cadillac Hotel, where someone in authority would be available.

Representing Midland Steel at the Book–Cadillac was a little man, an attorney whose name I do not remember. I recall two things about this man. He smoked cigarettes through a long holder, and his vocabulary consisted of the one word *no*. If his vocabulary was wider than that, no one could prove it.

We went into an all-night session. The weather was cold, and the windows were all closed. In spite of the lack of fresh air, everyone except myself began to smoke cigarettes. In a short time, the atmosphere became impossible, and I left the room for air. I walked down the hallway and heard a man call me. I turned, and there was a man of about middle age who said, "Mortimer, why are you trying to crucify me?" I said, "I didn't know I was trying to crucify anybody, but who are you?" He said he was the owner of Midland Steel. He added that he had just come from Cleveland, where Bob Black had told him I was a very fair-minded and decent person. (Bob Black was President and General Manager of White Motor.)

The hallway was populated with the usual crowd of newsmen, and they began to surround us. He invited me into his suite, which adjoined the room in which we had been negotiating. I went into his room, and he was almost in tears. The substance of his remarks was that he would concede everything the union wanted, but he begged not to be asked to sign anything. He said, "If I sign that contract you have presented to me, I will be out of business tomorrow. I will not be able to buy one pound of steel."

He was right. The Steel Institute was a part of the National Association of Manufacturers' bitterly anti-union policy, and it held the power of life and death over any member or manufacturer that went beyond the narrow guidelines set by their highly paid but stupid attorneys.

I asked him to meet with us in the next room. He agreed, and when his position had been discussed among the bargaining committee, it was agreed to call off the strike. He signed a contract, but it was a contract acceptable to the Steel Institute. The real settlement was verbal, and contained substantially everything demanded by the union. The name of this man who owned Midland Steel escapes me, but if my memory serves me right, and I think it does, he was Chairman of the Republican National Committee at that time.

CHAPTER NINE

THE GREAT GENERAL MOTORS SIT-DOWN

Late in October, something occurred that revealed that our organizing efforts were bearing fruit. Two brothers named Perkins were fired for union activity in Fisher #1. The workers, led by Bud Simons, Walter Moore, Joe Devitt, and Jay Green, stopped work. A committee was selected to meet with the plant manager, Mr. Parker, and demand the immediate rehiring of the Perkins brothers. It was at this meeting that Bud Simons made the now-famous remark, "Mr. Parker, you may not know it, but you are talking to the union right now!"

Every worker refused to resume work until the two fired men were back on the job. General Motors ordered the Police Department to find and bring these two men back to the job. The Flint radio station broadcast spot announcements urging them to return. No work was done, however, until the Perkins boys walked into the plant and resumed their jobs. One of them had gone to the show with his girlfriend, so by the time they were found and brought back to the plant, it was 10:00 P.M.

This incident had a terrific impact on the rest of the workers. A mass meeting of Fisher #1 workers was called for the following evening in the union hall on Saginaw Street. I came up from Detroit to attend the meeting and was overjoyed to see the results of a lot of hard work by Travis and the organizing committee. I also felt a sense of gratification at the results of my own work.

The dark clouds of fear that had hung over Flint were rapidly disappearing. The auto workers were now feeling their strength and power. Fear of the boss had evaporated to the point where the workers were openly talking union. People were now crowding into the office to sign application blanks. Our plans to strike GM around January 1, 1937, were developing nicely.

I made frequent trips to Cleveland, where I conferred with the officers of local 45. I recall meeting with Charles Beckman, John DeVito, Paul Miley, John Troeter, and others. I kept in touch with them constantly. Our reasons for setting the January 1 date were threefold:

> A strike prior to the Christmas holidays would be very bad psychology. We did not want the union going down the workers' chimneys on Christmas Eve with a bag of troubles instead of toys.
>
> General Motors had announced a Christmas bonus of $50 to be paid all its employees on December 18, and a strike would, in all probability, cancel this out. Fifty dollars was a lot of money in 1936. Together with the last pay a family could scrimp along for nearly a month on that.
>
> Frank Murphy would be sworn in as Governor of Michigan on January 1, 1937, and we felt the union would receive better treatment from him than we could expect from his predecessor, Frank Fitzgerald.

Murphy impressed me as a kindly, humane person. I am sure his sympathies were with the auto workers, the people. Fitzgerald, I am sure, would have used the police powers of the State to crush the sit-down strike, but Murphy refrained. Here, I think, was the real test of the man. Murphy was under enormous pressure. He was being attacked from many sides by those who benefit from the status quo, but he knew that the time had come for change in employer–employee relations. While all the legalities of the State, built up over many years, gave the employer tremendous advantages over the working people, Governor Murphy was able to block these advantages and give the auto workers an even chance in their struggle.

There are those who occupy positions of power who will sit on the safety valve until an explosion occurs and its destructive force scatters debris far and wide. But Frank Murphy was not one of these. He knew the tremendous upsurge of the CIO, and the sit-down strikes were something more than just another labor dispute. He knew they were the result of a generations-long orgy of greed and exploitation resulting from a social system whose driving force was profit.

Murphy unquestionably believed in and supported the profit system, but he also believed it must be controlled. Otherwise, like an engine without an operator, it would destroy itself. The best control would be a strong labor movement, and Murphy was for it.

The Big Strike Begins

On December 26, 1936, I was with Bob Travis and Henry Kraus in Travis' room in the Dresden Hotel in Flint, when Louis Spisak, President of the Fisher Body local in Cleveland, telephoned, very excited and obviously upset. He managed to tell me that Fisher–Cleveland was on strike, that they were sitting down. Spisak was a weak leader, and I realized immediately that unless responsibility was taken out of his hands, the whole strike could be lost. I assured him I was leaving for Cleveland at once and that he was to sit tight, make no commitments whatsoever to anyone until I arrived on the 6:00 P.M. train. Upon my arrival in Cleveland, I was surrounded by newsmen. They wanted to know if I had come to settle the strike. Would I meet with Mayor Burton? Would I meet with the Fisher Body management? "No! That is all out!" I told them. However, I was told that Louis Spisak had already met with Mayor Burton, and that he wanted to settle the strike. I said, "President Spisak does not have the authority to settle this strike. The whole matter is now in the hands of the international union."

I went at once to the Fisher plant on Coit Road. The building was surrounded by hundreds of mounted police, who refused entry to anyone. The workers were in possession of the plant, and their morale was exceedingly high. I spoke to them over a public address system, and told them the international union would support them all the way. I said, "Keep up the fight, fellows, we are going to win this one!" I arranged a meeting with the Executive Board of the local at once.

Present were Spisak, Charles Beckman, John DeVito, and Jerry Strauss who had all come out of the plant to attend. Paul Miley remained in the plant in charge of the strike. We lost no time in coming to a decision. We issued a press statement to the effect that the strike could and would be settled only as a part of a national agreement with the General Motors Corporation, and that there would be no talks with local management or city officials.

The die was cast. The strikers were elated. At long last, the discredited leadership of the AFL had been discarded. The auto manufacturers could no longer count on the collective dotage of a moribund AFL Executive Council to help them out. Now the accumulated grievances of half a century of the open shop would be fought out.

I called Bob Travis in Flint and told him to close down Fisher #1, as soon as possible. Before going to my daughter's home for the night (she was now Mrs. Duaine Stewart, and living in Cleveland; Margaret and I had moved to Detroit), I received a wire from John L. Lewis, congratulating me on the press statement and pledging all-out support.

GM Gives Us an Assist

On December 29, 1936, the General Motors Corporation secretly began to remove important dies from Fisher #1. The purpose was to get them out of this union "hotbed." One of the workers on the night shift, John Ananich, called Travis and said, "They are going to move the dies out, Bob!" Travis, who was quick to make decisions, told Ananich to get some of the other union men and to stop the dies from being moved. Travis then called the office girl, Hazel Simon, and told her to put the flicker on. The flicker was a two hundred watt bulb over the union hall across the street from the plant. When it was on, it meant that something of importance was happening, so at lunchtime the workers came streaming across the street to the union hall.

The meeting was short and to the point. Travis told them that the dies meant their jobs, and if they permitted the dies to be taken away, many of them would be unemployed. The workers decided to strike the plant, and to sit in and protect their jobs. It was a crucial decision, since if the workers went home over the weekend, and New Year's Day following, they would be leaving their jobs unprotected and the dies could be moved without opposition. The workers went directly from the meeting and took over the plant. They shouted from the windows to Travis and Kraus, "She is all ours, Bob." The strike started in Cleveland had now been confirmed. Thus began the historic forty-four-day sit-down strike, on December 30, 1936. A fine story of this great struggle was written by Henry Kraus in his book, *The Many and the Few*.

With the two key body plants solidly on strike, the long-planned battle was on. With the Cleveland Fisher Body plant under the able and militant leadership of Beckman, DeVito, and Miley (Spisak, having proved too weak, was bypassed), there was no possibility of the struggle being short-circuited by local maneuverings and negotiations such as Mayor Burton had attempted. I returned to Flint and Detroit.

I had no illusions about the struggle we were in. It was certain that so powerful an enemy as General Motors, supported by every open-shop employer in America, would use every weapon at its command including the courts, the police, the newspapers, the radio, and demagogues like Father Coughlin who joined Frank Norris, the howling Baptist from Fort Worth, in denouncing the union and its leadership as Reds.

The sit-downers in Fisher #1 immediately began to organize the strike. They held an election. Walter Moore, a Communist, was elected Mayor, with a council of ten. Mayor Moore appointed a Chief of Police, whose duty it was to maintain order. The strikers' police chief immediately asked the company police to leave. They complied and the entire Fisher #1 plant was now controlled by the strikers. A Sanitary Engineer was appointed to see that everything was kept clean and orderly. It is a widely accepted fact that the factory was kept cleaner and more orderly than it ever was before.

A restaurant owner near the union hall turned over his kitchen and all the equipment to the strikers for the duration. The union employed a professional cook, Max Gazan, from the Detroit Cooks' Union. Each day a detail of strikers was sent to help in the kitchen, to serve as bus boys, to wash dishes, and to prepare the food. The strike was conducted like a well-run household. Liquor was banned from the plant and every precaution was taken to prevent disruptive elements from causing trouble. The sit-down strike aroused immediate and worldwide attention. Every news agency and publication of consequence had reporters stationed in Flint and Detroit. Many stories went over the wires about this remarkably effective strike, which within a few days paralyzed every General Motors plant in the United States.

Some stories were true. Some of them were half true, and some were downright falsehoods, written to create dissension between strikers and their wives. The *Flint Journal* printed a story to the effect that a flu epidemic had broken out among the strikers. Understandably, many of the wives were deeply concerned. The union promptly sent in a doctor and a nurse, who examined every man in the plant. Their report revealed one man with a slight cold but no evidence of flu whatsoever. Other stories hinted darkly about women of easy virtue entering the plant at night. All such attempts at destroying unity and morale were quickly exposed.

Help was given generously to all in need. Money for this purpose came from the Mortimer–Travis account. Food, clothing, coal, rent, medicine were readily available. President Lewis wired the union that unlimited funds would be available in support of the strike. Thousands of dollars came from the United Mine Workers, the Amalgamated Clothing Workers, the Rubber Workers, and many other unions.

The strike was less than a week old when Judge Edward D.

Black, of the Detroit Circuit Court, issued an injunction ordering the strikers to vacate the plants. Brilliant work by attorneys Maurice Sugar and Lee Pressman revealed the fact that Judge Black was a heavy owner of General Motors stock, over $200,000 worth, in fact. Under a Michigan law prohibiting any judge with a financial interest in any case from sitting on it, Judge Black's injunction was null and void.

The Battle of Bulls Run

The strike was peaceful. Too peaceful, in fact, for General Motors. The corporation needed violence, some reason for police action that would force the hand of Governor Murphy. Murphy had not used the police power of the State against the strikers, contrary to all previous practice. The police had always been used to club and intimidate striking workers, whether strikes were peaceful or not. The Flint police and in fact the entire city government were subservient to General Motors, and they precipitated the first violence of the strike, when on January 11 they stopped a truck carrying food to the strikers in Fisher #2, a small plant that had quickly followed Fisher #1 in sitting down.

Travis immediately mobilized all available pickets around this plant. Picket lines had now been strengthened by many hundreds from other shops. Joe Ditzel, for example, had brought well over a hundred from as far away as Local 12 in Toledo. A battle began between the strikers and the police when the police attempted to force their way into the plant. This battle has gone down in American labor history as the "Battle of Bulls Run."

The strikers inside the plant drenched the police with high-pressure fire hoses, and pelted them with bottles, automobile door hinges, and anything available. The pickets outside joined the battle. The temperature was near zero, and the drenched police quickly retreated to the Chevrolet plant across the street. Another wave of police attempted to gain entry but met the same strong resistance. They, too, were swept off their feet, drenched by fire hoses. Their uniforms quickly froze on their bodies and they, in turn, withdrew. Thirty-six police were sent to Hurley

Hospital suffering from light to severe bruises, while five of the strikers were wounded by gunfire. The battle lasted about six hours, when the police finally withdrew, licking their wounds.

Injunction #2

On January 25, General Motors went into the court of Judge Paul V. Gadola, asking for a mandatory injunction, which, if issued, would compel immediate evacuation of the plants. Keep in mind the fact that the Supreme Court of Michigan had previously ruled that there was no such thing as peaceful picketing, thereby outlawing picketing as a weapon in labor's hands. This injunction then, if granted, would leave the union legally defenseless and unable to prevent the corporation from reopening its plants.

Judge Gadola issued a show cause order and set hearings on the injunction for Monday, February 1. Representing the union at the hearing were Maurice Sugar and Lee Pressman. It was clear from the first that Judge Gadola would issue the injunction, and he did. Then began an intensive discussion among the international union officers over what course to pursue.

President Martin had summoned attorney Larry Davidow for a legal opinion. Why Martin had summoned Davidow mystified me. We already had the two best labor lawyers in America and they were doing a fine job. I listened to Davidow's advice and was amazed. Davidow's plan to beat the injunction was to take the case out of Judge Gadola's court and transfer it to the Federal Court in Bay City. I objected. "Larry," I told him, "I am not an attorney but it appears to me there is a better answer than that. I want another opinion on this. I want to talk to Maurice Sugar."

President Martin asked Davidow whether he had any objections to Maurice Sugar coming in, Davidow said he had none, and I immediately phoned Sugar. George Addes and Ed Hall had supported my position. We knew that Maurice Sugar was tops as a labor attorney. His practice was overwhelmingly labor and civil rights cases. I was at a loss to understand why Martin was maneuvering Sugar out of the picture and replacing him with Davidow, who had far less labor law experience and ability.

Sugar came right over to the international office in the Hofmann Building, and Davidow explained the plan. Sugar disagreed with the proposed strategy. "This present injunction," he explained, "depends on Governor Murphy for enforcement. If the matter is taken to Bay City, we will be dealing with the Department of Justice and the Federal marshals. Now, in which of the two would we have the fairest hearing? My advice is, let's leave the case where it is. I know Frank Murphy. We were graduated from law school together, and, believe me, our best chance is with him."

Davidow lacked that quality that inspired confidence in people like Addes, Hall, and me. He was too devious, and his legal advice was questionable. But had I not raised an objection, and had I not been supported by Addes and Hall, Martin would assuredly have taken Davidow's advice, and the consequences would have been disastrous.

Sit-down in Plant #4

The union's answer to Judge Gadola's injunction and the back-to-work movement begun by GM was a sit-down strike in plant #4 of Chevrolet. This was the engine assembly department, and while the entire General Motors empire would still be paralyzed by the strikes in Fisher #1 and Fisher–Cleveland, this strike in plant #4 demonstrated the union's ability to spread the strike wherever necessary. It was the chief factor that caused General Motors to reply favorably to a letter from Governor Murphy requesting a meeting between the company and the union.

During the six weeks of the strike, I was in frequent contact with John L. Lewis in Washington. I kept him informed of developments almost daily, and during the "Battle of Bulls Run" I was in hourly contact with him.

GM Agrees to Negotiate

Following General Motors' agreement to negotiate, as requested by Governor Murphy, President Lewis arrived in Detroit. The corporation designated as its representatives William F. Knudsen, John Thomas Smith, and Donaldson Brown. Knudsen was president of GM and John Thomas Smith was its attorney, while Donaldson Brown represented the Du Pont Corporation. Representing the international union was Homer Martin, and John L. Lewis represented the CIO. Lee Pressman, CIO attorney, also participated in the negotiations.

At the end of the first day of negotiations between the union and Governor Murphy (the GM representatives refused to meet with, or even enter the same room with, the union representatives until the last day, just before an agreement was reached), Lewis was visibly perturbed. He told Addes, Hall, and me that he could not continue in negotiations with "this man Martin." He said, "He is totally unpredictable and I never know what foolish remark he will make next. He is, after all, the President of your international union and could wreck everything. Isn't there someone else that could represent the union?"

The three of us decided it was necessary for Martin to go on a speaking tour of the various locals to "build up morale." Martin readily agreed, as he did not enjoy the long tedious hours required as a negotiator. He left immediately for Kansas City, St. Louis, and other points. Ed Hall accompanied him to make sure he stayed on the road until the strike was settled. I replaced Martin, joining Lewis and Pressman.

Negotiations began February 3, 1937, in Judge George Murphy's court. Judge Murphy was the brother of the Governor Frank Murphy. As I have said, the representatives of General Motors refused to enter the same room with the union representatives, claiming that it would constitute "recognition of the union." They demanded, too, that Governor Murphy enforce the injunction issued by Judge Gadola, by the use of the National Guard, if necessary.

Murphy was in a difficult position. Down deep inside I believe his sympathies were with the union. Frank Murphy came from a long line of Irish revolutionaries and this was evidently a strong influence in his life. Moreover, his name had been widely mentioned as the successor to Franklin D. Roosevelt as President of the United States. To use the armed forces of the State to evict courageous men struggling for human dignity and a chance to live decently would not add luster to his name.

Murphy's position was that since, at long last, the corporation and the union were in communication with each other, nothing would be gained by enforcement of the injunction. Only bitterness would result and the war between GM and its workers would be prolonged indefinitely. Since the three corporation representatives refused to enter the same room with us, it was necessary that Murphy be a go-between, meeting first with one group, then with the other. He carried messages between us for several days.

The corporation's position was that the union had "seized" its property, and they would not discuss a settlement until we had returned that property to its rightful owners. I replied by saying, "We have not seized anything. Every man sitting down in these plants entered onto company property with the company's knowledge and consent. All the strikers can be accused of is that they have not yet gone home. The property is still the corporation's, and is being better cared for now than it has ever been."

Murphy took exception to this line of reasoning. "But, Mr. Mortimer, you are fully aware of the fact that your remaining in their plants is illegal, are you not?" "Governor," I replied, "is it not true that the Supreme Court of the State of Michigan has ruled that there is no such thing as peaceful picketing, and therefore whatever we do would be illegal?" The Governor nodded, "Yes, that unfortunately is true." "Well, then, Governor," I said, "since there isn't anything legal we can do, we are forced to do the one illegal thing that is the most effective." The Governor did not carry the matter further.

Governor Murphy was a tired and harried man. To settle this strike without violence or bloodshed, a strike that had captured the imagination of the whole world, would be an outstanding accomplishment. But he was under tremendous pressure from the other side. To witness the ordeal he was going through aroused my sympathy at times. President Roosevelt, too, was pressing for a settlement, and were it not for his insistence that the meetings continue, I felt that General Motors would have broken off negotiations at several points. One critical issue in the negotiations was the duration of the contract. We were insisting on a contract of one year, but it was obvious to us that we might have to compromise on this point.

I made a trip to Flint one evening, and with Travis entered the Fisher #1 plant. We discussed this point with the strikers. It was they, after all, who would be called upon to make the necessary sacrifice in winning the strike. Moreover, I wanted their participation in decisions of this sort. I wanted to know their opinion on the duration of the contract. I told them that President Roosevelt was urging us to sign a thirty-day contract but that the union was still demanding a contract of one year's duration. It was possible, however, that a compromise might have to be made, and I wanted their reaction to the matter. The sit-downers agreed that the union must insist on a contract of one year's duration, but that we must not under any circumstances agree to less than six months. We all agreed that we could build a real union in less than six months and that was the important thing. To force General Motors to sign a contract (something they had so often avowed would never occur), a contract of sufficiently long duration that would ensure us enough time to solidify our position would be a tremendous victory at this juncture in American labor history.

Returning to Detroit, I told Lewis of my meeting with the sit-downers in Flint, and of their conviction that we must continue to demand a one-year contract, but in case of necessity, that we could compromise on six months. "That is what I like about you fellows, you certainly know what you want," Lewis said.

During the course of the negotiations, Murphy came to us with a huge pile of telegrams he had received that morning. He said, "I have received five thousand so far today." The telegrams were for the most part highly critical of him and of the way he had failed to enforce the injunction against the strikers. Many of them were very abusive. This flood of telegrams continued for days. It was the result of a campaign conducted by the National Association of Manufacturers and the National Chamber of Commerce, to pressure Murphy into using the armed forces of the State against the strikers. Looking over the pile of telegrams, President Lewis said, "Why, Governor, I didn't think you would be influenced by this sort of thing. If it is telegrams you want, I will see that you get a million." The Governor replied, "No, no! Don't do that! I am not influenced by them, but I did want you to know what was going on."

A day later, the Governor came into the room and said, "John, Washington wishes to speak to you." Lewis picked up the phone, motioning to me to listen in on the extension. President Roosevelt said, "John, I just had a talk with Sloan [Alfred P. Sloan] and I think I can get him to sign a thirty-day contract." Lewis replied, "Mr. President, it must be a six-month contract." Roosevelt said, "Maybe I can get him to agree to a two-month contract, I don't know, I will try." Lewis again answered, "Mr. President, it must be a six-month contract." Roosevelt was obviously irked. "Come, come, now, John, this is no time to quibble." But again Lewis said, "Mr. President, it must be a six-month contract." The next voice we heard was that of Secretary of Labor, Frances Perkins, who related the facts of the meeting with Sloan. She, too, then hung up.[19]

The AFL Executive Council pursued its disruptive efforts to the end. Learning that General Motors was on the verge of capitulating to the UAW–CIO, William Green sent a telegram which was signed by every member of the Executive Council. It was addressed to Knudsen and demanded that the corporation refrain from negotiating a contract with the UAW–CIO, since such a contract would "destroy the rights of AFL members in the General Motors plants." It threatened to strike the plants of the corporation in the event a contract was entered into with the UAW–CIO.

Governor Murphy showed us the telegram. After we had read and discussed its contents, Lewis arose, reached for his hat, and said, "I would suggest, Governor, that you summon Bill Green to Detroit, and see if he can get these men back to work." Murphy became flustered and hastened to assure us that we were the proper people to negotiate with. Murphy said, "They have given me this telegram, and are trying to use it as an excuse for not coming to an understanding. They are claiming to be the innocent victims of a war between two rival unions."

After several days of negotiations by remote control, with Lewis, Pressman, and me in one room of Judge Murphy's court, and the representatives of General Motors and the Du Ponts in another, Murphy came to us very much worried. It was about 1:00 P.M. and the Governor said, "They have not removed their hats or coats. They are demanding that the strikers vacate their plants. They told me you have a half-hour to decide, and if you do not comply, they are leaving."

"They will not leave, Governor, they wouldn't dare," Lewis replied. The half-hour passed and they were still there. An hour passed, and they did not leave. Lewis then said, "Governor, invite them in here, and let us talk to them man-to-man."

The Governor conveyed this invitation to them, and after a short period, they came in. Their whole demeanor revealed that they knew they had lost. We arose and shook hands with them, inviting them to sit down and remove their coats and hats. We all sat around a long table, our union group on one side, and the corporation's on the opposite.

Knudsen sat across from me. He leaned over and said to me, "This is a hell of a committee."

"Why? What do you mean?" I asked.

"It is all lawyers and coal miners," he said with a smile, "and only two auto workers."

This was true, since only Knudsen and myself were familiar with the inside working of an automobile factory. The company lawyers were totally ignorant of the complicated procedures in the manufacture of automobiles. They were concerned solely with legalities and the fourteenth-century ideas of the Du Ponts.

Knudsen was quite a different person. I am sure that if matters were left in his hands, the strike would have been of short duration. He was impatient with all the nebulous legal theories advanced by the two company attorneys and in private statements made to me, indicated that he wanted to get back to the task of making automobiles.

John L. Lewis was a tower of strength. He knew, as did we all, that to get these men's signatures on a contract with the union meant an enormous victory for the CIO and a shattering defeat for the open shop. The Du Pont–General Motors combine was the fortress that dominated the entire automotive industry, and we were at last face-to-face with the men whose decisions were final.

Governor Murphy withdrew and left us alone with these men for the first time. The three representatives of Du Pont–General Motors were now face-to-face with the representatives of their workers. It was an experience they did not enjoy and would not have endured had not grim necessity demanded it. We entered into serious discussions with them on the issues involved and made it crystal clear that the resumption of work depended entirely on their entering into a contract with the UAW–CIO. We finally agreed to the wording of an agreement with the exception of three items. These were: The duration of the agreement, the designation and number of plants to be covered by the agreement, and the workers' right to wear union buttons on the job.

The last point may seem trivial, but the corporation's attorneys did not consider it so. They insisted that wearing union buttons constituted intimidation against other workers. Heated arguments occurred also over the corporation's intention to arrest and punish a number of workers for violence during the strike. I strongly opposed this. "Let us get one thing straight, gentlemen," I said. "Everyone goes back to work without reprisals, or nobody goes back. If we are going to end this strike, it must be on the basis of letting bygones be bygones."

"But, what shall we do with a man who strikes his foreman?" Knudsen demanded.

"What shall we do with the foreman who calls a worker a son-of-a-bitch?" I replied.

"What foreman did that?" Knudsen asked.

"I am not naming names, Mr. Knudsen," I said. "But I think it is time the corporation understood that the union is here to stay. Over the years the General Motors Corporation has built up a supervisory staff, trained to drive the workers to the point of exhaustion, and at less than a living wage. You must begin to rearrange the furniture of your minds or this strike will become only the first of many more to follow."

Lewis raised the question of the Gadola injunction, still unenforced. He demanded that the injunction be withdrawn and all legal action initiated by the corporation against the union be halted. The corporation attorneys argued about whether or not Judge Gadola would agree to nullify the injunction, but they finally agreed.

It was now 2:00 A.M., February 10, 1937. We decided to meet at 2:00 P.M. in the Statler Hotel. President Lewis had developed a cold, and was running a temperature, so he went to bed and called a doctor to attend him. We met as planned at 2:00 P.M. At 4:00 P.M. we moved over to Lewis's suite. He was still confined to his bed and his wife had flown in from Washington.

I got a call from Travis in Flint, telling me that the corporation had shut off the heat, and it was unbearably cold in the Chevrolet #4 plant. Over the phone we decided that he should get all the men over into the heat treat department, turn on the gas in the furnaces, then open the windows in plant #4. I said, "Bob, I think this will bring a quick reaction." In about ten minutes, Governor Murphy came to me and said, "Mr. Mortimer, your people have opened the windows in plant #4, and the sprinkler system will freeze."

"Governor, it appears to me the corporation is showing very bad faith in shutting off the heat just when we are so close to a settlement," I replied. "We cannot tolerate their jeopardizing the health of our people. If the corporation will turn on the heat, we will close the windows."

The Governor shook his head. "Mr. Mortimer, don't you think it is asking a lot to have the corporation furnish heat while your people occupy their property?"

He left me and went to talk to Knudsen about the matter. Knudsen promised to turn the heat back on. Thereupon I called Travis, and said, "Bob, they are going to turn the heat on, so when you hear it come back into the radiators, be sure to close the windows." Travis promised to do so. Fifteen minutes later, the Governor again came to me and said, "Mr. Mortimer, the heat has been turned on but the windows are still open." I phoned Travis once more and asked him why the windows were still open. "The damned chain slipped off the pulley," Bob explained, "but a man is fixing it." Thus ended the episode of the open windows.

There were still three remaining matters in the dispute to be handled. About 5:00 P.M., corporation attorney Smith came to Lewis's bedside and once again raised the question of a thirty-day contract. Lewis arose on his elbow, and in his most sonorous voice asked, "But, you want your plants to reopen, do you not?" Smith replied, "Yes, yes, of course!" "Well then, it is six months!" Lewis said, turning his back on Smith. The latter stood looking at Lewis for a few moments. "Very well, then, Mr. Lewis," he said, and left the room.

Mr. Knudsen and I went into an adjoining room, and before we sat down, he said to me, "Mr. Mortimer, let your people wear a button, ten buttons, a hundred buttons, a thousand buttons, I don't care a damn. Let us get back to making automobiles."

Knudsen was thoroughly disgusted with all the interminable legal arguments. He wanted to get back to the practical things of life. After consultation with Bob Travis and Henry Kraus, I had prepared a list of the seventeen plants to be included in the contract. There was some slight argument about Guide Lamp, but this was quickly decided in our favor. Knudsen readily agreed to the list I gave him, and the negotiations were over. The great victory of the GM sit-downers was officially sealed.

It was embodied in a one page document which said:

GENERAL MOTORS AGREEMENT

February 11, 1937

Agreement entered into on this 11th day of February, 1937, between the General Motors Corporation (hereinafter referred to as the Corporation) and the International Union, United Automobile Workers of America (hereinafter referred to as the Union).

1) The Corporation hereby recognizes the Union as the Collective Bargaining agency for those employes of the

Corporation who are members of the Union. The Corporation recognizes and will not interfere with the right of its employes to be members of the Union. There shall be no discrimination, interference, restraint or coercion by the Corporation or any of its agents against any employee because of membership in the Union.

2) The Corporation and the Union agree to commence collective bargaining negotiations on February 16th with regard to the issues specified in the letter of January 4th, 1937, from the Union to the Corporation, for the purpose of entering into a collective bargaining agreement, or agreements, covering such issues, looking to a final and complete settlement of all matters in dispute.

3) The Union agrees to forthwith terminate the present strike against the Corporation, and to evacuate all plants now occupied by strikers.

4) The Corporation agrees that all of its plants, which are on strike, or otherwise idle shall resume operations as rapidly as possible.

5) It is understood that all employees now on strike or otherwise idle will return to their usual work when called and that no discrimination shall be made or prejudices exercised by the Corporation against any employee because of his former affiliation with, or activities in, the Union or the present strike.

6) The Union agrees that pending the negotiations referred to in Paragraph Two, there shall be no strikes called or any other interruption to or interference with production, by the Union or its members.

7) During the existence of the collective bargaining agreement contemplated pursuant to Paragraph Two, all opportunities to achieve a satisfactory settlement of any grievance or enforcement of any demands by negotiations shall be exhausted before there shall be any strikes or other interruption to or interference with production by the Union or its members. There shall be no attempts to intimidate or coerce any employes by the Union and there shall not be any solicitation or signing up of members by

the Union on the premises of the Company. This is not to preclude individual discussion.

8) After the evacuation of its plants and the termination of the strike the Corporation agrees to consent to the entry of orders, dismissing the injunction proceedings which have been started by the Corporation against the Union, or any of its members, or officers or any of its locals, including those pending in Flint, Michigan and Cleveland, Ohio, and subject to the approval of the Court to discontinue all contempt proceedings which it has instituted thereunder.

GENERAL MOTORS CORPORATION
William S. Knudsen
J. T. Smith
D. Brown
UNITED AUTOMOBILE WORKERS
Wyndham Mortimer, First Vice President
Lee Pressman, General Counsel, CIO
John L. Lewis, Chairman, CIO
Frank Murphy and James F. Dewey

It was signed by John L. Lewis for the CIO, myself for the UAW, and Lee Pressman as the Union's attorney.

CHAPTER TEN

THE UNION IS BUILT, THEN ALMOST DESTROYED

In keeping with the February eleventh agreement ending the sit-down strike, negotiations between GM and the international union began on February 16, 1937.

Representing the corporation were William F. Knudsen, President; Charles E. Wilson, Vice-President; Mr. DuBruel, Research Department; and Harry Anderson, Personnel Department.

Mr. Knudsen did not attend all sessions, but participated at times.

Representing the UAW–CIO were John Brophy, CIO; Ed Hall, UAW Vice-President; and Wyndham Mortimer, UAW Vice-President.

These negotiations were a milestone in American labor history. Whereas the February eleventh agreement dealt mainly with recognition of the union and the procedure to be followed in getting the plants of the corporation in operation, we were now negotiating a complete agreement, practicing collective bargaining, something the huge automobile companies had vowed would never happen.

Since we were blazing a trail and were walking where no auto worker had walked before, every forward step was difficult. We had to deal in fundamentals. Things that today are taken for granted were not accepted by the corporation at that period in the union's history. They had to be fought for and won.

Every meaningful demand put forward by the union was regarded as a challenge to the corporation's authority, to their property rights, which they regarded as sacred. To illustrate this, I made a remark to the effect that the profits of General Motors were such that they could well afford to raise wages substantially, whereupon Harry Anderson, his face livid with anger, said, "Mr. Mortimer, our profits are none of your God-damned business!"

Another example of the corporation's thinking was their insistence upon an aggrieved worker's taking the grievance to his foreman first rather than to his shop steward. The corporation's legal advisers argued that for the foreman to deal with the shop steward was tantamount to giving up one of the employer's age-old prerogatives, namely the right to discipline, to run his own business. The union's position was that the aggrieved worker must first take the grievance to the steward. Our members were instructed to deal only through their shop stewards. The steward would then discuss the matter with the foreman and try to get the grievance adjusted. But the foreman had received instructions to deal directly with the employee and would therefore refuse to discuss any grievance with the steward. Our position was that since the foreman could, and usually did, intimidate the individual worker, it was mandatory that all grievances be handled by the official representative of the union. Unless we insisted on this procedure, the union would be circumvented from performing its duty, its main reason for existence. The corporation's refusal to deal with the stewards was one of the reasons so many work stoppages occurred during 1937–1938. There were other reasons, of course, such as the arrogant supervisory staff, who stubbornly refused to recognize the changed situation. They now had to readjust their thinking, which in some cases was very hard.

Then there was the question of seniority. For many years the automobile manufacturers had adopted a seniority formula that was a complete negation of seniority itself. Their formula was based not only on seniority, but also on merit, skill, and dependability. The corporation being the sole judge of the last three factors, the result was a total denial of the first. We contended that seniority meant length of service and nothing more. It was our contention that the years of service given the employer earned the worker a right to the job. It was a right that accrued to one that had given the most productive years of his life to an employer or to an industry.

It challenged the idea that the job belonged to the boss, to do with as he wished. It also challenged the open-shop employer's practice of discharging employees without cause and filling their places with younger men whose youth and agility could be turned to greater speed-up, and therefore greater profit.

All the above arguments and more were put forward with as much force as we were capable of. The very colorful vocabulary of Ed Hall was used to good advantage. His description of an arrogant foreman was an original. Speaking to Mr. Wilson and Mr. Knudsen on one occasion, he compared a certain foreman to a "stud duck." Mr. Knudsen asked, "A stud duck? What is that?" Hall answered, "You know what I am talking about. Don't act so innocent."

The presence of John Brophy was helpful since he represented the CIO, and at that juncture in labor history, the CIO meant John L. Lewis, whose reputation for observing contracts was well known. Moreover, Brophy's long experience in the mining industry was invaluable.

Agreement was reached and ratified March 12, 1937. It covered grievance procedure, recognition of shop committees (stewards), wage adjustments, six-month probationary period, lay-offs and rehires by seniority, seniority retained in transfers, and posting of seniority lists.

It was a very modest accomplishment when compared to agreements reached years later, but given the powerful adversary we faced and the weak organization we had in 1937, the wonder is that we did so well.

In 1937, we were recognized as the bargaining agent in only seventeen plants of the vast General Motors empire. We were the bargaining agency for our membership only. There was yet the task of organizing the many thousands of other GM workers, not to mention the huge Ford operations, and also of completing the organization in the Chrysler Corporation. In other words, we had a membership of about 75,000 out of a potential of one million. Clearly, our most urgent job was to complete our original plan to bring unionism to the entire auto and parts industry. This agreement of March 12, 1937, was a step in that direction.

Sit-down Strikes Galore

Following the victory of February 11th and the ending of the sit-down strikes in Flint and Cleveland, and while we were engaged in negotiations with General Motors, there occurred a wave of sit-down strikes unparalleled in the annals of American labor. The storming of the GM citadel had set in motion a wave of revolt against the open-shop employers that could not be contained. Sixty thousand Chrysler workers in Dodge and Plymouth alone sat down. At one point, eighteen sit-down strikes were going on simultaneously in Detroit. Auto factories were not the only ones involved. Others included cigar factories, meat packers, leather workers, and Woolworth's. Altogether, the spring of 1937 was a hectic one. I was kept busy going from one sit-down strike to another, and seemed to spend all day every day trying to keep up with the unbelievable upsurge of sentiment for the CIO.

Police Brutality

In early April, the Detroit police began a "get tough" campaign of ousting sit-down strikers from their plants. They began by throwing a few girls out of a cigar factory. The daily papers were alerted, and news photographers were there to take pictures of the strikers being ousted. They went from one struck plant to another, in what was clearly a dress rehearsal of what they planned to do at Dodge and Plymouth. The strikers were always pictured as being a band of thieves who had stolen the employer's property, and the police were always the brave knights in shining armor who would save America from the horrible Reds.

The union demanded that the police raids cease. But it was clear that in the absence of some kind of counteraction by the union, the raids would continue until there would no doubt be a clash of major proportions between the strikers and the police.

The Power Strike

Another interesting event of that hectic spring was my involvement in a strike which, by rights, should not have been my concern at all, but which, as things stood at the time, fell under the jurisdiction of the UAW. This strike was also the occasion of my first meeting with Wendell Willkie, for whom I was to develop a certain admiration.

On May 19, 1937, I arrived at my office in the Hofmann Building, and was given three telephone numbers to call. My secretary told me that there was a strike in the Consumers Power plants, and that all of Michigan from Pontiac north was paralyzed. The three phone numbers were those of John L. Lewis, Governor Frank Murphy, and William F. Knudsen.

They had all been trying frantically to reach President Martin, but he had left the day before and had not said where he could be reached. This was his usual practice. I called Lewis first, and he was extremely anxious and disturbed over the strike. He wanted me to do everything within my power to get the current back on. I promised him I would do whatever I could. I then called Governor Murphy, who was also very agitated and wanted to know where he could reach Martin. I could only tell him that I did not know, but that I was leaving immediately for Saginaw and the strike headquarters. I called Mr. Knudsen, who was very upset because every GM plant outside of Detroit was shut down. I could only tell him what I had told the others.

One might ask at this point how the UAW got mixed up in this power strike. The answer is simple. Along with other mass industries, the power industry had been open shop. And, like thousands of non-union workers elsewhere, they rushed to join the CIO. They joined the UAW because it was the only CIO union thereabouts. An international union had not yet been chartered by the CIO that would have jurisdiction over the power industry. Consequently, we found ourselves involved in a strike that had very far-reaching implications. Streetcars stopped. Elevators jammed between floors. The farmer's lights went out in his barn and his feed chopper didn't work. The effect was that of a general strike.

I reached Saginaw as quickly as possible and met with the union committee. Robert Travis was in Saginaw when I arrived. Governor Murphy had ordered both the company representatives and the union committee to meet in his office the following morning. It was decided to call off the strike and restore power at once; afterward, with the Governor in on the negotiations, the grievances of the power workers would be taken up. The direct cause of the strike was the miserably low wages paid; some workers earned as little as $45 a month. Top wages were $135 a month.

Negotiations were resumed in the offices of Governor Murphy in Lansing, but it was abundantly clear that the representatives of the Consumers Power Company did not have the authority to sign a contract. Someone higher up had this power, but we did not know who it was at this time.

After several days of fruitless talks, both sides returned to Saginaw and it appeared that another strike was inevitable. A disturbing factor on the union side was that several members of our negotiating committee were convinced that no one in the leadership could be trusted, from John L. Lewis down. This made negotiating very difficult, and it was clear to me that these men would be satisfied with nothing less than another strike. They hoped to turn such a strike into a catastrophe by opening the sluice gates of the power dams and releasing all the water.

Two of these men actually started toward the dams, but were headed off by Bob Travis and Henry Kraus who demanded that they return to Saginaw. It was in this sort of atmosphere that I received a phone call from John L. Lewis. President Lewis said, "Wyndham, I want you to go to the Blackstone Hotel in Chicago. You will make contact there with a Mr. Wendell Willkie. Mr. Willkie is the man who can settle your difficulty. Go and see him at once."

We went to Chicago, to the Blackstone Hotel, and found Wendell Willkie there. It was a stinking hot day, and he was sitting in his room, dressed only in his BVD's drinking a tall lemonade, and sweating.

I introduced myself and the committee, and he said, "Yes, yes, come in."

That was the first time I had met him, but he impressed me as a very fine person, and I met him again several times. He came right to the point and said, "Look, we will recognize your union as the bargaining agent; we'll sign a contract with you; we'll give you a ten percent increase in pay." He went on to enumerate the things he would agree to. "But," he said, "you'll have to meet me in New York."

Arriving back in Saginaw, I had another phone call from President Lewis. He said, "Wyndham, bring your committee to the New Yorker Hotel in New York. A settlement will be worked out there with Mr. Willkie." We left Saginaw at once, and took a train for New York. When we arrived at the New Yorker Hotel, we were met by the same Consumers Power representatives we had left in Saginaw. With them was Mr. Wendell Willkie. During talks there with Willkie and the Consumers Power representatives, at which the major issues were being resolved, we received a phone call from John L. Lewis asking both sides to meet with him in the United Mine Workers building in Washington. The meeting in Washington resulted in a contract covering wages, hours, and working conditions, and an increase in pay of ten percent. There was also an agreement to reclassify upward everyone covered by the contract.

During the Washington negotiations, two members of the union negotiating committee were absent. I searched for them, but they were nowhere to be found. During the period of signing the contract, these two men had phoned the union headquarters in Saginaw, told the workers that they were being betrayed, and ordered them to shut down the power again.

The union committee chartered a plane and flew back to Flint, where Travis had called a meeting of the striking workers. I appeared at this meeting with a copy of the contract. I read it and explained every clause in it, and advised them to accept it. The contract was accepted overwhelmingly, and the power was turned back on. It was a long step forward for the power workers, their first escape from open-shop conditions.

Eventually the CIO chartered the Utility Workers

International Union. Under this charter a drive was conducted by the CIO to bring the union to all workers in the power industry, and the Consumers Power workers were transferred to the jurisdiction of this new organization.

Cadillac Square Demonstration

Our relations with the police continuing to be unsatisfactory, we decided to hold a demonstration of mass proportions in Cadillac Square. In cooperation with the Detroit Federation for Civil Liberties, we distributed 100,000 leaflets calling upon the working people of Detroit to converge on Cadillac Square at 4:00 P.M. on Friday, February 4, 1938. I spent several days contacting the local unions in and around the Detroit area, making sure that the workers would march directly from their work to the mass demonstration. The police threatened us with force if such a mass demonstration were held.

Some of the leadership in our own ranks was shaky. Among these were Homer Martin and Adolph Germer. Germer would stop me, point his finger at my nose and say, "But you do not have a permit. You are organizing another Haymarket riot."

"Adolph," I replied, "if my history is correct, and I am sure it is, the Haymarket mass meeting *did* have a permit. But, permit or not, when fifty thousand auto workers march down Woodward Avenue, the Detroit police will do nothing."

Germer shot back, "But will you be marching with them down Woodward Avenue?"

I said, "Watch me, and see."

With locked arms, Dick Frankensteen and I led the demonstration down Woodward Avenue to Cadillac Square on that day.

The number of workers in the square was at least two hundred thousand. Some estimates were as high as five hundred thousand, but I think this would be too high. On the day of the demonstration, all business places were shut down and the employees told to go home because there would surely be bloodshed. Many of them stayed and joined the demonstration. President Martin was nowhere to be found. He was hiding out for fear there would be trouble. But when the vast square began to fill up and he felt the police would not dare attack such an outpouring of workers, he arrived in a taxi and delivered one of his usual "militant" speeches.

This enormous mass meeting demonstrated beyond question the power of labor in Michigan, and especially in Detroit, where a fascist-minded Chief of Police, Heinie Pickert, would have crushed the CIO in a bloodbath if he could.

The morning following the mass meeting in Cadillac Square, John L. Lewis came to Detroit. Along with George Addes, Ed Hall, and Homer Martin, I met him at the B. & O. depot. Lewis had come to participate in the negotiations that ended the Chrysler strike. I showed him a picture of the mass meeting in the *Free Press*. He was highly pleased. "Adolph" [Germer], he said, "has been sending me daily reports and pouring his fears into my ears. But I felt you fellows knew the situation and were aware of what you were doing."

Factionalism

The situation among the top leadership was deteriorating. Homer Martin, sensing his own inadequacy for the high office he held, had formed an alliance with the Lovestonites, a small political group that had been expelled from the Communist Party. They were led by one Jay Lovestone, who was without doubt the most professional disruptionist to be found anywhere. For the period extending from the summer of 1937 until the Cleveland convention in 1939, Lovestone was in reality the President of the UAW.

In a short time the international office was overrun by members of the Lovestone faction. Henry Kraus, the editor of *The United Auto Worker* from its inception, and a person of great ability, was fired. In his place, Martin appointed a very colorless person, a Lovestonite, William Munger. *The United Auto Worker,* the official paper of the international union, now became a weapon against the real, honest leadership, who were trying to build a powerful industrial union in the auto industry.

The policy of Lovestone was to divert the attention of the auto workers away from their real enemies, the auto manufacturers, and rivet their attention on a man six thousand miles away, Joe Stalin. Now Stalin had many shortcomings, but by no stretch of the imagination could he be regarded as an enemy of the auto workers of America, or of the working people generally. Even if, through some mental gymnastics and a lot of flag-waving, one might be convinced of Stalin's enmity, the danger was not immediate, while the question of organizing Ford, GM, and Chrysler was a task that demanded all our energy and attention. If Stalin was a problem, he was the problem of the Russian people, not the American working man. Anyone opposing the Lovestone policy of witch-hunting and urging that our attention be concentrated on the problems close to home was labeled a "Stalinist," an agent of Moscow, a termite. It was a case of the sinners calling the righteous to repentance, to quote Abe Lincoln.

To prevent objective discussion, there appeared to be an unlimited reservoir of issues raised in the meetings of the Executive Board, issues that were extraneous and foreign to the real problems facing the UAW. Correspondence between Martin and Lovestone, published a year later, revealed that Martin was completely under the influence and direction of Lovestone. For example, on Lovestone's orders, Martin would raise such questions as the sinking of the gunboat *Panay* (an American gunboat sunk by the Japanese). A resolution was introduced by Martin in the Executive Board, criticizing and condemning our government for sending the *Panay* into Chinese waters. There was not one word of criticism leveled at the Japanese, who were also invaders of Chinese territory.

I criticized Martin's resolution on the grounds that it was extraneous and did not serve the interests of the auto workers. Moreover, the resolution was one-sided. If our government had no business in China, then neither did the Japanese. I proposed an amendment condemning any and all foreign invasions of the Chinese mainland. This was called "Stalinism" and it was implied that I was carrying out orders from Moscow.

A line of cleavage was developing inside the Executive Board. Issues were not being decided by debate and open discussion. Factional lines were hardening and no question or issue could be decided on its merits. The welfare of the membership was being sacrificed to appease and implement the anti-working-class policy and program of Jay Lovestone. The majority of the Executive Board were being swayed by the hysteria engendered by this professional factionalist.

The Milwaukee Convention

On Monday, August 23, 1937, the second annual convention of the UAW was held in Milwaukee. It was called to order at 10:00 A.M. by President Martin. There was every reason for this convention to have been the most joyous and happy gathering that any similar body ever had in the history of American labor.

In the brief fifteen months since the South Bend convention in April, 1936, we had grown from a membership of about 20,000 to over 400,000 dues-paying members, as represented by the almost two thousand delegates present. We had stormed and taken the most formidable fortress of capitalism, the General Motors–Du Pont combine, whose influence dominated the entire automobile industry. We had captured the secondary ramparts of the auto industry, the Chrysler Coropration, had helped set in motion a tidal wave of unionism that swept from coast to coast. We had delivered a death blow to the open shop, and that hateful institution was now breathing its last. Yet this second convention of our international union was torn by dissension. The virus of factionalism injected into the blood stream of the union by the Lovestone cabal found us a divided organization that was in danger of being torn asunder.

The officers who had led and built the union were under an unprincipled attack. Specifically these were George F. Addes, Secretary–Treasurer; Ed Hall, Second Vice-President; Board members Leo LaMotte and Dick Reisinger, and me. We were scheduled to be replaced, and the international union was to have its claws clipped, its teeth pulled, and was to become as harmless as a domestic kitten.

Lovestone was in attendance at the convention, and from the anonymity of his hotel room, directed the hand of President Martin throughout. It will be asked why, in view of the disruptive role being played by Lovestone and his group, he was not exposed before the delegates. This is a logical question, and its answer is to be found in the fact that *proof* comes before exposure.

I knew the role being played by the Lovestone–Martin cabal, as did Hall, Addes, and the others, but we lacked documentary proof. In all probability, had it not been for the intervention of John L. Lewis, there would have been a split in the international union at this convention. Lewis appeared as the principal speaker and in the course of his remarks, pointed out the tremendous and unparalleled growth in membership and influence of the UAW in the short space of fifteen months. He asked, "What do you want of your officers? They all look good to me." It was both a plea and a piece of advice on his part to re-elect the officers, and for all to go back to work to build the UAW and the CIO. What Lewis did not know at this juncture was the role being played by the Lovestone group, or, if he did have suspicions along this line, he, too, lacked the evidence necessary to expose it fully and completely.

I returned from the Milwaukee convention with mixed feelings. I hoped the advice of Lewis would be taken seriously, and that we could again go forward in building the UAW and the CIO. But I knew or felt this was wishful thinking while the Lovestone cabal existed. I was afraid the statements of Lewis, together with his tremendous influence, had only diverted, not stopped the plans already laid to seize complete control, to place Lovestonites in every key position, and to destroy the UAW as an effective weapon against the employer. Time would prove the correctness of this suspicion.

My Fears Confirmed

Immediately following the Milwaukee convention, Bob Travis, Victor Reuther, and Roy Reuther were fired. These three young men had played a commendable role in the Flint sit-down strikes. It is not an exaggeration to say that Bob Travis was the most brilliant strike leader and strategist the UAW or any other union ever had. Local 156 in Flint was placed under the administratorship of Jack Little and Burt Harris. Harris was an officer in the Black Legion. A huge man physically, Harris played the same role in local 156 as he had played in the Black Legion, as a gangster and hatchet man.

Ed Hall and I were both refused any meaningful assignments, and although the union's constitution was plain, saying "It shall be the duty of the Vice-President to assist the President in the performance of his duties," neither Hall nor I was ever consulted on any problems whatsoever. Instead of utilizing our experience, all of us much older and more experienced union men, Martin, on the orders of Lovestone, hired a man named Francis Henson, a Lovestonite from New York, to be his administrative assistant. Henson knew nothing of the problems of the auto workers or of the auto industry. He was placed in the international union offices to be the eyes and ears of Jay Lovestone, which he did faithfully. He made a daily report, some days two reports, to Lovestone in New York, giving in detail everything that happened in the international offices: who the visitors were; who talked with Martin and what they talked about; how long they stayed, he even made a record of the telephone calls. On one occasion, Henson asked me to lunch with him, and I accepted. I knew he was fishing for something, so I was careful of my conversation. He reported this luncheon meeting to Lovestone, and remarked that "Mortimer is a poker face."

Another questionable person was George F. Miles (alias Alex Bail). Miles was the editor of the *Workers Age,* the official organ of the Lovestone splinter group. Miles wrote the editorials that appeared in *The United Auto Worker*. He too was in daily touch with Lovestone. Still another person was Saul Held, who was a staff writer under Munger, but whose real duties were those of an overseer, to make sure Lovestone's instructions were carried out. Held was in touch with Lovestone by letter and phone, and contacted him several times a day. Then there was Eve Stone, the wife of George Miles, whom Lovestone ordered Martin to place in charge of Women's Auxiliaries.

All of these people were on the payroll of the international union at good salaries, a percentage of which found its way into the treasury of the Lovestone organization in New York. In addition to the above, there were a number on the organizing staff. The treasury of the international union was without doubt the financial mainstay of the Lovestone group.

Insurance Swindle

In May, 1938, I had an occasion to go to my office in the international union one evening to finish up some correspondence and other matters. Board member Fred C. Pieper, accompanied by a man whose name was William Tepper, a certified public accountant, arrived a short time later. They proceeded immediately to go over the financial records of the international union. My interest was aroused, so I inquired about the purpose of such an examination. Such a study had not been authorized by the Executive Board as far as I knew. Tepper said that it was a study in preparation for an insurance program that would give coverage to the membership, and that the study was authorized by President Martin.

I felt that here was something that should be looked into. I told Addes, Hall, and Frankensteen about the activities of Pieper and Tepper. I inquired of the Executive Board as to the details of the insurance scheme, and warned against getting involved in something beyond our proper sphere of activities. We were after all, a labor organization, and the sad experience of other labor unions that had plunged in over their heads in this and similar schemes was fresh in my memory. The Brotherhood of Locomotive Engineers, for example, had become involved in an insurance deal, and also in Florida real estate. It not only bankrupted the organization, but the membership were compelled to make good the loss. I personally knew of men who were paying fifty dollars a month dues for years to liquidate their debt and responsibility.

I had not the slightest confidence in Pieper, nor do I believe anyone else did, even including President Martin. Martin once told me that he was sure Pieper was a stool pigeon.

Yet he was now joining with him in putting across a gigantic swindle under the guise of an insurance plan.

William (Bill) Tepper, the public accountant, had aroused suspicion when he was discovered going over the financial records of the international one night, together with an accountant from the General Motors accounting department. George Addes ordered him fired from the payroll of the international union, but this order was countermanded by Martin and Pieper as head of the Finance Committee.

On June 8, 1938, the international Executive Board met in Detroit on call of President Martin. The Executive Board was called in session to consider the insurance plan. Since this special meeting of the Executive Board was very expensive, and unnecessary as well, it was decided to add several other subjects to the agenda. The proposed added subjects were the following:

Insurance:

BE IT RESOLVED: that the question of insurance be referred to the CIO for a complete and thorough study, and

BE IT FURTHER RESOLVED: that all members of the international Executive Board stand instructed personally to investigate all angles of insurance, and

BE IT FURTHER RESOLVED: that such recommendations as may come from the CIO, together with any recommendations of the international Executive Board members be combined in a resolution, and that this resolution shall be submitted to the next convention of the UAW.

William Tepper:

BE IT RESOLVED: that the President stand instructed forthwith to discharge and terminate the services of William E. Tepper.

Finance and Audit Committee:

BE IT RESOLVED: that the Finance and Auditing Committee shall convene not more than ten days prior to the Board meetings, and shall depart for their districts not later than one week after adjournment.

This last resolution was very necessary since Pieper and his associates on the Finance Committee had been in continuous session in the international office for over a year, while his district (Southern) was the poorest organized and the least cared for in the international union. Pieper planned on making and had actually made the chairmanship of the Finance Committee a full-time job, when in fact the duties of that office required not over ten days' time throughout the year.

The Executive Board decided by a vote of thirteen to five to add these resolutions to the agenda. President Martin, despite the fact that he had called the Executive Board into session, did not attend the meeting. He professed to see in the thirteen to five vote a conspiracy against him. What he feared was the open discussion of the subjects raised in the increased agenda, and the thirteen to five vote against his program. It proved the Board was not completely under his control, and this must be changed somehow.

Expulsions

Accordingly, on June 9, President Martin expelled George F. Addes, Ed Hall, Walter Wells, Richard Frankensteen, and me. We were charged with conduct unbecoming officers of the international union, and conspiring to turn the international union over to the Communists. We had believed for some time that Lovestone's plans envisioned the removal from office and from the staff of all those who had done the spadework in building the international union, and the replacement of them with others who would be governed by his instructions and advice. With the expulsion order, he had succeeded in severing from the staff and from elected office nearly everyone whose name was linked with the most glorious period in the history of the international union. There still remained several members of the Executive Board who had played a good role—such men as Dick Reisinger, Paul Miley, Ellsworth Kramer, and others. Walter Reuther was also a member of the Executive Board, and usually voted with us against Lovestone, but Walter was never a very trustworthy ally. He tried to keep one foot in each camp, so that he could easily switch sides just in case. Now removed from the staff and from office were the following:

Robert Travis: The real leader and strike strategist of the Flint sit-down strike.

Henry Kraus: The founder and editor of *The United Auto Worker,* whose services to the UAW, much of it without pay, were greater than many of those now in the leadership.

Victor Reuther: A very courageous international representative who played a most commendable role in the Flint struggle.

Roy Reuther: Brother of Victor and Walter, who also played a constructive and valuable role in the Flint strikes.

George F. Addes: The international Secretary–Treasurer. One of the stalwarts and founders of the UAW from Toledo, Ohio.

Ed Hall: Second Vice-President of the international union, and also one of the original founders of the UAW.

Richard Frankensteen: Member of the Executive Board, who came to the international union from the Chrysler Corporation, bringing with him an already organized independent union.

Wyndham Mortimer: First Vice-President of the international union. My contribution to the UAW–CIO is largely what this book is all about.

With the expulsions came widespread confusion throughout the international union, and there followed ten months of bitter struggle, during which time the union was torn by dissent, and there was a real danger of its being weakened to the point where it would become impotent and lose its value to the auto workers and to the CIO as a weapon against an arrogant, monopolistic capitalism. It could even be destroyed altogether.

The union's constitution provided for trials of officers accused of wrongdoing, but in the hardened factional situation created by the Lovestone influence, and in a trial where the accuser is also the judge and jury, only a simpleton could believe that such a trial could or would be fair and impartial. Moreover, regardless of the outcome of such a trial, I knew the final decision would have to be made by the membership. I had had ample opportunity to observe the strange and unpredictable behavior of Homer Martin since I first met him in the Fort Wayne Hotel at the 1934 conference of federal unions in Detroit. Martin was a dishonest and abysmally ignorant person where trade unionism was concerned, and, under the guidance of Lovestone, would go to any lengths to achieve his purpose. It was in this situation and atmosphere that the trials began.

Trials

On July 25 the proceedings against me and the others began. We had engaged Maurice Sugar as our attorney. To dignify what followed by referring to it as a trial would be to do violence to the English language, and to insult our Anglo-Saxon system of jurisprudence.

As we got off the elevator at the eleventh floor of the Griswold Building (the offices of the international union) Attorney Sugar and I were surrounded by a group of about twenty Negroes. They were very belligerent, threatening Sugar with violence. One of them was the largest man I had ever seen. I asked him what this demonstration was all about. He said that Sugar had referred to them as "gorillas."

They had been told that Sugar had made a speech in which he referred to them in that way. No such speech was ever made. Sugar asked them, "Who told you this foolish story?" They revealed that Martin had talked to them. Obviously, Martin had planned this demonstration in the hope that bodily harm would come to our attorney, and perhaps to the rest of us as well.

I still admire the cool and calm way in which Maurice Sugar handled this very difficult and dangerous situation. As I recall, he asked them why they allowed themselves to be used in this way. He asked these men if they had ever heard of James Victory. Some of them had heard of this case. Sugar told them, "I am Maurice Sugar. It was I who fought and won freedom for James Victory. It was I who fought and won the right of the Negro people to enter the cemetery by the main entrance instead of through the back alley."

These men parted and made way for us to enter the offices.

The long corridor along which we had to walk was lined solidly on both sides by men with clubs. A curious arrangement was that all the Negroes were on one side, while all the whites occupied the other. A Jim Crow goon squad.

The trial began with Sugar asking for a bill of particulars. What was our crime? When and where did it occur? Martin and his attorney, Larry Davidow, refused the request. Under our American and Anglo-Saxon system of law, the accused is entitled to know what he is accused of. All the allegations are spelled out, and the accused is furnished with a copy. With this information in his possession, the attorney can then proceed to build up the defense. It was clear that the Martin–Lovestone cabal had no such facts with which to convict, but such trifles would not be permitted to stand in the way of our execution.

After days of argument and questioning of one witness (F. J. Michel) Martin ruled that there would be no more cross-questioning of witnesses, and that we must submit our arguments for the defense in the form of briefs. The Executive Board would render a decision after studying these briefs.

Leaving the trial room, I noticed the Negro who was of such huge size bending over and drinking from the fountain. I walked over and said, "Well, pal, what do you say?" He first glanced around very quickly, and whispered to me. He said, "You tell Mr. Sugar not to worry about us; we know the score." I learned that a Reverend Hill, a Negro minister, had contacted this group of Negroes and had given them some of the facts of life. From that day on, although Martin did not know it, these workers would have defended us in the event of violence.

After about a week of futile effort trying to conduct the "trials" on a legal and acceptable basis, we were informed by a member of the Executive Board of a plan to use violence and have our attorney and the five officers beaten up. We were advised to stay away. For this reason, and also because the rules governing the trials did violence to all concepts of reason and justice, we refused to proceed further with the so-called trials. Moreover, we were convinced that the final decision would, and indeed must, rest with the membership, and what the

Martin–Lovestone crowd did or said would be of no consequence. We decided to take the dispute to the membership, and to the national CIO.

The Martin–Lovestone Letters

Shortly after our decision to remain away from the farce in the international offices, the correspondence between Homer Martin and Jay Lovestone fell into our hands. Here was the evidence we had been looking for. These letters between Martin and Lovestone and his numerous informers inside the international union revealed an amazing web of intrigue and double dealing. They showed not only the conspiracy to weaken and possibly destroy the UAW, but a conspiracy between Lovestone and his agents inside the international office to undermine Martin himself.

In reading these conspiratorial documents, one could not escape the conclusion that Lovestone was, in fact, the real President of the international union. It was on his orders that so many of the men who had led the great sit-down strikes, and who had brought the membership from just over 20,000 in 1936 until it reached 400,000 in 1937, were all removed from the staff and the offices of the international union.

Once we had the damaging Martin–Lovestone letters in our possession, it was imperative that this evidence of Martin's duplicity be made known to the membership and the CIO as a whole as quickly as possible. The revealing correspondence was photostated, and Henry Kraus was given the task of preparing and editing a special edition of our paper. The paper was sent to every local union in the international. It revealed the essential facts and details of the conspiracy that had brought the UAW to the brink of disaster. The original correspondence was placed in the hands of President Lewis of the CIO.

The publication of this correspondence caused consternation in the ranks of the Martin–Lovestone cabal. Martin first denied any knowledge of, or acquaintance with Lovestone. Lovestone was not so shy. He admitted his correspondence with Martin was missing, and all the letters from Martin to Lovestone were written on the stationery of the international union and signed by Homer Martin himself.

The local unions' membership had but to compare the signature on the letters with Martin's signature on their local union charter. There could be no mistake. In addition to all his other faults, President Martin was a liar.

The Cleveland Convention

In April, 1939, a special convention of the UAW was held in Cleveland, Ohio, with headquarters in the Hollenden Hotel. This convention was called to terminate the factional war that had almost destroyed the union despite the fact that this Martin–Lovestone group represented only a small fraction of the membership. Martin and his small coterie held a separate convention of their own. At the Cleveland convention Martin was expelled from the union for ninety-nine years.

At this convention our caucus had about eighty-five percent of the delegates, but we had not yet decided whom we were going to elect President. It was generally understood to be a tossup between George Addes and me. Personally, I would have been just as glad to have had George selected, since he was a very trustworthy man. He was also much younger than I, and I was never ambitious anyway. It was a terrifically responsible job.

Attending the convention were Sidney Hillman, President of the Amalgamated Clothing Workers, and Philip Murray, Vice-President of the United Mine Workers, both claiming to represent John L. Lewis and the CIO. The name of John L. Lewis carried tremendous weight with the delegates and was decisive on crucial questions.

Philip Murray, a devout Roman Catholic, was strongly influenced by the teachings of his church. He was guided more by the encyclicals of Pope Leo XIII than by the principles of American trade unionism. We were not aware that Hillman and Murray were determined that neither Addes nor I should become President. We were also not aware that neither Hillman nor Murray spoke for Lewis.

Murray and Hillman supported R. J. Thomas for the UAW Presidency, a man who, up to that time, was practically unknown.

He had been put in as Vice-President of the international union by the Martin–Lovestone clique but had never shown anything that would justify his choice for this enormously difficult post.

I was approached by Sidney Hillman and Philip Murray and was asked who my choice was to succeed Homer Martin. They indicated their preference for Thomas. I declined to support Thomas. I said that I would support whoever was the choice of the Unity Caucus. Hillman indicated that he had talked to Earl Browder, and that Browder was for the election of R. J. Thomas. I said that I did not care who Browder was for and that I was opposed to R. J. Thomas. I said further that it appeared to me that the new President must be one who had made a contribution to the international union. I said, "R. J. Thomas was the last man to desert Martin and Lovestone. He has done nothing and has said nothing to deserve such an office and would still be a Lovestonite except that he is being groomed for Martin's replacement. I cannot support him."

The following day the Communist Party appeared in the persons of Louis Budenz, Bill Gebert, Roy Hudson, and Earl Browder. I was approached by Budenz and urged to support the CIO and R. J. Thomas. I refused. I was then contacted by Roy Hudson who tried to tell me that Thomas was the choice of Lewis and the CIO. I told him I did not believe this and I would not support Thomas. I knew Lewis did not want R. J. Thomas as president of the UAW and I felt that Hillman and Murray had their own fish to fry. I had, and still have, the highest respect and regard for John L. Lewis. In my opinion he has done more for American labor than any other individual to date.

Murray addressed the convention and launched into a Red-baiting tirade directed at Ed Hall, George Addes, and me. Now George Addes could by no stretch of the imagination be labeled a Communist. He was the most devout Catholic I ever knew in my life. And Ed Hall was a thirty-second degree Mason. Murray said, ". . . and now this Red Shylock is demanding its pound of flesh." His meaning was clear. He was determined to push aside the officers who had saved the union from the Martin–Lovestone conspiracy, and to place into office a man who would take orders, and who would attack Lewis, in the developing struggle for power in the CIO.

I went to Phil Murray. "What do you mean by referring to us as a Shylock demanding our pound of flesh? What do you mean, a pound of flesh?" He said that Ed Hall, George Addes, and I had become too controversial. "You men have made too many enemies."

What we did not know, and what the delegates did not know, was that there had already developed a split in the CIO, and the struggle to unseat Lewis had begun. Sidney Hillman was already very close to the White House and had the ear of President Roosevelt. The quarrel between Lewis and President Roosevelt had begun, and Hillman and Murray were on their way up, or so they thought.

Nevertheless, the tactics of Murray and Hillman caused great confusion among the delegates. Since it was thought that they were there as representatives of John L. Lewis and the CIO, many delegates felt that it was impossible to revolt against their recommendations. And so R. T. Thomas was elected President of the UAW by default.

The delegates were further advised to abolish all Vice-Presidencies and give more power to the President. This was the set-up in the miners' union and in the Amalgamated Clothing Workers. The delegates did go along and abolish the Vice-Presidencies. They did elect their own Executive Board, however, instead of following the example of the Amalgamated Clothing Workers. George Addes was elected as Secretary–Treasurer, but Ed Hall and I were no longer Vice-Presidents. John L. Lewis was quite upset over the election of Thomas, but we were not aware of this until much later.

Murray used Thomas to attack Lewis, since he did not have the courage to do so himself. Were it not for the interference of Murray and Hillman at the Cleveland convention, a far different CIO would probably exist today. George Addes or I would have unquestionably become President of the UAW and the union would have played a far more militant and decisive role in the years that followed.

The CIO convention in 1939 burst out into an open break

between Lewis and Hillman. This is one of the best-kept secrets I know of. I am telling it now because more than a quarter of a century has elapsed since then, and I can see no reason why it should not be told.

Lewis stopped me in the lobby of the Whitcomb Hotel and said, "Wyndham, there is to be an enlarged meeting of the Executive Board at two this afternoon. I would appreciate it if you would be there." I assured him that I would be present. The meeting began promptly, and Lewis announced that he would not be a candidate for re-election as President of the CIO. This was a closed meeting and the announcement was not released to the press. The announcement was a bombshell and brought forth an avalanche of pleas and protests from everyone present. Lewis was obviously very angry about something. Philip Murray paced the aisle, a very worried man.

Hillman arose and said, "Without John L. Lewis the CIO is impossible." Lewis turned to Hillman and said, "Since you have entry to the White House and I do not, and since you have the ear of the President and I do not, and since the President thinks I no longer speak for the CIO, I think you may be able to do more for the membership than I can."

It was clear that Lewis resented Hillman's frequent White House conferences, and President Roosevelt's practice of bypassing him. After all, Lewis was the elected spokesman for CIO, and to be pushed aside on important conferences with the White House was something he refused to tolerate.

After a three-hour heated session filled with repeated pleas and protests from everyone present, Lewis agreed to remain as President, but he insisted that it would be the last term that he would serve.

Hillman walked out of the meeting as Lewis was speaking, and the following year, in 1940, Murray became President of the CIO at the November convention in Atlantic City.

CHAPTER ELEVEN

THE AIRCRAFT ORGANIZATION CAMPAIGN

In July, 1939, Margaret and I left Cleveland for Los Angeles, where I had been assigned the task of organizing the aircraft industry. We left Cleveland early in the morning of a warm sunny day. We had just bought a new car (a bright red 1939 Buick), and looked forward to a long and pleasant trip. Our daughter, Irma, rode into town with us, and when we dropped her off at work in downtown Cleveland, Margaret could no longer hold back her emotions. It was hard for her to leave these familiar surroundings and our only daughter for the long separation. She began to cry and continued to cry until we had passed Elyria, Ohio. She then became reconciled to what appeared to be the inevitable, and regained her composure.

The trip took us five and a half days. When we finally arrived in San Bernardino and the San Gabriel Valley, the orange groves were a welcome sight after so many miles of barren desert-like country that contained only sagebrush and tumbleweed. The day was very warm, 109 degrees. We drove through Pasadena and turned south on Figueroa Street to Third and Spring Streets, where the UAW Regional Office was located. We were very glad to end the long drive and to begin the job of organizing the aircraft industry.

The Organization Drive Begins

I had first to familiarize myself with the size and scope of this vital industry I had come to organize. It extended from San Diego, California, north to Seattle, Washington, with the heaviest concentration in the Los Angeles area. With a potential membership of 150,000, this huge body of workers was almost completely without a union of any kind.

Boeing in Seattle, Consolidated in San Diego, and Lockheed in Burbank had "sweetheart" agreements with the International Association of Machinists (IAM), but few if any workers were members of the union. The UAW–CIO had very few members but they made themselves heard in the Douglas and North American Aviation plants and elsewhere.

The IAM had made no effort to organize aircraft, contenting itself with such agreements as it could get by way of the back door without the participation of the workers. At Lockheed, for instance, the corporation printed all the IAM leaflets on their offset presses. Such collaboration was common and it was intensified immediately upon my arrival. The press and radio sprang to the defense of the aircraft industry in its efforts to keep the open shop wide open. Red-baiting was their principal weapon. Everyone from John L. Lewis on down was an "agent of Moscow." We were said to be in a conspiracy to wreck our government's war preparations, to sabotage the national defense.

The amazing thing was that so many underpaid aircraft workers were influenced by this nonsense. Men and women working for fifty cents an hour (twenty dollars a week or less) would argue over the "Red" issue and be diverted from the real question. Men working for fifty cents an hour and taking home a pay check of $19.40 a week, after Social Security deductions, were on the ragged edge of hunger and starvation, and yet were often swayed by the propaganda of the *Los Angeles Times,* the Hearst *Examiner,* and other mouthpieces of monopoly.

The most noticeable thing about the aircraft workers was their youth. Shift change resembled a high school dismissal. In fact, most of the workers were in their late teens or early twenties. The aircraft companies had conducted a recruiting campaign throughout the nation that had resulted in a tremendous migration of young men to southern California. Representatives of Lockheed, Douglas, North American, and Boeing were located in such eastern cities as Cleveland, Chicago, Detroit, Philadelphia, New York, and others. Their task was to entice young people to California through false promises and advertising. The aim was to flood California with a huge surplus of unemployed and potential workers who would be driven by poverty to work for a pittance.

"Learn Aircraft Engineering" was the slogan. A young man would be urged to buy a course in aircraft engineering costing him, in some cases, as much as $600. Upon his arrival in California he would be taught how to use a rivet gun, and after a short training period would be put to work in an aircraft plant at fifty cents an hour (Walsh–Healy minimum wages). I tried to expose this racket, but I did not have access to the daily press. Moreover, the press is not likely to expose or injure their advertisers, so the flood of young people continued and there was an oversupply of vigorous young men seeking jobs and careers in aircraft.

I decided to publish a weekly paper called the *Aircraft Organizer*. This paper was distributed regularly at Vultee, North American, Lockheed, Ryan, and Consolidated. I arranged with the Workers Alliance to take charge of the distributions. The first distributions were met with insults and abuse. The CIO was charged with being a Communist organization. Everyone from John L. Lewis to Harry Bridges was labeled an "agent" of the Kremlin.

It was again the same old red herring used by the open-shoppers in the East. However, as in the East, I felt the union would prevail because it had the answer to the problem of low wages and bad conditions. The fifty cent wage was not caused by the Kremlin, and no amount of Red-baiting would raise wages so much as one penny. The worst offender in Red-baiting was the IAM. Its leadership was mentally bankrupt, permitting the organization to be used as a bar to real unionism in the aircraft industry. The contracts signed between the IAM and Consolidated Aircraft, Douglas, and Boeing were concluded between the management and the IAM officials without the knowledge or consent of the workers, and in fact without any membership in these plants. These contracts were then used as a bar to organization by the UAW–CIO.

The IAM was the first labor organization to break the solid front in opposition to the Taft–Hartley Act in later years, and signed the required "non-Communist" affidavits in the expectation that it would benefit thereby. This wrong policy led the IAM from one defeat to another, and the benefits it sought by cravenly complying with the Taft–Hartley law finally resulted in its total loss of prestige among the aircraft workers.

The Vultee Strike

After about three months of our campaign, the workers at Vultee were clamoring for a National Labor Relations Board (NLRB) election to win UAW certification as the bargaining agent. I was perhaps over-cautious but I was not so sure of winning an election in so short a time.

In November, 1939, Vultee employed approximately 600 workers. New workers were being hired rapidly and by February, 1940, 4,000 workers were employed in the Downey plant. Many of them were from the cattle ranges of New Mexico, Arizona, and Nevada, young men to whom fifty cents an hour was a fabulous wage. In fact, some of them freely admitted to me that they felt they were overpaid. They were convinced the aircraft companies were a sort of benevolent society that lost money on their labor. No amount of argument could convince them otherwise. It was this sort of atmosphere that caused my hesitation in asking the NLRB for an election.

Another and a different factor caused me finally to ask for an election. This was the age of the workers. A very large proportion of them were of marriageable age, and they could not afford to get married on a take-home pay of $19.40 a week. This proved a most important factor and was one of the most potent reasons for our winning the election.

Following the election victory, I addressed a letter to the

Vultee management asking for a meeting, the purpose being to negotiate a collective bargaining agreement. A meeting date was set, but management did not appear, only an assistant personnel director. He was without authority of any kind and could not conclude an agreement.

After six weeks of this run-around, it was evident that something drastic was necessary. A strike vote was ordered. The vote was overwhelmingly in favor.

In the summer of 1940 the aircraft workers at the Vultee (Downey) plant had reached the end of their patience and could no longer endure their miserably low wages. In Los Angeles, fifty cents had begun to look not so good after all.

The Aeronautical Chamber of Commerce had decided that the Walsh–Healy Minimum Wage Act, which set the fifty cents per hour minimum, should be regarded, not as the minimum wage, but as the maximum beyond which they would not go for new employees. The result of their decision was that the average wage paid in aircraft in the year 1940 was fifty-two and one-half cents per hour.

This low wage meant the aircraft worker had a take home pay of about twenty dollars per week for forty hours. A strike vote was overwhelmingly in favor of a strike and accordingly, on November 15, 1940, a picket line closed the Vultee plant, and one of the most significant struggles of the aircraft workers began.

On the day preceding the strike, November 14, I had called the international union office in Detroit to advise President R. J. Thomas of the impending strike and to obtain his sanction, but he was not in his office. He was on his way, by car, to the CIO convention in Atlantic City. I then called CIO President John L. Lewis in Washington. I explained the situation to him and he gave his personal approval for the strike, saying, "Go ahead, I will support you." Lewis also said, "You must get rid of President Thomas, Wyndham." I knew that Lewis and Thomas were not on friendly terms and that Lewis had recently referred to Thomas as a "dunderheaded blabbermouth," so I replied, "I am inclined to agree with you, John, but my immediate concern is this strike." He repeated his promise to support the strike.

Lewis kept his promise, even though the entire weight of the press, radio, and others were mobilized against us. R. J. Thomas, influenced by Hillman and Murray, was on the verge of calling the strike off and would have done so except for the opposition of Lewis, Addes, and others.

The strike was one hundred percent effective and stopped the production of training planes for the armed forces. This fact aroused all the reactionary elements in America and the flood of abuse and vituperation that descended upon the union and upon me in particular was something to behold. There was no criticism of the industry for paying starvation wages while doing business on a cost-plus basis. The entire weight of the propaganda machine was directed against the CIO and the UAW.

Once again we found men in the leadership who rated "respectability" above the needs of those who live by work. Philip Murray and Sidney Hillman, both of whom had basked too long in the White House sun, exerted all the pressure and prestige of their offices to drive the Vultee workers back to their jobs at the impossible wage of fifty cents an hour. All of their influence was directed toward Thomas, urging that he order the men back to work and demanding also that I be removed from California. I was kept informed of this through telephone conversations with Addes and Lewis, who both supported the strike.

During a mass meeting of the strikers across Lakewood Boulevard from the Vultee plant, a slender dark-haired woman came to me and asked, "Are you Mr. Mortimer?" I assured her that I was, and she asked me to meet with two men from the War Department who were at the Biltmore Hotel. I said I would meet them, but not alone, I would bring Lew Michener, UAW–CIO Regional Director, with me. We went to the Biltmore.

One of the men we met wore a colonel's uniform. His name I do not recall. The other was in civilian clothes. His name was Major Sydney Simpson. The colonel immediately asked me to order the strikers back to work pending negotiations. I refused this suggestion and said I thought the government should bring its pressure and influence to bear against the aircraft companies instead of against the union. He left the room at once and I did not see him again.

I told Simpson that the company officials had not met with us at any time and the first step must be to arrange a meeting between the union and the company. Simpson did arrange such a meeting for 10:00 A.M. the following day. I appeared, with the negotiating committee, promptly at 10:00 A.M. and met with Mr. Harry W. Millar of the Vultee company. Even though both the union and the company were present and ready to proceed, Major Simpson, the War Department conciliator, did not appear.

After a wait of several hours, Mr. Millar left the room, giving me a phone number where he could be reached. When Simpson did not appear after several days, I went looking for him. During all this time the daily press was carrying on a vicious anti-union campaign, blaming us for the delay in settling the strike.

When I arrived at the Biltmore Hotel lobby, I ran into the slender dark-haired lady who had approached me several days earlier near the Vultee plant. I asked her where Simpson was and she pointed to the bar. I found him there, too drunk to stand up. I was angry and contacted Walter Smethurst, a union representative. We both went to the press room and exposed the fact that the Federal conciliator was too drunk to participate in negotiations. The newspapers ran big headlines to that effect, and Simpson was recalled immediately. The union and the company then proceeded to negotiate without a conciliator, and arrived at a settlement.

The agreement was the best in the aircraft industry at that time. The greatest gain achieved by the union was the smashing of the fifty cent minimum. The starting wage became sixty-two and one-half cents. This was a real victory at that time since it destroyed the ruling of the Aeronautical Chamber of Commerce which had fixed the Walsh–Healy fifty cent minimum as the maximum starting wage in aircraft. This victory gave the organizing drive a real boost and we knew that we would soon be able to move against Ryan in San Diego.

Shortly before the scheduled contract-ratifying meeting of

the Vultee local, I received a telegram from R. J. Thomas instructing me to delay signing the contract until he arrived. "R.J." wanted his picture in the papers showing him signing the contract that brought peace to the aircraft industry, even though all the work had already been done by the negotiating committee.

I met Thomas at the airport and drove him to the Biltmore. Upon entering the hotel lobby, we were surrounded by the press. They immediately began to question Thomas about newspaper stories of "Communist influence" in the Vultee strike. R.J.'s answer was a classic, an example of stupidity personified. He said, "You boys notice that nobody is calling *me* a Communist, don't you?" The implication was that charges against others, me in particular, had some foundation. Leaving the lobby and walking down the corridor to the meeting rooms I told Thomas, "Tom, that was the worst chicken shit statement I ever heard!" He did not answer me. News photographers dutifully snapped his picture while signing his name to a blank sheet of paper and his desire for publicity was satisfied.

CHAPTER TWELVE

THE NORTH AMERICAN STRIKE

In the fall of 1940, I petitioned the National Labor Relations Board for an election to determine the bargaining agent at North American Aviation in Inglewood. I presented signed application cards totaling thirty-five percent of the employees then working at the plant. The IAM petitioned the NLRB for a place on the ballot. This was granted. There followed a vicious campaign of slander and epithets.

The IAM was led by James Lynch, an unimaginative person whose whole campaign was conducted negatively. He was against the UAW. He was against the CIO. He was against Harry Bridges, John L. Lewis, and Wyndham Mortimer. In fact, he was against everyone except the North American Aviation Corporation. What the IAM under his leadership was *for* we never found out. Lynch tried to convince the North American workers that we were agents of the Kremlin and that Joe Stalin was the enemy. Red-baiting, name-calling, and all the usual outpourings of a small mind were used to confuse the aircraft workers and prevent the spread of industrial unionism to the aircraft industry.

The election was ordered for February 20, 1941. The campaign took place during the rainy season, and passing out literature was a messy operation at times. We used our sound equipment to good advantage and carried on a vigorous campaign inside the plant. My policy was to point out to the workers that it was the aircraft manufacturers who were paying the low wages, that it was the Aeronautical Chamber of Commerce who fixed those wages, and that Joe Stalin and the CIO had nothing to do with it. The campaign became a contest to see which union would be most effective in getting its message across.

The campaign lasted about two months. We were putting out our paper twice a week, the IAM was putting out a big paper twice a week, and in addition to this we were both putting out mimeographed leaflets each day. Five other newspapers were being distributed, issued by commercial interests, just an advertising attempt to reach the aircraft workers' market. The workers would come out of the plant, thousands of them, and no sooner were they out of the gate than they would have an armful of paper. If it was raining, which it frequently was during that period, the papers would get wet and many of them would just throw them down and walk away.

I mentioned to Philip M. (Slim) Connelly, who was head of the CIO Council in this area, that we would have to stop putting out so much paper. He said, "You can't walk off the field and let them have it alone." I told him that I did not intend to do that.

The first thing we got up was a little booklet. It had probably twenty pages. We called it "Facts for Aircrafters." It was filled with information vital to aircraft workers. For instance, the first page would have what they call "decimal equivalents." You take an inch and it is divided into thousandths of an inch. How many thousandths of an inch are there in 360 seconds, and so on. Alongside of that would be some factual information regarding their work, the chemical composition of Duralumin, how to do various things. For example, we printed one table in the booklet called "Bend Allowances." This information was difficult for most workers to obtain; it was contributed by an engineer who belonged to the union. Across the bottom of the page would be printed VOTE CIO. This booklet went over big with the fellows. Many of them, not even members of the UAW, came to the union office to ask for them.

On one occasion we had six girls dressed up in red berets and blue capes, and each one had a big basket of little penny suckers. On the paper of the sucker was printed, "Don't be a sucker—Vote cio." One of the girls was my daughter and she said that a lot of the fellows would come back to her and say, "Give me two, I've got two kids. Give me two more."

We had something like that each week. Another time, through the efforts of one of our organizers, John J. (Scotty) Orr, we arranged for a bagpipe band, and the Scottish women paraded during the shift change, playing the bagpipes and beating the drums.

In the meantime, the IAM kept up their drumfire of Red-baiting. The day before the election was the real payoff. They had put out a leaflet baiting the CIO, me, Bridges, Lewis, and of course Joe Stalin was in on it too. I told Kraus, who was working with me, that we would have to do something startling on election day.

I had noticed that on the bottom of their leaflet they had printed, "This leaflet was handed to you by a real 100 percent American." I suggested we go to Hollywood and see if we could find some real, original Americans. So we did. We went and hired about eight Indians. We asked them to come dressed in the clothes they would wear back on the reservation.

When the whistle blew, we had two of these fellows at each gate. One of them had on a loin cloth, and a feather sticking in his hair. He had a deep bass voice and looked like a bronze giant. He just kept handing out these leaflets and saying to the workers, "VOTE CIO." All that was printed on the leaflet was "This leaflet was handed to you by real 100 percent original Americans!" Everybody stopped and looked. Traffic was paralyzed. This, I think, was what clinched the whole thing. It made the Machinists' Red-baiting arguments look so silly. The election took place the next day and we won. Our margin was only sixty-five votes, too close for comfort, but considering the hysteria in the country at that time, it was a notable victory. And the North American workers joined the ranks of the UAW–CIO.

We now had a good nucleus on the West Coast. My plans

were to bring the entire aircraft industry into the UAW–CIO and we were well on our way to accomplishing this when, as so often happens in the labor movement, jealousy and factionalism reared their ugly heads. There followed one of the most shameful pages in labor history.

Banished to Seattle

Immediately following the North American election I received a telegram from R. J. Thomas instructing me to stay away from North American Aviation. I could not understand this, since it was plain that the workers there had confidence in me. But it was apparent that R. J. Thomas and Richard T. Frankensteen and other people in the international office were apprehensive about our success, worried about the publicity that comes with success. If I succeeded in organizing 200,000 aircraft workers, as indeed it seemed I might now do, they could only see me as a dangerous threat to their jobs. As a result of Thomas' order, I did stop going to North American. Frankensteen came out to the West Coast soon after and ordered me to Seattle, where the Boeing workers were in revolt against the IAM. The Machinists had expelled the local union leaders and the entire membership rose in protest.

My wife and I drove to Seattle and into one of the worst situations I ever experienced in all my years as a labor leader.

We registered at the Roosevelt Hotel about 10:00 P.M. The next morning, going into the coffee shop, I bought a copy of the *Post Intelligencer*. Big black headlines across the front page read, "COMMUNISTS INVADE SEATTLE." The article declared that I had arrived in Seattle the previous night, accompanied by thirty-nine carloads of goons. (It must have taken a mighty imagination to expand my little, 110-pound wife into thirty-nine carloads of goons!)

After breakfast, I went to the office of the *Post Intelligencer* and asked to speak to the editor, Mr. Boettiger (F.D.R.'s son-in-law). I was told he was not in. The attack on me continued. On the basis of this first slanderous story, a storm of threats was launched in my direction. Dave Beck, Teamsters

Union President, threatened to have me thrown in the Snohomish River. The District Attorney promised an investigation of my activities. The police shadowed me, and it was impossible to find a meeting hall. I had often heard and read of cities being controlled by gangsters, but now I was experiencing the real thing. The entire business community was terrified of Dave Beck.[20] If I had not experienced this I would not have believed it possible.

I had brought our sound equipment from Los Angeles, but found it impossible to rent a garage to house it. I rented the Civic Auditorium for a mass meeting and the police appeared and padlocked the doors. Our deposit of $900 was returned. I arranged a meeting at the Fishermen's Hall and the Fire Department promptly condemned the building.

The *Post Intelligencer* had said that I was ordered into Seattle by the Communist Party. The District Attorney wired R. J. Thomas, asking him if I was in Seattle on his orders. Thomas wired back saying that he knew nothing of my whereabouts. It was possible, of course, that Thomas did not know where I was, because I worked on the organizing staff under Frankensteen at that time. But he could have readily found out where I was by just going into Frankensteen's adjoining office. It appeared to me that upon receiving a telegram from the District Attorney he should have been alerted to something out of the ordinary. The incident revealed either his ineptitude or his bad faith.

I petitioned the National Labor Relations Board in Seattle for an election at Boeing. They would not process the petition. The Dave Beck forces owned the Democratic Party in Washington and it was futile to expect action of any sort.

Someone threw acid on our sound equipment, and every time it was taken out to be used it would be shot full of bullet holes. The police refused to act. Appealing to the police was an exercise in futility.

The Boeing company fired everyone who was active in the UAW and many others who were merely critical of the IAM.

My wife and I were getting uneasy because of the violence which was going on. One morning I noticed two men by the elevator. They were Filipinos. They followed me into the coffee shop and walked behind me all the way to the CIO office. The secretary of the CIO was there and I said, "Harding, what's happening around here? There are two fellows following me around and they followed me here. They are in the lobby now. Who are they?"

He laughed and said, "Dave Beck won't bother you as long as those fellows are around. They make their living gutting fish." They were well-known to the thugs and were experts with a knife. They followed me everywhere I went while I was there, for about a month, and nothing happened to me. I have often recalled this striking silent demonstration of union solidarity.

In this situation, where the entire city and even the NLRB were controlled by the Dave Beck machine, I decided to return to Los Angeles, where other important developments were brewing.

All this time, the situation at North American was growing worse and worse. Frankensteen had taken over the negotiations and had made many speeches. He had the workers all hopped up and ready to go on strike. My wife and I headed for home and as we neared Bend, Oregon, we heard on my car radio that the North American workers had voted to strike.

Frankensteen's Responsibility

It had been Frankensteen who had set the original deadline for the strike, and just before the negotiations broke off, Frankensteen had said to the company's representatives: "We won't settle for anything less than seventy-five and ten (seventy-five cent minimum and a ten cent general raise), and if we don't get that by Wednesday (May 28), we hit the bricks!" It was Frankensteen, moreover, who at the time of the strike vote proposed that the power to call the strike be left in the hands of the local negotiating committee. When asked at this time about authorization for a strike, he replied to the committee, "Don't worry about that, that's only a piece of paper and I can fix that up!" Frankensteen had thus assumed the basic responsibility in working up the strike sentiment at North American and in preparing the entire groundwork for such action.

On the day that negotiations broke off, Frankensteen announced to the committee that he had asked the National Mediation Board to take over the case. This announcement was received with misgivings by members of the committee since the record of the Mediation Board in strikes occurring on the West Coast had been exceedingly bad. John L. Lewis also had issued a warning about the Board's strike-breaking record. Nevertheless, through Frankensteen's action, certification of the case to the Mediation Board was more or less an accomplished fact and the committee reluctantly agreed to go along.

On May 27, the three members of the negotiating committee who had gone to Washington, together with Frankensteen and Lew Michener, the UAW's Pacific Coast Regional Director, reached an agreement with the North American management, postponing the strike deadline in return for a concession by the company of a retroactive pay clause. This agreement contained the following points:

1. Any raises or other concessions would be retroactive to May 1.

2. The union would not strike until three days after the Mediation Board had published its findings.

3. In case it did strike prior to this time the retroactive pay clause would be lost.

These terms plainly indicated that the union was holding firmly to its option to strike at any time the negotiating committee felt that it was necessary or advisable to do so. It was not a no-strike agreement. The terms merely held that if a strike did take place, the retroactive pay clause would be lost.

The representative of the Mediation Board gave assurances to the negotiating committee that there would be absolutely no delay in pushing the negotiations. Nevertheless, it was fully six days before a Board panel was obtained to hear the case. Here again the same story of delay and stalling was repeated, with the company adamantly refusing to make the slightest concession above the fifty cent minimum.

It should be mentioned that, in this final crucial period of negotiations, Frankensteen was not present at a single one of the sessions. He excused himself by stating that he was busy with the Chrysler negotiations.

The negotiating committee decided that further parleying of this sort was simply a waste of time. It was the same old policy of delay, linger, and wait that had been used for so long to maintain this unbearable fifty cent minimum. The six members of the committee who were still in Inglewood contacted the three members who were in Washington by telephone and they decided unanimously for an immediate strike.

This decision was fortified by the report of the six men at North American that further delay would be perilous to the continued strength of the union, since many men were quitting the organization and others were beginning to heed the call for wildcat action coming from provocateurs and other dubious elements in the plant. It became a question of either striking unitedly with the full force of the union behind such a strike, or allowing wildcat actions to dissipate the strength of the union.

When I arrived home on Sunday, I called Lew Michener. His wife told me a mass meeting was scheduled in the CIO Building for that afternoon and asked me to attend. Michener, Elmer Freitag, and Walter Wiitenan (leaders of the NAA local) had just returned from Washington, D.C. They made their reports, but were not able to calm the workers. They were impatient to strike. Michener asked me to assist the negotiating committee in its efforts to postpone strike action from June 4 to some indefinite date. I took the floor and urged the workers to be governed by the wishes of the regional director and their own committee. I urged them to exercise patience, and to remove the Tuesday strike deadline. They voted to do so. The meeting adjourned and I felt the immediate crisis had passed and that perhaps a strike could be averted.

The following evening I learned that the situation was again at the boiling point. My daughter worked in the office of the local, and she called me to say, "Pop, these fellows are going to go on strike tonight."

I said, "There isn't much I can do about it. Who's out there?" She told me that Bioletti and Althof, two union representatives, were both there. I spoke to Ross Althof and requested that he and Bioletti use the sound truck to speak to the workers at lunchtime and urge them to stay at work. Neither Althof nor Bioletti went near the men at lunchtime and the strike began.

On Thursday, June 5, at 3:00 A.M., as the night shift left work, they set up a picket line which, at 6:00 A.M., was swelled by the thousands of day-shifters coming to work. Even the Hearst papers admitted that this was the largest picket line in California's history. It was entirely peaceful; not a man sought to enter the plant. The company locked the gates and the strike was on.

I was still under orders to stay away from the NAA plant, but since the strike had begun I went out to the headquarters and set up a kitchen where the pickets could get coffee and food.

The strike proceeded on its peaceful course. Everyone who came in contact with it admitted that it was a model of organization and rank-and-file control. However, on Saturday, June 7, Frankensteen flew into town and without warning summoned the negotiating committee and the international representatives to appear before him. At this meeting he issued his command that the strike must be terminated immediately and that the workers must return to the plant, even though they had not received so much as a promise that the company would grant anything above the fifty cent wage.

At the meeting with Frankensteen on June 7, I told him I did not agree with him. I pointed out that he was as much to blame for the situation as anyone, and that to raise the question of strike sanction at this time sounded very funny to me, since he was responsible for as many unauthorized strikes in our organization as anyone. I asked him who authorized the GM sit-down strike. It was not authorized until long after it occurred. Who gave sanction to the Chrysler strike in 1937? Nobody did, until after it was an accomplished fact. Who authorized the recent Vultee strike? Actually, it was not authorized until several days had elapsed and then Thomas gave it reluctant sanction. He agreed that he had helped to manipulate many strikes without sanction, but maintained that this one was different.

Frankensteen did not confine himself to reasoning. He threatened every possible punishment in case the local leaders refused to obey his edict. Meanwhile, upon his request, a membership meeting of all strikers had been called for the following day (Sunday), at which time he was to bring his proposals before them. Imagine our shock, then, when that very Saturday evening we heard Frankensteen on a nationwide radio broadcast (donated by whom and for what reason?) denounce the strike and its leaders in terms that exceeded the attacks of the Dies Committee in virulence and falsehood![21]

Frankensteen sent me a wire asking me to meet him at the Biltmore Hotel. I went to the hotel and met with him, Mike Dragon, and two other men, one of them Frankensteen's press agent. Frankensteen said, "The strikers must go back to work." I asked, "On what terms?" He answered, "No terms, they just go back!" I was told to go out to the picket line and order them back to work. He knew the men had confidence in me. I refused.

My refusal precipitated an argument during which I told Frankensteen that I had spent the past two years telling the aircraft workers that the UAW would raise their living standards and benefit them in many ways, and that I had meant every word of it. I would not now betray them.

He said, "Well, Mort, you know what that means?"

I assured him I understood.

By the time I arrived back home there was a telegram firing me from the international staff.

So ended my years as a UAW organizer.

How and Why the Union Was Destroyed

I am not prepared to analyze the minds of Richard Frankensteen and Sidney Hillman, in denouncing the strike at North American and in calling it "Communist-led and -inspired." Nor can I understand how men who aspire to the leadership of labor are able to sacrifice labor's interests in favor of the Democratic Party. I cannot understand men to whom a visit to the White House is more important than getting the workers out of the dog house.

Moreover, I could not spend two years with the aircraft workers, preparing their minds for the acceptance of the UAW–CIO as their bargaining agent, and then reverse my position on orders from someone in Washington, D.C. (because there can be no doubt that the command to end the strike came from someone high up in the government), who either did not know or did not care what the consequences would be to the aircraft workers. I could not bring myself to betray these young people.

I could not spend two years telling them to organize and fight for a better life, and then, when they accepted my promises and were in the midst of the struggle, withdraw that support and betray the young men and women who had given me their confidence.

Frankensteen got his orders from Hillman. I have this on excellent authority. Hillman was so close to the White House that the glare of publicity blinded him and he was unable to see the woods for the trees.

My two years' effort had accomplished the thing I had set out to do. The entire aircraft industry on the West Coast was ready to fall into the lap of the UAW–CIO like a ripe plum. And now, I could see all this work was lost.

For the international union to claim that the strike was unauthorized was a ridiculous argument. Actually, up to then, there had not been one authorized strike by the UAW since its inception. Nevertheless, the international union had never before refused to support a strike of one of its locals on the flimsy excuse that it lacked authorization. Yet this was the reason now given for its betrayal of the North American strikers.

The following morning, Monday, there was a picket line around the plant that was ten thousand strong. Over a thousand police were sent to the plant to break the line and allow a handful of scabs in. But all such attempts were quickly crushed, despite a barrage of tear gas. It was only the unprecedented order of President Roosevelt for United States troops to take over the plant that finally broke the strike. Such extreme action on the part of the Administration would never have been possible were it not for Frankensteen's public denunciation.

After the troops arrived and broke the lines and escorted scabs into the plant, and arrested the strike captains, Frankensteen immediately issued a statement praising the troops and condoning their actions and offering to gather a scab army to help them. He said, "In the event the deliberate failure of certain skilled workers to return to their jobs should create a bottleneck in the supply of skilled labor, our organization will cooperate with the Federal government to supply the necessary skilled union workers from organized plants throughout the country."

What were some of the actions of the troops at North American to which Frankensteen so glibly gave his blessing?

The forceful smashing of all picket lines; the illegal arrest of sixteen strike captains by the troops and their detention in an army camp where they were stripped, fingerprinted, mugged, and third-degreed at great length; the subjecting of all neighborhoods in which NAA workers lived to an armed patrol by army trucks loaded with machine guns; patrolling of meetings of NAA workers even after they had formally decided to return to work. Most serious of all were the actions of the troops inside the plant. They were posted everywhere, bristling with arms and marching up and down all aisles. Numerous workers were forced to tear up their union cards and to remove their union buttons. The officer in charge of the plant, Colonel Branshaw, posted a notice calling for an unlimited speed-up in production. Workers were subject to dismissal without possibility of redress.

Over twenty-five union officers, chief stewards, and stewards were fired, and as they were fired they were immediately reclassified by their draft boards and made eligible for induction into the army. All this occurred before our country was involved in the war.

The members of the NAA negotiating committee were fired from their jobs when they were suspended by Frankensteen, and these men have remained blacklisted ever since! They were forced to leave their work in aircraft and go into other lines of work, many of them hounded by the blacklist and government investigators throughout these many years.

Although more than twenty-five years have passed since the North American strike, the international union has stubbornly refused to process the grievances of Elmer Freitag, Walter Wiitenan, and ten others who were blacklisted from the industry and have been harassed ever since. The UAW, by its refusal to seek justice for these men, has become a partner in their persecution.

What followed the strike at North American can only be understood if we know something of what was going on in the top echelons of the CIO.

John L. Lewis was under attack by Sidney Hillman and Philip Murray, both of whom sought to displace him as the CIO voice at the White House. Both wished to bask in the sun of publicity that surrounded the Roosevelt presence.

Hillman had a special concern with the spread of fascism. The Hitler massacre of the Jewish people was unparalleled in history, and Hillman regarded the strike at North American as weakening the defense effort and this country's help to those fighting Hitler.

The split between Roosevelt and Lewis had begun some time back. I met Lewis at the UAW convention in St. Louis in 1940 and I asked him to tell me what his differences with Roosevelt were. He told me that he wanted certain promises from Roosevelt in the form of concessions to labor, in return for labor's continued support. Roosevelt would not make any commitments because he had been told by Hillman and Murray that Lewis no longer spoke for the CIO.

Lewis finally endorsed Wendell Willkie for the Presidency because Willkie had promised to grant concessions to labor. But so great was the Roosevelt influence among the workers that no one, not even John L. Lewis, could persuade them to follow Willkie. In my opinion, Willkie was a more liberal-minded person than Roosevelt, but this fact was unknown to the average working man or woman. Undoubtedly, Roosevelt was widely accepted by American workers as their friend. When he had assumed the Presidency, F.D.R. was confronted with the overriding problem of saving capitalism. Our "American way of life" had collapsed, with somewhere around twenty million unemployed. If, in his efforts to get the economy back and functioning, a few crumbs in the form of WPA and CCC fell to labor, it was incidental and not because F.D.R. was basically pro-labor. In my opinion, he was pro-private enterprise and differed from other Presidents merely in the way he carried out this fundamental loyalty. F.D.R. will go down in history as the man who saved capitalism from itself, after Hoover and other apostles of *laissez-faire* had all but killed it.

I have dealt with President Roosevelt only because millions of American workers regard him as labor's friend. Certainly, destroying food and plowing little pigs under ground was not the work of a friend when hunger was widespread in the land. We should understand that "friends" of ours are not found among millionaires.

John L. Lewis has done more for American labor than all the politicians in Washington. We must recognize this if we would keep our thinking straight. Lewis gave us the most powerful weapon American labor ever had. With this weapon, we destroyed the open shop and raised our living standards.

American labor, and especially its leadership today, is afflicted with a virulent disease known as Respectability. It is wedded to the racket of free enterprise, the right of the few to rob the many. The Executive Council of the AFL–CIO believes in and advocates a system by which private capital has monopolized the earth and robbed the common people. Its president, George Meany, is one of America's most blatant warmongers. His right-hand man, Jay Lovestone, is reported to be a CIA agent.

Aftermath

Out of a job, my wife and I moved back to our little cottage in Cleveland, Ohio. I was there about fourteen months without a job of any kind. I was offered two jobs by different corporations who wanted me to become a labor relations man, but I told them, "No, my whole life has been spent on the other side of the table, and I see no reason why I should switch now." Both corporations made very nice monetary offers.

After fourteen months, at the 1942 union convention in Chicago, a number of delegates went to Frankensteen and Thomas and asked them what was happening with me. They also told the two regional directors from Ohio, Paul Miley and Dick Reisinger, that if I was not put back to work, they would not go back as regional directors. They in turn put pressure on Thomas and Frankensteen.

Frankensteen came to me to tell me how sorry he was for what had happened in California, and that it had been a big mistake. He told me how much he appreciated the great efforts I had made and that I was undoubtedly the outstanding organizer in the UAW. He said I could go back to work on his staff. I said, "That is fine, but where?" He said, "Well, you can go back out to Los Angeles if you want to and continue in aircraft." I asked how Thomas would take that, to which he replied, "It doesn't matter what Thomas says, I'm putting you on my staff." I told him I was going in to see Thomas, since Thomas could block it if he wanted to do so. He would have to sign the checks. While money is not the most important thing to me, I did have to eat!

I went in to see Thomas and told him I had just talked to Dick and that he was going to put me back on his staff. I said, "I would like to know what your position is on it." He said, "I am opposed to it." When I asked on what grounds, he hesitated a minute and then went back to the Homer Martin days and said, "During the Homer Martin days you and I were on the opposite side of the fence." I said, "Yes, that's right. But what were we fighting about, Tom?"

"Well," he said, "we had an argument about collective security." I said, "Yeah. I thought collective security among anti-fascist nations was a good idea then, and I think it is now. What do you think now?"

By this time we were in the war, and of course he was in favor of it now. I said, "Well, then what is the argument about now?" He said, "You also called me a dumb son-of-a-bitch." I said, "Tom, I never called you a son-of-a-bitch. I thought you were plenty dumb a lot of times, but I never called you any names like that."

After a few more words of little consequence, he said, "All right, you write me a letter and tell me that you want to go back on the staff and I will let the Executive Board make the decision and I will not vote one way or the other. If they want to put you on, all right." I said that was fine with me. I went into the next office and had the girl type up a letter requesting to be returned to the staff, saying that Frankensteen had agreed to put me on his staff organizing in aircraft. I took it in and put it on his desk. He went to a Board meeting in Philadelphia the next week. This was right after the Chicago convention, and I fully expected that it was in the bag and I would be going back to work.

After the Board meeting in Philadelphia, Thomas had not yet returned when I called George Addes and asked what had happened in Philadelphia. He said, "It is all set. You are going back on the staff. I am just waiting for Thomas to come in and sign the paper." I waited a few days and nothing happened. I called Detroit again. Thomas was still not there. In the meantime I got a telegram from Allan Haywood, of the national CIO, asking me to come to Washington to report to his office as soon as possible. I went to Haywood's office in Washington and he handed me a credential saying that I was on the staff of the CIO, not the UAW. I said, "How come? I am supposed to go on the UAW staff." He smiled and said, "We will not release you." I did not understand him, so he said, "Oh, you've been on our staff for over thirty days."

This was obviously a gimmick. What had actually happened was that during the Philadelphia meeting, the Detroit papers, the *Free Press* and the *News* had come out with big stories about the convention in Chicago, and saying that Thomas was paying off his political debts to the Communist Party, and that I was to go back on the payroll while a man named Devereau was to be fired. (Devereau was a professional anti-Communist.) Thomas was afraid to go back to Detroit, so he had gone to Washington and asked for Murray's help. The Board had voted to put me on the staff and he could not refuse. If he put me on, it would look as though the newspaper stories were correct. So Murray had taken him off the hook by putting me on the CIO staff.

I didn't know whether to take the job or to tell them to go fly a kite. I called my wife and asked her what she thought. She said I should do whatever I thought was best. I talked to Mike Quill and several others, including George Addes. They all thought I should take the job and wait until the heat was off Thomas, when we could change it. So I took it.

They sent me to Denver, Colorado, where there was absolutely nothing for me to do. It is sheep-raising country with little industry. As for my duties, there simply were not any. I spent several months just riding around the beautiful Rocky Mountains, doing nothing. I kept writing to Haywood asking him to transfer me to someplace where there was work I could do, but he kept making excuses and saying there were no openings anywhere.

I wrote, finally, and said that I could just as well be doing nothing at home, as fifteen hundred miles away from home. But, he still refused to assign me to an industrial center. In the industrial centers like Cleveland, or Detroit, they would contact the leadership before assigning an organizer, and say, "What about so-and-so?" Apparently I had worked up such a reputation as an organizer that people like Thomas, Reuther, and others looked upon me as a potential threat. I had somehow managed to be the center of discussion in too many newspapers, and in their book this was not good.

So I continued to spend time wandering around Denver. I went through the coal fields in Colorado, down to Ludlow where the massacre had taken place. I visited that place several times and saw where the women and children had been burned to death. The Miners' Union had erected a statue of a coal miner with his pick and shovel. He had one arm around his wife and the other arm around a little child. I became well acquainted with the sights and scenes of the Rocky Mountains.

Finally I was told to go to Salt Lake City, Utah. The Steel Workers director there, a fellow named Varrow Jones, was a bishop in the Mormon church and he wouldn't touch me with a ten-foot pole. He was wasting his time trying to organize a plant that had about 800 people, about 600 of them women. Jones would call a meeting on Sunday and I'd go to the meetings and sit there. I noticed there was not one woman at the meetings. I asked one of the fellows there, "How do you expect to organize this plant unless you are able to reach the women?" He didn't know. "That is up to Jones," he said.

I mentioned this to a fellow from the Mine, Mill, and Smelter Workers and said there should be at least one woman on the organizing staff. He took me to his home, where I talked to his two daughters who worked in the plant. They were fed up with Jones and the whole works. One girl said she had never worked in a plant before, and yet they put her on a drill press right away. One day she was having trouble, and asked one of the men to help her get the drill out to have it sharpened. His reply was, "You're getting as much money as I am, take it out yourself." He was a union representative. She said, "They'll never organize those women. Never." I raised this question with Jones. He spoke very curtly about women's place being in the home and why didn't they stay where they belonged. They never did organize the place, of course.

The only thing I was able to do in Salt Lake City was to help the CIO regional director. He was a little Italian named Bonacci. He spoke with an accent, and occasionally had trouble among these clannish people in Utah. He would say to me, "You talka better English, maybe you could do something with them."

We were in the war, of course, and there was bitter feeling among the people against the Japanese. A packing house in Salt Lake City had gone on strike because the workers were refusing to work with the Japanese. The union had received a telegram from the CIO in Washington demanding that they go back to work because the war effort needed meat. Bonacci asked me to go into the meeting and talk to them. There was a lot of criticism of the Japanese, a lot of name-calling.

I finally asked the chairman if I could say a few words. I introduced myself and told them the purpose of my visit. I pointed out to them that many of them had sons in the armed forces and they would not want to do anything to deprive them of a piece of meat just for the sake of their emotions and feeling for the Japanese people. I also pointed out, "The war with Japan was not caused by the common ordinary people of Japan, any more than it was caused by you." I spoke against prejudice and as I talked they all listened very intently. The meeting lasted for about two hours and the heat finally died down. They voted to go back to work. When I went back out to the car, Bonacci was still sitting there. He had been sitting there all that time. He asked what happened, and I said, "Well, they're going back to work!" He was very impressed.

The internal struggle was still going on between the UAW and the CIO, with everyone building their various political machines, and I was still stuck in the Rocky Mountains. From Salt Lake City I again wrote to Haywood and said, "Allan, if you can't transfer me to someplace where there is a job for me to do, someplace where I can become active and render a service for the money I receive, I am going to have to quit and go home." He wrote back saying that he was very sorry but that he could not find an opening for me.

In the meantime, while I worked in Utah, my wife and I had decided to move to Los Angeles permanently and had sold our Cleveland home. We no longer liked the winters in Ohio. We had decided I could be "away from home" in Los Angeles as well as Cleveland, so Margaret had gone on to Los Angeles to establish our home there. Our daughter was living in Los Angeles with her baby daughter while her husband was in the Army and on his way to Europe.

I quit the job and headed for Los Angeles. Soon after I arrived the State, County, and Municipal Workers, CIO, asked me to take over their office here. By this time many of the organizers were being taken into the armed forces. Almost the entire staff of the Mine, Mill, and Smelter Workers union had been called to war, and I was asked to take over their office. I left the State, County, and Municipal Workers and went to work for Mine, Mill until the war was over. In 1945, the union fellows were coming back to their jobs, so I quit that job, and my wife and I hopped in our old Buick and went back East for a visit with her folks and mine.

That was my last union job, although I am still very much interested, of course, and still write articles for the union papers and keep up a large correspondence with union members and old union friends, like John Anderson, Cap Kenny, Charlie Beckman, Bill Dieter, and many, many others. Many of those I used to know have died, and I am now looked upon as a relic of the past. But I still enjoy going back and seeing the fellows and finding out what's going on and where they are going from here.

CHAPTER THIRTEEN

THE PROBLEMS BEFORE LABOR

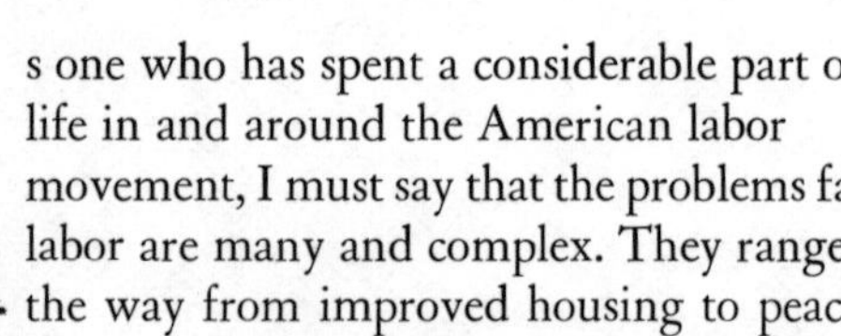

As one who has spent a considerable part of his life in and around the American labor movement, I must say that the problems facing labor are many and complex. They range all the way from improved housing to peace and disarmament. The question of war or peace casts its shadow over all other matters, for unless we avoid a nuclear war there will be no problems to solve. And prosperity based on war, such as the war in Vietnam, is a dangerous and horrible illusion! But in the minds of millions, the most immediate problem that demands an answer is the question of unemployment. A job is an absolute must, and without it, the future is bleak, hopeless, and worrisome.

We have two major causes of unemployment today aside from the usual one, erroneously called "overproduction." The first of these is called "automation," and the second is the flight of jobs to the low wage areas of the world.

If one wishes to view the future awaiting millions of working men and women, it can be seen in that industry where automation has been developed to the greatest degree—the coal industry. Large areas in the coal regions of Pennsylvania, West Virginia, Ohio, and Illinois have become depressed areas. Thousands of unemployed coal miners have been existing on pitifully inadequate amounts of corn meal, beans, rice, and other foodstuffs, doled out by the Surplus Commodity Corporation. This poverty is not caused by a decline in the coal industry. On the contrary, coal production has reached an all-time high.

This same condition is rapidly developing in other industries. Time was when we could expect new industries to take up the slack, and the men and women displaced in one industry could eventually find work in another. This is no longer true. It is not true because investment capital is not being plowed back into new industries in America in anything like the amount required to employ the millions now being displaced by automation. When investments are made, it is in automated plants and factories where fewer workers, not more, are employed. Capital is, of course, international. It seeks the highest profit, regardless of geography. While capital is international in its outlook, the practice of industry to channel production into low wage areas has been accelerated tremendously since the end of World War II. It has gone much further than most of us realize. Perhaps a few examples will help us to understand something of the importance to labor of this development.

Whole industries have fled to such low wage areas as Japan, Italy, Germany, and elsewhere. The plywood mills of Oregon and Washington are closed down, and the huge logs of spruce, redwood, and ponderosa pine are towed in huge rafts to Japan, where they are made into plywood and are sent back to America at lower cost than if they were made here.

Westinghouse and General Electric have bought or built plants in Italy and Japan, where radios, TV sets, and other electric gadgets are made. They are then sold here under the old familiar trade names. The old familiar names of sewing machines like Singer, New Home, and White, are being almost totally manufactured in Japan. They are then sold here under the same names that have been household words for many years.

The old clichés about American know-how are as dead as the dodo. We no longer have a monopoly on the techniques of mass production. New factories being built abroad by American capital are just as modern and up-to-date as anything here, while wages paid are but a fraction of ours.

It appears to me that the two factors of automation and the

flight of our boasted technology to other highly developed industrial nations have brought about a change that calls for some new thinking on the part of labor and its leadership. Our much touted American way of life cannot be maintained for long unless we in the labor movement also think and act internationally. Common cause must be made with labor everywhere, not to pull our standards down but rather to raise them up.

It is no solution to advocate a return to the oxcart days of production, nor will it solve anything to insist upon investment capital staying at home. It has no home. Its home is the whole earth or whatever part of it offers the highest return on its investment.

What is needed is not to quarrel or bicker with the workers of other lands over who is to perform certain jobs or tasks, or to argue that automobiles should be made here in America rather than in Britain, France, Germany, or Italy. The time has come to convince the workers and common people of America that we must produce wealth to *use* and not to make people rich. I am well aware of the fact that we in America have been brainwashed and intimidated until such words as peace and socialism are never mentioned in polite society. But these two words must be heard loudly and constantly.

Nature is bountiful, and the ingenuity of man is very great. The problem of how to produce in abundance for all has been solved. It has been solved for some time, but only that portion of our production is distributed which enables someone somewhere to get back more than he contributes. Profit is the sacred cow of our society. It is long past time for this bovine to be turned into steaks. Whatever its merits may have been in generations past, its continued existence is an anachronism. It stands athwart the highway of progress and bars the way to an economic paradise that is now within our grasp.

I said we must make common cause with labor everywhere throughout the world, but how is this to be done by a leadership that is wedded to things as they are? In their denial of the class struggle they disown the only reason for the existence of a labor union. For if the interests of the worker and the employer are mutual, then what possible reason can there be for the existence of the AFL–CIO?

American labor is no longer living in a vacuum. To an increasing extent the standard of life in America will be determined by the standard of life elsewhere. The American auto worker will not earn comparatively high wages for very long when the British, German, and Italian auto worker is making seventy cents an hour. The American metal miner cannot maintain his wage levels and compete with the copper miners of Peru who earn seventy cents a day. These problems of automation, low wage areas, and peace can be solved only if American labor will unite with labor everywhere. We must work with and not against the workers of the Soviet Union and the world's largest labor federation, the World Federation of Trade Unions (WFTU).

Red-baiting has done tremendous damage to the labor movement in America. It has destroyed some of the finest leaders the union ever had, particularly in the CIO. Since labor cut off its left wing in 1949 the old bird has been flying around in circles on those rare occasions when it has been able to get off the ground at all. At the 1949 CIO convention, Walter Reuther spearheaded the Red-baiters. He had started on his way to respectability and to becoming acceptable to capitalism. Only a fool could believe that the CIO was strengthened by purging the left wing unions, which represented almost a million members. Reuther was not always a Red-baiter. Indeed, he was once very much a left-winger himself and it was then that he made his most important contribution to the UAW. I first met him shortly after he and his brother Victor had returned from a trip around the world. They had been in the Soviet Union, where they had spent a considerable time working in a Soviet auto plant in the city of Gorky. Both of them were starry-eyed over what they had seen and were loud in their praises of the Russian workers who, they said, were building a "Socialist society."

But Walter Reuther forgot all about his past. Perhaps some of his memory lapses were due to expediency and some to extenuating circumstances. Unfortunately, he forgot many other things, as well. I mention these things now to illustrate the lack of principle that has animated Walter Reuther all throughout his life. When principle was in conflict with ambition, principle was always the loser.

As one who lived through, and participated in the beginnings of the UAW and the CIO, I have only contempt for those who now attempt to rewrite history to substantiate false claims of being the founders of the international union. The theme of a recent UAW convention in Long Beach, California (May, 1966), was "Thirty Years of Progress." The thirty years, of course, began at South Bend in April, 1936. But the UAW began *before* April, 1936! It began in the shops. It began when the open shop was supreme. It succeeded because at each critical point the rank and file rejected all divisive forces.

Presently, as in the past, the greatest hope of American labor is in the rank-and-file membership, the men and women who pay their dues and who maintain unity and solidarity at the bench, the lathe, and the assembly line. When a little more experience has taught them a few more facts of life, they will decide they have had enough. The leaders who have forgotten their origin and mission will be swept aside. Their places will be taken by younger and more militant leaders, fresh from the shop, mill, and factory. Rest assured, this new and younger leadership is already in the making. We may not yet have heard their names but to doubt that these future leaders exist is to doubt the whole of American labor history.

As human beings we have come a long way since man climbed down out of a tree and walked erect. We have come up through savagery, barbarism, feudalism, and now capitalism. Many have taken the next step and entered socialism. At each successive step on our upward climb, the beneficiaries of the old order have opposed the new. It is so today, but we shall not stop here.

This changing world includes us too. The future belongs to us, and there is one grand thing about the future—there is lots of it!

A PERSONAL AFTERWORD

have been urged many times to give my views on religion, and to relate my experience as I developed or evolved from the primitive religion of my childhood until I grew to reject all so-called "revealed" religions.

I was born into a devoutly religious family of the Protestant persuasion. On the parlor table of our home there were two books, the Bible and Bunyan's *Pilgrim's Progress.* Both were brought from Wales by my parents, and both were printed in the Welsh language. Since I could not read Gaelic, I contented myself with looking at the pictures. There was a picture of God in *Pilgrim's Progress.* He was a benign-looking old man with long whiskers who sat on a throne beside a river surrounded by a host of angels. There was also a picture of the Devil. He had horns, a forked tail, and cloven hoofs.

To the men and women of that generation, both of these impossible creatures were *real.* We were taught that God knew our innermost thoughts and was listening to every conversation. God was everywhere. The Bible was the word of God. It must not be questioned under peril of eternal punishment. As a small boy about eight years old, I asked my father why, since God was everywhere, no one had ever seen him. Dad replied, "With God all things are possible," and said that we must not doubt the Bible's teachings.

We were told that the Devil, too, was everywhere, and that he never stopped trying to lead us astray. We must be on guard all the time lest he lead us into some sinful activity. So, between these two deities, we children had our minds filled with fear and trepidation.

I did not seriously question all this until I was about fourteen years of age. I had heard about Colonel Robert G. Ingersoll, who had toured America during my younger years. I had never seen him nor heard him speak, but his influence was great. His lectures against Christianity drew enormous audiences. He filled the largest auditoriums and his attacks on Christianity were devastating. His ideas and statements were repeated by those who had heard him and the attacks upon him by priests and ministers were loud and long. His soul was assigned to everlasting fire and brimstone.

My doubts were first aroused by a man older than myself, a Swede named Friedhof Whitman. Whitman had seen and heard Ingersoll and would tell me some of his criticisms of Christianity. They seemed true and did not do violence to my reason. The arguments of Whitman and Ingersoll destroyed to a great extent my beliefs in the miraculous. There was still a lingering thought, however, that perhaps there was a God somewhere in the far-off universe. But such thoughts were vague and I ceased to fear this nebulous creature that no one had ever seen nor made contact with. I did not make my doubts known because I did not wish to disturb my parents, but I continued to grow away from the orthodoxy of the time.

I continued attendance at church. It was the only recreation available in the coal-mining patches of Pennsylvania, and after six days under ground, Sunday was a welcome interlude to the hard and dirty toil of a coal mine. I played piano at church and Sunday school. I sang the old Christian hymns. It was one place the boys and girls all gathered, and in fact was a sort of social assembly where gossip was exchanged.

When I left the coal fields and moved to Ohio, I was already what I would call a freethinker. After I moved to a larger community and came in contact with a more progressive element, I was introduced to the *Age of Reason*. This book was written by Thomas Paine, the "most famous immigrant ever to step on American soil," as Ingersoll called him. The book was loaned to me by an Englishman whose name was John Fauldon, a worker in a steel mill. He was a voracious reader and he introduced me to the works of Darwin, Bradlaugh, and Ingersoll.

But the final blow to Christian dogma in my thinking and to the impossible creeds and teachings of Christianity was *God and My Neighbor* by Robert Blatchford. Blatchford was an English Fabian-Socialist who had mastered the art of putting great thoughts into simple words and phrases. Never having gone to the university or college, he had not learned how to "darken counsel with a multitude of words." His language was simple and direct. Like Ingersoll and Paine, Blatchford's logic was devastating. He took the dogmas and creeds apart, scattering the myths and allegories of Christianity to the four winds. He said, "If God is responsible for man's existence, He is responsible for man's imperfections. Man cannot sin against God, since man can only act as God had foreseen and intended that he should act."

Blatchford received a letter from a Christian who wrote about an animal called the "aye-aye" and denounced Blatchford's articles on religion. The Christian said:

> There is a little animal called an aye-aye. This animal has two hands. Each hand has five fingers. The peculiar thing about these hands is that the middle finger is elongated a great deal . . . to enable it to scoop a special sort of insect out of special cracks in the special trees it frequents. . . . In this, as in scores of other instances, is shown the infinite goodness of God."

Blatchford replied,

> The infinite goodness of God to whom? To the animal whose special finger enables him to catch the insect? Then what about the insect? Where does he come in? Does not the long finger of the animal show the infinite *badness* of God to the insect?

> If a man fell into the sea and saw a shark coming, I cannot fancy his praising the infinite goodness of God in giving the shark so large a mouth. The greyhound's speed is a great boon to the greyhound, but it is no boon to the hare.

Blatchford spoke of many things, such as ". . . if God made Adam weak, and Eve seductive, and the serpent subtle, was that Adam's fault or God's?"

It was criticism like this, taking in the entire range of myth and miracle that comprised the body of Christianity, that finally swept all the cobwebs from my mind. The dogmas of original sin, the Virgin birth, the story of creation, Noah's Ark, predestination, transubstantiation, were simply not true. My mind at last was free, and I have never felt a need for such superstitions since.

My position now is that outside of nature there is nothing. It is true that we are surrounded by mystery, and one of the most profound mysteries is the human mind.

What is life? What is thought? What is the subconscious mind? In an effort to find answers to these mysteries, many universities throughout the world are conducting studies of the many supernormal occurrences that have attracted widespread attention. What do they mean? I am glad that science is devoting a small portion of its time to unraveling these mysteries. I have personally had some very baffling psychic experiences. They were beyond explanation by any of the known laws of nature. Yet I am sure that nature has the answer. It is up to science to unravel the mystery. Two of the baffling experiences contained what can be called "evidence" of survival. I do not say proof, but evidence, yes!

I am getting old. As I write these lines in December, 1965, I am nearing my eighty-second year. At this age, and although my general health is good, I am aware that my life's span is not long, but to the question, do I fear the end, the answer must be no. The same Mother Nature that put me here will also remove me in good time. Why should one fear that which will come to all that is? In regard to death, there are two or three things I think about. There is first the question of pain. I hope that my end will be painless, or nearly so. Then there is the feeling of reluctance at leaving loved ones and friends. The thought of annihilation is distasteful to one who has experienced and enjoyed life. These thoughts have gone through my mind many times.

Death has dropped a curtain of mystery between us and those who have passed on. No theologian knows, or ever did know, any more about this mystery than we know ourselves. Is it wise, then, to sell even a fraction of our liberty of thought for a promise the Bank of the Future may fail to honor? As for me, I will

> So live, that when my summons comes, to join the innumerable caravan that moves to that mysterious realm where each must take his chamber in the silent halls of death, I go not like a quarry slave at night, scourged to his dungeon, but, sustained and soothed by an unfaltering trust, I shall wrap the draperies of my couch about me and lie down to pleasant dreams.

APPENDICES

APPENDIX—LETTERS

After he had been separated from active leadership in the labor movement, Mortimer retained his contact by becoming a tireless letterwriter and pamphleteer. At least two of his pamphlets were published, and for years he maintained a series of letters on current labor problems sent to a large regular list of union activists. He also wrote a series in *People's World*. Many other letters appeared in the regular daily and weekly press on a variety of subjects and gained attention. Altogether, his miscellaneous writings would fill a volume or two. The following is a more or less random sampling.

June 18, 1941

Mr. Philip Murray, President
Congress of Industrial Organizations
1106 Connecticut Avenue
Washington, D.C.

Dear Brother Murray:

As the President of the Congress of Industrial Organizations I feel you are entitled to a word or two of explanation on what transpired at the North American Aviation strike, and the part I played in it. Also I feel as one of the pioneers in building the United Automobile Workers of America I am entitled to an opportunity to state my case to you.

I think it is only fair to say that I had nothing to do with the calling of the strike. For five weeks prior to the strike, and while all this strike preparation was going on, I was in Seattle, Washington, on the Boeing situation, and had nothing whatsoever to do with the incidents leading up to the strike. Once the strike was called, I did all I could to help the men win. I also opposed Dick in his efforts to drive the men back to work as I felt then and feel now that had he endorsed the strike, the troops would not have come in and we would have won this strike.

As a matter of fact, the strike was lost and it was Dick's denunciation of the strike and the strike leadership that gave the signal for the attack which I feel has set back organization in aircraft for many a day. I feel it is only fair to say also that I did have a lot to do with persuading these men to return to work and have therefore kept in contact with them to the end that the threads of organization may be mended.

I was told by Lew Michener at least six weeks ago to stay away from the North American situation as there was great danger of a strike developing there, and since I have been a point of attack for a long time he felt it best that I remain out of the picture. I carried out Michener's instructions to the letter and took no part in the matter except as I was told to assist the negotiating committee in its efforts to postpone strike action from June 4th to some indefinite future date.

I took the floor and urged the workers to be governed by the wishes of the Regional Director and their own committee. We were successful at that time in postponing strike action, and I again withdrew from the picture on instructions of Michener. I carried out Michener's instructions to the letter and took no part in the developing strike crisis as it progressed from day to day. I think even Frankensteen will agree that this was true.

It is no exaggeration to say that the strike psychology built up in the minds of the young workers in the North American plant is the result of Frankensteen's handling of the situation, since in my opinion he did more than anyone else to create the atmosphere out of which developed the strike.

It was Frankensteen who raised the slogan of "75 and 10 or else . . ."

It was Frankensteen who authorized the strike vote.

It was Frankensteen who set the original deadline for the calling of the strike.

It was Frankensteen who spoke to the North American workers prior to his departure for Washington and told them in ringing words that he would get them "75 and 10" or "hit the bricks!"

It was Frankensteen who agreed to the proposal that the power to call the strike should be left in the hands of the negotiating committee or at least there is no record of his having opposed such a procedure.

It was Frankensteen who told the North American workers that he didn't have much faith in the Mediation Board, and that he was taking the matter to them just as a necessary move, but that he would not permit a delay of more than a few days, etc.

When asked "How about authorization for a strike?" he replied to Elmer Freitag, "Don't worry about that—that is only a piece of paper and I can fix that up."

On the morning of June 7th, Frankensteen called a meeting of all the International Representatives in the C.I.O. building, and told us that the strikers would have to go back to work Monday morning or he would go on the radio and denounce the negotiating committee as "irresponsible, impetuous, inexperienced," etc., and would denounce the strike as a "wildcat."

Lew Michener told him the matter could be arranged if he would agree to wait another day or two, so it could be done without injuring the morale and destroying the organization, but Frankensteen was adamant and said they must go back to work Monday.

Five members of the negotiating committee were willing to support Frankensteen in his efforts to get the men back to work, as was Michener also, and the reason these men did not continue to support Frankensteen was because he went on nationwide radio hook-up and denounced them as "irresponsible, inexperienced, etc.," and said the strike was called by the Communist Party before he had even talked to the workers in the mass meeting called for that purpose.

Now it seems to me that Frankensteen is due for some severe criticism for his actions in denouncing to the whole world the negotiating committee before he had even talked to the North American strikers, and his claims that the whole thing was engineered by the Communists is just so much hogwash! *There isn't one Communist on the negotiating committee and Frankensteen knows it!*

IF HE COULD COME TO THE BEAN FIELD MASS MEETING TO TALK TO THE STRIKERS AFTER HE HAD DENOUNCED THEIR LEADERSHIP AND THEREBY ALIENATED THEM, WHY DIDN'T HE COME AND TELL THE STRIKERS WHAT HE HAD TO SAY BEFORE HIS RADIO SPEECH AND VICIOUS PRESS RELEASE?

It was a publicity seeker's holiday and Frankensteen took full advantage of it by denouncing and blaming the "reds" for a situation that he was as much, if not more, to blame for as anyone else.

Now a word more about my reasons for taking the position I did. I am not trying to make any excuses, and am not trying to get back on the payroll of the International Union. In fact I am preparing to go back to work in the shop where I will be able to say my life is my own at least after the day's work is done.

At the meeting with Frankensteen on June 7th, I told him I did not agree with him because there were several factors in the problem that he was completely ignoring. I pointed out to him that he was as much to blame for the situation as anyone else, and to raise the question of strike sanction at this time sounded very funny to me since he was responsible for as many unauthorized strikes in our organization as anyone I could think of. I asked him who authorized the GM sit-down strike. It was not authorized until long after it occurred. Who gave sanction to the Chrysler strike in 1937? Nobody gave it sanction until after it was an accomplished fact. Who authorized the recent Vultee strike? It was not authorized until several days had elapsed and then Thomas gave it reluctant sanction. Who authorized the recent Ford strike? I am not certain, but it certainly did not have sanction before it happened. He agreed that he had helped to manipulate many strikes without sanction, but this one was different, etc. Now I am willing to leave it to your good judgment as to whether or not this argument of strike sanction has much validity in our organization where strike sanction is the exception rather than the rule.

Now, Philip, I felt then and I feel now that had Frankensteen given his sanction to this strike we would have achieved a victory in aircraft comparable to the victory in auto in the 1937 sit-down strikes. Out of this North American strike we could have set in motion a wave of organization sentiment that would have swept the entire aircraft industry and brought it into the CIO just as we did back in 1937 with the automobile industry but Dick's interest was not in doing this necessary thing, but rather he raised such questions as "strike sanction," "National Defense," etc. I think I am at fault in not trying to get in touch with you to find out your thoughts on the matter, but after all it was Saturday afternoon here, and three hours later in Washington. The next day was Sunday and for this reason (although I realize now that an attempt should have been made to reach you) I did not try to call.

At Sunday's meeting in the bean field Frankensteen read a telegram from R. J. Thomas urging the men to return to work, but did not read one from you. By this time the resentment against Dick was so great that we had difficulty in getting him safely away from the field. His statements about an organized booing squad are not true; the feeling against him was the result of his own mishandling of the situation, and rushing to the press and radio to denounce the men these strikers had just elected to represent them. After all, the committee had just come from Washington where they had been under attack by the Dies Committee, and they no sooner arrived home than they are again attacked by Frankensteen for the same reasons. Now I submit to you, is this the proper thing to do?

Dick's press statements praising President Roosevelt for sending in the army, and his praising the army for the wonderful way in which they broke the strike has destroyed whatever influence he had among the aircraft workers out here. The army not only broke the strike, but they tried desperately to smash the union as well. I think you have reports on their actions that will substantiate my statement on this. Picket lines were smashed and driven a mile away from the plant. The union headquarters were invaded by the military and everyone driven out. Eighteen picket captains were arrested without warrant or authority in law and were taken to a camp in San Pedro about twenty miles away where they were stripped naked and questioned for hours by the F.B.I. They were then released about midnight and told to "get going." They had no money for fare back home, and had to make their way back as best they could. This is the procedure that Frankensteen lauded to high heaven in his press releases and over the radio.

To understand this problem it is necessary to know something of the background. In my judgment it is wrong to try to govern a new organization composed of very young elements in the same way we would with an old established union composed of men who are older and more experienced. Moreover, these aircraft workers have had two previous bitter experiences with the UAW and are highly suspicious of any person that comes out to them from away back East and tells them one thing today and another thing tomorrow. They tasted false leadership in the Douglas strike in March 1937, and again in the spring of 1938 in the Northrup strike. In both of these strikes they were betrayed in a most flagrant manner.

After two years of hard and unceasing effort we have at last succeeded in building an organization, to the point where we had every reason to hope of completely organizing the aircraft industry on the West Coast. Under Frankensteen's leadership the whole thing is crumbling. As an evidence of the truth of this statement, I want to tell you that whereas before the strike we were collecting on an average of $300 per day in dues and initiations at North American, now since the men have been forced back to work we have averaged about two dollars a day.

The only possible solution to the problem now is to restore the confidence of these workers in the CIO. This can best be done by allowing them to carry through our democratic processes, as provided for in our International Union's Constitution.

After much urging, we persuaded the negotiating committee to go and talk to Frankensteen in an effort to compose their differences. He was adamant in his determination to go to Washington with a committee that he would *appoint*. The negotiating committee then offered to withdraw from the picture if Dick would agree to accept a committee elected by the membership. This he refused to do, and since the Constitution of our International Union specifically states that negotiating committees must be elected, this has only added fuel to the fire.

There are many things in connection with this whole sad business which cause the aircraft workers to wonder, and ask such questions as these:

Why didn't Frankensteen come to our mass meeting before he called us "communists" instead of after?

Who paid for the nationwide hook-up over which Frankensteen denounced our strike—and if it was donated, who donated it and why?

Why did the International and Frankensteen join in with the Dies Committee in an effort to discredit and destroy our confidence in our elected leadership while at the same time join in singing the praises of the U.S. Army for doing such a good job of smashing the strike?

Why did Frankensteen give out press statements lauding the President of the United States for sending in the troops and stating it was necessary to use the Army in unauthorized strikes?

Why did Frankensteen violate the Constitution of the International and give out press releases saying that "he" had suspended the negotiating committee, and then the North American Aviation Corporation fired these men and they have been unemployed since?

Now, Brother Murray, these are just some of the questions the boys at North American and elsewhere are asking and it is tearing the union down.

In addition to this the AFL is taking advantage of Dick's red-baiting press statements and they are at the present time intensifying their efforts and are meeting with some success. We can yet salvage the organization if this silly red-baiting is stopped, and the democratic processes are allowed to operate in our own union. After all, red-baiting is a badly frayed weapon out here on the West Coast where it has been used against Bridges to the point where it has become a nauseating odor in the nostrils of every honest person. I don't say there are no Communists on the West Coast. I know there are some here, but to say this strike was precipitated by them is just not true. The only real subversive element in the whole strike situation is the fifty cents per hour paid in the aircraft industry, and the Communists are not responsible for that situation.

I regard the actions of Frankensteen as a setback to organization in aircraft, but the situation is not hopeless if we but make some effort to understand the problem and approach it intelligently.

I am coming East in a short while, and would appreciate a meeting with you at which time we can discuss this matter fully.[22]

Fraternally yours,
Wyndham Mortimer
450 West 48th Street
Los Angeles, California

ims
uopwa
cio

August 11, 1949

The Editor
Ammunition
28 West Warren
Detroit, 1, Michigan

Dear Sir and Brother:

After reading the article, "Ideas Come to a Head" in the July issue of *Ammunition,* I feel somewhat ill.

I have been a working man all my life, and if there is any one loyalty I have, it is to the working class. Since I went to work fifty-three years ago at the age of twelve, I feel I am qualified to speak from experience. Early in life I learned certain lessons and I have not forgotten them.

I learned that the boss pays the worker to work eight hours, but does not pay him for eight hours' work. If this were not true, no wage-earner would be employed. The worker earns his pay in about two hours. The other six hours, he works for nothing; this is known as "surplus value." This is the tribute we must pay for an insecure and precarious livelihood. Is this not true? If it is true, then what can be the purpose of the article, other than to "darken council with a multitude of words"?

According to your article, this six hours of surplus value taken by the boss is only interest on his investment, or a "fair" profit. The fact is, it is a form of burglary. The capitalist is about as necessary to the general welfare as a bedbug. If all the capitalists in America were to die tomorrow, our productive capacity would remain unchanged, and we would learn of their deaths only by reading the papers. Like pirates, they live by levying tribute. It is as simple as that.

To fool the working people, big business is using the kind of arguments by which, as Lincoln said, "A man can prove a horse chestnut to be a chestnut horse." No amount of word-juggling will make a chestnut horse out of a horse chestnut. And no amount of propaganda can make capitalism fit the needs and hopes of the auto workers or the masses of American working people.

Unpaid labor, or surplus value as Marx terms it, is nothing

new. Capitalism hides it. Unpaid labor is not out in the open for all to see, as it was in other systems, such as feudalism or chattel slavery. That is why we don't see it until we begin to add things up.

Lincoln also said, "It has so happened in all ages of the world, that some have labored, and others, without labor, have enjoyed a large proportion of the fruits." He was speaking of the slave under chattel slavery, the serf under feudalism, and the wage-earner under capitalism.

The serf was able to spend part of his time working his own acreage, but most of his time was spent on the land of the feudal lord. The paid and unpaid labor was easy to see. In order to pacify the serf and keep him working, they invented the alibi of "divine right," and told him that God willed it that way. If the serf questioned the alibi and was courageous enough to say so, his future on this planet was short and extremely rough.

Suppose the present-day worker worked his paid labor in one building and his unpaid labor in another. He'd start to work at eight A.M., and by ten o'clock he'd have made his wages. Then he'd go to another building and produce six hours of unpaid labor. Everyone would see what was going on, and all this hocus-pocus about a "fair profit" would be known for what it really is—just an alibi for someone to get something he did not earn, because someone had earned something he did not get.

To say that the present-day auto worker agrees to a "fair" profit or a "fair" return on investment is just another way of saying that the poison injected into his mental bloodstream has had its effect. When all he reads in the daily papers, hears over the radio, or sees in the movies is a line of propaganda designed to foster the notion that we are living under the best of all possible economic systems in the best of all possible countries in the best of all possible worlds, it would be strange indeed if some of this lethal gas did not find its way into his ears and out of his mouth. Should this same auto worker seek enlightenment from his union publications, he would receive another dose of the same poison, liberally sprinkled with anti-Soviet propaganda.

Moreover, what the auto worker may or may not think today is no indication or guarantee of what he may think tomorow, especially when he learns, as learn he will, of the way in which he is robbed, of the way some of his leaders have learned to talk nonsense in a most clever way.

Under our so-called "American way," or "society of free men," or whatever fancy name we decide to use, the hard, cold fact remains: the worker, who must sell his labor power in order to live, can sell it only if a boss can be found, and only when he gives three-fourths of that labor power to the boss.

Moreover, the wage-earner without a job, and therefore without visible means of support, has no legal right to life. What sort of a "free" society is it where one man must beg another for permission to work? Permission to earn his livelihood? The fact is, the right to earn a livelihood does not exist for the wage-earner. He has only the right to ask permission to earn a livelihood. The right to work is fundamental. There is no real freedom where this right does not exist.

You say, "British socialism is not abhorrent to UAW members." Again, you say, "Most UAW members believe in a future non-Marxist world that includes privately owned corporations, paced by cooperatively owned activities and government-owned authorities—the so-called mixed economy, like Sweden, like Britain, but with the UAW and Roosevelt and Senator Norris added."

Now, isn't that a precious piece of nonsense? Roosevelt and Norris are dead. They have been succeeded by Truman, who shows his cynical indifference to labor and the common people by appointing Tom Clark to the Supreme Court to replace Frank Murphy.

I would remind you that surplus value would be perfectly safe with either Roosevelt or Norris. Their crime, in the eyes of monopoly, was that they saved capitalism from itself. Instead of looking forward to electing another Roosevelt, it would be more in keeping with reality to expect another Harding, another Hoover, or, God forbid, another Truman.

The so-called mixed economy of Britain is something about which the less said the better. While I believe that the British workers have benefited somewhat from increased pensions, free medical and dental care, and hospitalization, the fact remains that the same King issues the same decrees; the same British Army is called in to scab and break strikes; and, as Strachey says, "The Socialists are in office everywhere and in power nowhere."

The British coal baron who formerly held a million pounds in coal securities, upon which he earned two percent per annum, is now the holder of a million pounds in government bonds upon which he is guaranteed six percent. Is this what you call a "middle" economy? In what way does it get a fat parasite off the backs of the British people? The same royal family and the same aristocracy are still in the saddle, but their seat is more secure.

Bevin shows the same tender regard for the Shell Oil Company as did Churchill. The British Army is ordered to shoot the poverty-stricken workers of Malaya, Africa, and elsewhere. A "Labour" government, committed to the policy of "gradualism" cannot come to power. It can only come to office.

I believe it is the purpose of your articles to create an atmosphere of sympathy for the mistaken policy of gradualism that has led to the farce we are witnessing in Britain today. I am quite aware of the sincere desire of some Labour Party members to keep their promises to the people, but these sincere ones are rapidly finding themselves on the outside looking in. I refer to such men as John Platt-Mills, Robertson, Zilliacus, and others.

For my part, I am waiting to see what the social democratic government now in office will do in the present economic crisis. Will it drop its policy of gradualism, and tackle the emergency on socialist lines? Or will it drop all thought of socialism in order to reassure Wall Street, thereby getting another billion dollars and a breathing spell? My guess is that it will forget the British working class. It will seek to transmute the gold of working class militancy and revolt into the lead of passivity and subservience.

Social democrats in general show a touching faith in the infallibility of capitalism—a faith not shared by the more shrewd and clear-sighted capitalists themselves. The younger capitalists are quite able to see the extreme difficulty of their position; but they are determined to make another attempt to save the system that has done so much for them. They know they have at least one great asset, and that is the above-mentioned faith of social democracy in capitalism.

The middle economy you refer to is a cruel delusion. It is a dead end street that leads the working class nowhere.

The history of the American labor movement is a story of leaders who, in the main, have forgotten their origin and mission. They rise to power and leadership by militantly attacking the few who rob the many. Once in power, they concentrate on two things—to remain in power, and to defend the status quo. If you think this is an exaggerated statement, read the speeches of Sam Gompers, Bill Green, Philip Murray, and Walter Reuther before and after they reached the top. The metamorphosis of labor leaders is an interesting study.

In the August, 1948, issue of the *American* magazine, Philip Murray denies the existence of a class struggle in America. If there is no such struggle, then why the CIO? Why the United Steel Workers? Moreover, just what in hell has Phil been doing for the past fifty years, if not engaging in the struggle?

I have a vivid memory of a young redheaded fellow who had recently returned from the Soviet Union back in 1934. He was all afire over what he saw there, and regarded a soviet America as the goal of his ambitions. His speeches then and now are very interesting. He has now reached a very high place of leadership and power. His two objectives are to remain in power and to defend the status quo. I refer to Walter Reuther. If you don't believe me, ask him.

I have never been to the Soviet Union. I only know what I am told, but out of all the welter of information and misinformation, I think certain things are obvious and true. I believe they were the first country on earth to abolish Tsars, dukes, earls, barons, bankers, capitalists, and landlords. The Soviet worker no longer donates three-fourths of his labor power to a boss for the right to live. The standard of life is steadily and rapidly rising, with wages going up and prices coming down. They enjoy complete and free medical, dental, and hospital care. They enjoy economic security, and a future without worry.

To me, all this spells progress, and it is difficult to understand just why the publications of my union should direct their main attack against the Soviets, and not against capitalism. Why should they go out of their way to attack the system that has ended the robbery of the working class, while at the same time defending the status quo in America?

With every good wish, I am

Fraternally yours,
Wyndham Mortimer,
Local 32
5459 Fourth Avenue
Los Angeles, California

September 8, 1949

To the Editor
Long Beach *Independent*
236 East Third Street
Long Beach, 12, California

Mr. Editor:

After reading your editorial, "Robeson Affair" in yesterday's *Independent,* I am impelled to make a few comments. It appears to me that as one grows older and older, he learns less and less about more and more. Moreover, most editors seem determined to learn it the hard way.

Your editorial says, "It was the Robeson affair that caused the trouble," implying that the Legion-sponsored hoodlums' right to throw stones takes precedence over the right of the Civil Rights Congress to hold a meeting, and over Robeson's right to sing. It is obvious that you are not concerned that our Constitution and Bill of Rights were violated, but you are concerned only because such violation "plays into the hands of the Communists." As Abe Lincoln would say, "It is a case of the sinners calling the righteous to repentance."

If you were living up to your responsibilities as the Editor of a widely circulated newspaper, and if your love for America were as deep as you would have us think, you would condemn this Legion-sponsored assault upon our Constitution and Bill of Rights. You would put the blame where it belongs. It was not the Communists or Robeson who violated our Constitution. It was people who never tire of telling us what good Americans they are, and what poor Americans others are. They remind me of Shakespeare's virgin who "protesteth her virtue overmuch." Good Americans, like virtuous virgins, do not have to advertise the fact. And I have heard it said that patriotism is the last refuge of scoundrels.

Your editorial says further, "About a year ago, Robeson was in Long Beach for a meeting put on by left-wingers. After the meeting, Robeson and two local left-wingers barged into one of our best restaurants with an arrogant, let's-start-something attitude. It was apparent they were looking for some incident on which they could pin the label of intolerance. They were frustrated because all that happened was that the piano player played 'God Bless America' and everyone but Robeson and his party joined in the singing." Now isn't that a precious piece of nonsense? Could it be that Robeson and his party were looking for something to eat? Could it be that "one of our best restaurants" practiced the un-American custom of refusing to serve Negroes? You do not say whether "one of our best restaurants" served Mr. Robeson or not. Isn't there something wrong when a great American of color is unwelcome anywhere in America? Isn't there something wrong when smugness and hypocrisy inspire the singing of "God Bless America"? Probably the reason that Mr. Robeson did not join in the singing was that he recognized it for what it was—a clean shirt over a dirty skin.

No attack upon Robeson or the left wing forces in America would be complete without an attack upon the Soviet Union. Your editorial is no exception. I have never been to the Soviet Union. I am an American and all my life has been spent in America, but I am not so naive or stupid as to believe all the hogwash printed in the Hearst press about the USSR. I think our American press is utterly incapable of presenting an unbiased, objective report on that country. I think, however, that if conditions in the Soviet Union were as bad as we are told, the present anti-Soviet hysteria would not exist. It is precisely because conditions are improving in Russia and deteriorating in the western democracies that there is a need for the present hysterical outbursts of little men who do not understand the problems confronting the capitalistic world today.

By any standards we use, Paul Robeson is a great man, a great American, and a great human being. He is a great athlete, a great lawyer, a wonderful actor, and the world's finest baritone. He is today the most powerful voice of the fourteen million American Negroes, determined to end the centuries of discrimination and Jim Crow. Of course he is loved by many and hated by some, but was it not ever thus? Have we not always crucified our saviors and crowned our oppressors? I am sure Paul Robeson will be remembered long after his traducers are forgotten, and that we will build a monument to his memory after he is dead, as we did for that other great Negro, Frederick Douglass.

You say, "The right of assembly and free speech must be protected in this country." With this sentence I heartily agree. It will not be protected, however, if men like yourself fail to live up to their responsibilities by blaming the victim instead of the criminal.

With every good wish I am

Respectfully yours,
Wyndham Mortimer
5459 Fourth Avenue
Los Angeles, California

September 18, 1962

To the Editor
Inglewood Daily News

Mr. Editor:

One of the most frequent contributors to the "Letter Box" is an extremely thoughtless man named Robert Wassman. After reading his various letters, I have reached the conclusion that Mr. Wassman is not too well informed on the world situation, nor, apparently, does he know the difference between Communism and Shintoism.

His advocacy of a Cuban invasion is a case in point. He is obviously unaware of the consequences of such a move. No intelligent person advocates war in this day and age, and I am glad President Kennedy has not talked in terms of using force up to this time. Another world war is equivalent to mass murder and suicide, and while glib talk about using force is very easy for thoughtless people, it does not serve the best interest of America or the world. Mr. Wassman appears to think that Cuba is necessary to the Soviet Union as a base for their rockets. I would point out that a nation that is able to hit the moon, photograph its other side, and to orbit the earth many times, would have little difficulty in hitting New York or any other American city from bases inside the Soviet Union itself. Not one of our own scientists or military leaders doubts this.

A world-wide struggle is going on between two economic systems, Capitalism and Socialism. Such are the conditions under which this struggle is waged, that our difficulties cannot be solved by war. Present-day weaponry makes a resort to war unthinkable and insane. I would point out that the Soviet Union was born out of World War I. World War II gave us a Soviet China, Poland, Czechoslovakia, Hungary, Roumania, East Germany, and now Cuba. The end is not yet. There is an excellent chance that World War III would give us a Soviet world.

There is but one answer to the H-bomb and other weapons of mass murder, and it is PEACE. The real patriots today are those who are talking, working, marching, and striving for peace.

What is the alternative? These dedicated men and women who are giving of their time and resources to keep another war away from America are deserving of the thanks and gratitude of every human being. Patriotism does not consist in waving the flag and advocating war at this point in time, nor will it ever be.

Respectfully yours,
Wyndham Mortimer

February 25, 1964

Rev. James W. Fifield, Pastor
First Congregational Church
First and Commonwealth
Los Angeles, California

Mr. Fifield:

After listening to the Sunday evening broadcast I have a strong urge to write you, and express my reactions. An increasing number of Americans do not accept your fantastic stories about the kind of life the Russian people live. One reason is that too many Americans have visited the Soviet Union, and an increasing number is doing so. They are learning that even ministers of the Gospel can tell tall stories. I, too, have been to the Soviet Union twice, and the things I witnessed there have nothing in common with the impressions you give over the air. The Soviet Union is not heaven, but it is not hell, either. Their standard of life is higher than the French, for instance, and there are millions of Americans who are worse off than the average Russian.

You have but to go through the industrial cities of our own country to see misery as great as anything to be found in the Soviet Union. There is no hunger in Russia. There are no houses of prostitution or peddlers of dope.

The Soviet Union realizes that a healthy child is a national asset. So they have socialized the medical and health resources of the nation. Every child in the Soviet Union is assured of the best medical care possible. They are assured, also, of a completely free compulsory secular education, without being bedeviled with parochial schools. The result is magnificent.

I am at a complete loss to understand how any informed person, in this day and age, can praise and even eulogize that medieval superstition that passes for a religion and is known as the Roman Catholic Church.

This so-called religion that claims a monopoly on God, has caused and still causes most of the ignorance and misery now being endured by what we call the civilized world. Spain, Portugal, Italy, and the South American countries are an example of what I mean. If you tried to practice your brand of religion in Spain, you would soon find out the kind of reptile on which you lavish your praise. Your political and economic philosophy would no doubt meet with the approval of Franco and the Pope, but I am quite sure religion would not.

You profess concern about the kind of world your daughters will live in. Let me say they will no doubt live in a much better world than the one envisioned by their Dad. Your "Freedom under God" society (whatever that is) appears to be nothing but a deep concern for the welfare of the upper crust, the scum on top, so to speak. People like you and Dan Smoot, Dean Manion, Eddy Rickenbacker, and others, have fallen victim to your own própaganda. You don't know what time it is, historically speaking. You have lost all contact with reality, and you live in a dream world. The Soviet Union and China are here to stay, and the world you knew a quarter-century ago no longer exists. To blame Harry Hopkins for giving the secret of the atom bomb to Russia is a ghoulish sort of thing to do. Accusing a dead man of treason is quite safe, since he is no longer around to defend himself. A corpse cannot sue for slander. Basing my predictions on the situation today, I will say that your children will be living in a socialist world, and it is too bad that men like you will spend their time and talents in struggling against tomorrow.

Yours sincerely,
Wyndham Mortimer

March 8, 1964

The Editor
Hawthorne Press

In passing the newly opened Goldwater Headquarters today, I noticed a sign in the window which said "Why Not Victory?" I do not know over who or what they expect to achieve this victory, but I assume they are referring to the cold war. If that is their aim, then I am quite sure that Barry Goldwater and the people supporting him are completely unaware of what time it is, historically speaking.

The cold war is a world-wide effort on the part of the beneficiaries of the status quo to contain the efforts of subject peoples fighting for freedom and independence. Any calm and realistic appraisal of the situation must agree that "victory," in the commonly accepted meaning of that word, is impossible. We are no doubt the world's most formidable military power, but we have already lost the war in Viet Nam. We lost the war in Korea. We lost the Bay of Pigs invasion of Cuba, because in each case we were not fighting the armies of these countries so much as we were fighting a whole people. Every man, woman, and child in Viet Nam is our enemy. Eighty percent of the land area is in the hands of the Viet Cong, and the government that we recognize dares not leave the city of Saigon.

Now if the Goldwater people wish to get involved in jungle warfare all over the world, I am quite sure the American people will not approve. If, on the other hand, they expect to be victorious in World War III, where they expect to be fighting China and the Soviet Union, they will have first to convince the American people that incineration is the most desirable way of shuffling off this mortal coil. Like people everywhere, we wish to live.

It appears to me that every rational person must know that war is not the answer to the world's troubles. Demanding and fighting for peace is not cowardice. It is just plain common sense, and anyone who thinks that nothing has happened in the last half-century to make peace a necessity had better begin to rearrange the furniture of his mind.

In my opinion, Goldwater with his seventeenth-century ideas has about as much chance of becoming our President as I have of becoming the Shah of Persia.

Respectfully,
Wyndham Mortimer

March 24, 1964

Editor
The Forum

Dear Sir:

I would like to comment, if I may, on the letters of Jessie Williamson and the Wassmans. These three correspondents claim to trace the origin of property in land back to the Bible and God. They have an advantage over me, since I have never been on such intimate terms with the Deity as these folks appear to be. I must rely on such mundane authorities as historians and anthropologists for such knowledge as I possess on the question of property.

If by property these people mean land, and that apparently is what they are talking about, then every inch of soil on the continents of North and South America is stolen property. Land titles in our southwest originated with King Philip of Spain. How did this rascal get title to American land? Why, he sent his "Conquistadors," more accurately described as butchers, here to slaughter the defenseless Indians. I seriously doubt that God had anything to do with such crimes. Moreover, I would suggest that they read the Forty-fourth and Forty-fifth verses of the Second chapter of *Acts,* which say, "And all that believed were together and had all things in common. And sold their possessions and goods, and parted them to men as every man had need." I submit, this quotation is a very poor argument for the institution of property.

I would suggest too, that these people read up on American history. Let them read *Tecumseh,* by Glenn Tucker, or *The American Indian,* by Hamlin Garland, who tells us that when the white man arrived, "The Plains Indians were the most magnificent specimens of the human race the world had ever seen." Yet today, they are reduced to beggary, living in concentration camps called reservations, on their own land. The land-hungry white man had no regard for anyone or anything, and to obtain possession of the land, he committed crimes such as those committed by Hitler or Attila the Hun. When people tell us that this was ordained of God, I can only answer bosh and nonsense.

The institution of property in land is a clever device whereby the owner of land is able to levy tribute from the landless. But just because one owns a piece of land, he has no right to deny others the same privilege. I am American enough to think that people are people regardless of their national origin or complexion, and when Mrs. Wassman denies that there is discrimination against the Spanish-speaking people and other minorities, one cannot help but wonder if she has been in a state of suspended animation all her life.

Respectfully yours,
Wyndham Mortimer

APPENDIX—NEWSLETTERS

#7 January 15, 1950

Fellow Members of CIO:

As was to be expected, one of the first and most significant casualties of the civil war within CIO is the fight against Jim Crow. The campaign against racial discrimination is being pushed aside until the next annual convention, when it will again be noted in nicely worded resolutions.

For instance, the Greater Los Angeles Industrial Union Council, which accurately reflects the thinking of CIO in this area, recently decided that there was nothing wrong about minstrel shows portraying Negroes as servile half-wits and morons, as long as tickets to such affairs were sold to anyone regardless of race or color. They can see nothing wrong in depicting a whole race of people as being inferior—mentally, morally, and otherwise. Discrimination can exist only when Negroes are denied the opportunity of buying tickets to such shows, where they will be allowed to see themselves through the eyes of Jim Crow.

The mentality that expels vast numbers from membership because of differences of opinion is the same mentality that sees nothing very harmful in discrimination because of color.

Jim Crow and Red-baiting are very closely related. They are different sides of the same coin. To deny one the right to work because of his opinion is not one whit different from denying one a job because of his color. Red-baiting is intended to divide labor along the lines of political opinion, while Jim Crow is designed to divide labor along the lines of color. Both are anti-labor, and both are used by monopoly as the most efficient weapons in their arsenal against all working people—black, white, yellow, red, or brown. The Red-baiting phase of these anti-union activities I will leave to another time, and will devote this letter to commenting on the question of racial discrimination.

I am not raising this question of racial discrimination because I am a sentimentalist or humanitarian, but rather from the most selfish of reasons. As a worker, I know that Jim Crow is a very profitable project to those who live by exploiting labor. Working-class unity is as necessary to labor's future as the air we breathe, and this unity is not possible while there is racial discrimination. To relax the fight against racial discrimination is to desert and betray the interests of all labor. This is why we must all feel concerned when this important question is pushed aside. All workers, of any race or color, have an identity of interest that rises above all else, and those leaders who would forget this paramount working-class interest in order to stoke the fires of the cold war must some day face an accounting of their stewardship.

If the present leadership is sincere in its claims of opposition to Jim Crow, a most convincing way to demonstrate its conviction would be to do something about abolishing discrimination inside the unions. It is not an accident that the two largest unions in CIO, the UAW and the USA, with several hundred thousand Negro members in their ranks, do not have ONE Negro in any elective post. The Negro membership is not represented because, in my opinion, the present leadership does not want them represented.

When the question of Negro representation is raised, too often the answer is, "These offices are filled on the basis of merit, and not on the basis of color." Or, "To elect a Negro to office because he is a Negro would be Jim Crow in reverse." The President of UAW becomes quite eloquent on this point. He has been able to convince even some Negroes of the soundness of his position, for I have heard some of them support him in his arguments against the best interests of their own people. Negroes who fall for this line about "merit," and who support this position on convention floors, are helping to block the progress of their own people, regardless of how honest or sincere they may be in their position.

Who is to decide this question of merit? The minority of Negroes who lack the votes to elect? Or the majority of whites, who have the votes but who can see no merit in being black?

A measure of our President's sincerity may be obtained from the fact that whereas he does not think the Negro membership possesses sufficient merit to justify a place on the UAW Executive Board, he does regard himself as having enough merit to sit as Vice-President of the NAACP.

The fact is—and the top leadership knows it—that the Negro will *never* receive recognition without pressure. When discrimination is abolished, it will be time enough to think in terms of merit, not before. It took terrific pressure to abolish chattel slavery. It required pressure to have the Fourteenth and Fifteenth Amendments to our Constitution adopted. It has required pressure from our unions before many employers would even hire a Negro. It takes pressure to keep them in their jobs. Is this not true?

The employers' excuse for not hiring Negroes is the same as that given for denying them a place in the top leadership. The employer says, "We hire people on the basis of fitness or merit, and not on the basis of color." In either case, the result is the same.

Satchel Paige has been a great athlete for many years. Major-league baseball had to be pressured to recognize this fact. A few Negroes, like Larry Doby, Jackie Robinson, and others, are receiving recognition only because of pressure. The rank-and-file of our large CIO unions must pressure some of the leadership also. They must learn that the Negro membership is entitled to representation precisely because they are Negroes. They must learn that the unity of labor depends upon equality of all working people, especially inside our own organizations. We must first abolish racial discrimination where we can—inside the house of labor.

The Negro is the last hired and the first fired. The Negro gets the hot, hard, and heavy jobs. It is the Negro who is lynched with sickening regularity, and who seldom gets a fair trial in court. Since all this and more is visited upon the Negro by monopoly's greed for profit, is it asking too much that the Negro be given recognition and representation in accordance with his number and importance? There can never be a return to the unity we enjoyed ten years ago while there is discrimination of any kind inside our own organizations.

In a white man's world, the Negro worker has every problem of the white worker—plus one more: he has the problem of color. No person of the white majority can ever possibly understand what this means. The claim that our Negro membership is adequately represented by an all-white Executive Board is a piece of brazen, chauvinistic nonsense, advocated by those who see nothing really wrong in racial discrimination and do not understand the harm it does the American labor movement.[23]

There can never be unity and civil war at the same time. The civil war must stop. It is a luxury we cannot afford. It has already cost us a fourth-round wage increase, and is now causing us to lose the fight against racial discrimination. The leaders who can see anything good in civil war need to have their eyes examined. They need to reread the Constitution of the United States, and especially the Bill of Rights of that Constitution.

If the Bill of Rights of our country's Constitution cannot find a refuge inside the CIO, then where can it rest? Where is it safe, if not with us? We grew to our present size and power because the Bill of Rights was a vital, living, and functioning part of our union. No honest working man or woman can really believe in the Bill of Rights, and at the same time tolerate racial discrimination.

Sincerely and Fraternally,
Wyndham Mortimer

P.S. While the response to our appeal for financial support is very encouraging, it is still not enough to cover the increased demand for a wider distribution of our letters. As we told you, these letters are being mailed to the rank and file in an effort to restore real democracy to our union. They have been financed by a small group of members who recall the early days of CIO, and who know something of the role played by the rank and file at that time. To be effective, we must expand. In order to expand, we must have help. If you think we are making a worthwhile contribution and effort, we would appreciate your help. In any case, show this letter to your sidekick in the shop, and if you would like others to receive it, send us their names and addresses. Mail all communications to the address on the top of this letter.

February 14, 1950

Fellow Members of CIO:

Many working people have difficulty in understanding some of the peculiar things taking place in CIO. They cannot understand why so many of their officers spend so much time flitting hither and yon, all over the earth, in support of the Marshall Plan, the Atlantic Pact, and so forth. We cannot understand why our top leadership can be so interested in destroying existing labor organizations in Europe, that were in existence long before any of them were born, and also why they go so far away when there is so much to be done at home.

Like every other question, the answer is simple when you know the facts. It is not mysterious at all. You see, folks, there is money in it. It really pays off in good old American dollars.

These dunderheaded blabbermouths that spend so much of their time and our money in attacking the so-called Reds, raiding sister unions, hunting witches, and looking under their beds at night, have found a way to make patriotism a nice paying proposition. Let me explain.

After V-E Day, our State Department made a very interesting discovery. They found out that the European working class, just out of the Underground and exerting tremendous influence and power, could no longer be bamboozled by the old-fashioned, striped-pants diplomat. The smooth-tongued, slick-mannered individual, working out of the State Department, doing the work of monopoly's cartels, could no longer deliver the goods. The job now required someone who talked like a worker, with the mannerisms of a worker, and who apparently represented the American working class, but who, in reality, carried out the orders and wishes of the State Department. To get men of this kind was not difficult. There was an ample supply of men in both the CIO and the AFL who would plant garlic on their grandmothers' graves for less money than monopoly was willing to pay.

Accordingly, the Congress passed an Act fixing classifications and compensations, known as the Foreign Service Act of 1946. This Act provides, among other things, for two categories or classifications of "Labor Advisors." One group is paid a yearly salary plus overseas allowance, plus transportation, plus other monies. The other group is paid on a per diem basis, plus expenses, plus transportation. This was clearly too good a thing to be ignored.

Most people pay good money for trips to Europe, Asia, and Africa, and here was an opportunity not only to get the trips free, but to be paid handsomely for making them. The only catch in the scheme was that they had to use the talents developed in the American labor movement to sell the French and Italian workers down the river. At sixty dollars per day, and salaries up to $15,000 per year, selling the European workers a bill of goods was not too hard a job. Sixty dollars a day, or $15,000 a year, *plus,* can salve a lot of consciences, especially a long way from home, and where the selling job could be hidden behind a lot of double-talk about fighting Communism and saving the American way of life.

As the first example, let us take Mr. James B. Carey. Mr. Carey is Philip Murray's "Secretary of State," and one of those rare individuals who has succeeded in making ignorance an asset. Carey was appointed to the President's Committee for Foreign Aid on June 22, 1947. He served for a period of four-and-a-half months at fifty dollars per day plus ten dollars per day expenses. We do not know if he continued to draw his salary [from the union] during this time or not.

On June 19, 1948, Mr. Carey was appointed to the Public Advisory Board of ECA. Up to October 24, 1949, he had attended fifteen meetings at fifty dollars a day plus ten dollars a day. Mr. Carey is also a member of the Trade Union Advisory Committee of ECA, and attended meetings of that Committee in London, England, in March, 1948, and again in July, 1948, at fifty dollars per day plus ten dollars per day, plus transportation.

Since then Mr. Carey has made numerous trips to Paris, Rome, Geneva, Moscow, and London, carrying out the interest of the State Department in disrupting the established trade unions in France and Italy. We do not know whether Mr. Carey drew his salary as Secretary–Treasurer of CIO during all these European trips or not, but it would be interesting to know. It is the same Jim Carey who is now trying to destroy the FE–UE, and the very same Carey who recently stated that we are now going to join with the fascists in a war against the Communists.

Another example is Mr. Allen Swim. Swim is the Editor of the CIO *News,* and judging by the honeyed words he uses in describing the Truman "promise and forget" administration, as well as the vile abuse he heaps on the left, he is trying very hard to earn the money he has so far received, no doubt in the hope that he will get some more. Mr. Swim has been appointed as a "consultant" to the ECA Labor Office, and he receives fifty dollars per day plus ten dollars per day, plus transportation. He spent five weeks visiting England, France, Belgium, Germany, and Italy in February and March, 1949. Whom he was consulting with, and what they were consulting about, Mr. Swim has never told us, but we can think, can't we?

Then there's Mr. Victor Reuther. Vic is the brother of Walter Reuther. He is the Educational Director of the UAW, and was appointed co-chairman (with Philip D. Reed of General Electric) of the United States branch of the Anglo–American Productivity Council. I am quite sure every CIO member knows just what "productivity" means. It is usually spelled S-P-E-E-D U-P here in America.

In the opinion of the State Department (who, after all, represent monopoly), the lazy workers over in Britain were not working hard enough, and it was decided to teach the louts to work faster. So this so-called "Productivity Council" was established, and who was better suited to teach these lazy Britishers than our own Victor Reuther? Nor was it a bad choice, because the Educational Department, under Vic's direction, makes "time study" a part of the educational program. It also put out very fine charts that proved that a wage cut under General Motors' escalator clause was only an illusion. It was not a cut at all.

Victor was appointed April 4, 1949, and has made three trips to Europe at various times, and covering various periods, for which he received fifty dollars per day plus ten dollars per day, plus traveling expenses. Victor hasn't told us what the reaction of the British has been to American speed-up, but knowing some British workers as I do, I will bet money it is considerably less than cordial. We do not know whether Victor continued to draw his salary as Educational Director during these lucrative trips or not, but it would be interesting to know.

Another "Labor Specialist" is Harry L. Martin, President of the American Newspaper Guild (shades of Heywood Broun). Mr. Martin is a Labor Information Specialist, with headquarters in Paris. His salary is $12,000 per year, plus overseas allowance of $1500 per year, plus transportation.

Clinton Golden, close friend of Phil Murray, now is a "Labor Advisor" at a salary of $15,000 per year, plus overseas allowance, plus transportation.

Harry Broglia from United Steel Workers is a "Special Labor Consultant" in Italy at a salary of $10,000 per year, plus overseas allowance, plus transportation.

Stanley Earl, of the Woodworkers, is now a "Labor Advisor" in Korea at a salary of $10,000 per year, plus overseas allowance, plus transportation.

D. Allan Strachan, former UAW representative, is now in Greece as "Chief of Labor Division" at $10,000 per year, plus overseas allowance, plus transportation.

The list of CIO "Labor Advisors" is too long for this letter, but they infest Europe and Asia like an army of locusts, spending their time and our money trying to weaken and destroy the organized labor movements of France and Italy. Their activities and depredations against the working people are a crime. But they are crimes that pay well for the time being.

Monopoly has always paid its servants very well, and patriotism is still the last refuge of scoundrels.

Fraternally,
Wyndham Mortimer

March 14, 1950

Fellow Workers of CIO:

I recently wrote a letter in which I accused the top leadership of CIO of being neutral in this fourth trial and persecution of Harry Bridges. I want to admit my error. I was wrong. They are not neutral, but are definitely on the side of the employers, the Immigration Department, and the FBI.

Any member of CIO interested in knowing just how putrid some so-called labor leaders have become should look over the testimony of one Marvin Rathborne, the latest stool pigeon to testify against Harry Bridges.

First it was Lew Michener, who testified that he discussed his appearing against Bridges with "officers of the UAW, including Roy Reuther [brother of Walter]." He said that they told him to go ahead and testify. Now it is Rathborne, former official of the California State CIO, recently turned real estate shark, who, if he can be believed, tells of conferring with Jim Carey, Joe Curran, and Phil Murray, all of whom urged him to testify against Bridges. If Rathborne is telling the truth on this point, then the silence of Murray, Carey, and Curran is understandable; if he is not telling the truth, their silence is still explainable. For them to deny such conversations with Rathborne would be to weaken and destroy the entire fabric of his lies and misinformation, and thereby to strengthen the case of Bridges. Their desire to destroy Bridges is greater than their desire for justice, hence their silence.

For purposes of publicity, and with a desire to throw dust in the membership's eyes, Mr. Murray and his Board issue pious statements about a "hands off" policy and about being interested only in seeing that Bridges has a "fair" trial. The testimony of Rathborne has put them on the spot. If he is telling the truth, then all their claims of fairness are revealed as traitorous hypocrisy. It reveals also the tie-up among the employer, the CIO, and the FBI. For the first time in American labor history, our top officials have joined with monopoly to harass, persecute, and imprison a man whom they could neither buy, bulldoze, nor frighten. A better example of collusion among the heads of a labor organization, the employers, and the government to imprison and exile an honest man would be impossible to find.

But, you may ask, why do the heads of CIO help labor's worst enemies to destroy this man who has done so much for the working people? Why should the Murray–Carey–Reuther–Curran crowd want to destroy the Bridges leadership and tradition on the West Coast? Is it because he has failed to fight for the membership? Nothing is further from the truth. Even the employers admit that Bridges is a hard bargainer and militant fighter. Is it because he has not obtained higher wages and better conditions? The wages are the highest, and conditions are the best, in the entire CIO. A longshoreman earns an average of a dollar and seventy-two cents an hour, with time-and-a-half after six hours and double time after eight hours.

Is Bridges a criminal? Has he robbed a bank or murdered a defenseless child? On the contrary. His life has been investigated more than that of any individual in all American history, and in spite of the combined snooping of the FBI and the police of city, county, and state, not to mention Scotland Yard, they have failed to uncover one unlawful act. Few men could stand this test, and yet we see the spectacle of Phil Murray, loudly proclaiming his Christian virtues on any and all occasions, joining with labor's worst enemies to imprison and exile one of the most capable and honest men in the American labor movement.

The fact is—and the Murray–Reuther–Carey–Curran crowd knows it—that Bridges is guilty of only one thing. He is guilty of building a union that is run by the membership, and not by Phil Murray. This is his crime. This is the issue.

If Harry Bridges had used his great prestige among the longshoremen to build a union controlled from the top instead of from the bottom, he would not now be on trial. He would, along with Murray and Reuther, be regarded as a "labor statesman" and the daily papers would mention his name with great respect. But since Harry thinks a union must represent and fight for the interests of the working people, and since he is determined the ILWU shall remain a rank and file union, and since he cannot be bought, bulldozed, or frightened, he is to be harassed, persecuted, and, if possible, imprisoned and exiled.

To be sure, the CIO accuses the ILWU of being "Communist-dominated," whatever that is. To charge it with Communist domination is simply Phil Murray's way of saying that the ILWU is run by the membership and not by Murray. A rank-and-file union will discuss and decide issues on the basis of what is best for the membership, and the working class as a whole. In Murray's vocabulary, this is un-American, Communistic, and a threat to our way of life.

The rank-and-file union will decide that human rights must come before property rights; that peace is preferable to another war; and that the billions being spent on arms and A-bombs would be better spent on pensions for the aged, blind, and physically handicapped; on schools, hospitals, and nurseries; and in a thousand other ways that would bring comfort and security to the people of America. To do this, however, would be regarded as socialistic or Communistic, and a threat to the foundations of the Republic. Imagine, if you can, one of Murray's steel unions deciding to adopt a resolution for peace, and calling for unity inside the CIO instead of civil war. Such a local union would immediately be placed under an administratorship, and the hunt for Reds would be on.

Under the Red-baiting barrage of the Murray–Reuther crowd, we have reached the place where it is subversive to talk peace. It is Communistic to hope that the burden of fear and want may be lifted from the shoulders of mankind. If we would earn the smile of Murray, we must think only of another war, think also of war inside our unions so that all power will be at the top and none down below.

This program of expulsion, disruption, and raiding, both here and abroad, is a device used by the enemies of labor to accomplish from the inside what they have been unable to do from the outside. Let us face facts. Who is to benefit from this program of expulsion and raiding? Will it benefit John and Mary Jones, who earn their bread by the sweat of their brows? Will it put more bread, milk, or meat on their table? Will it buy the kiddies more shoes, or pay the rent? Will it help to abolish Jim Crow, and the criminal discrimination against minority groups? Will it do any of the things that MUST be done if we are to escape another calamity such as we endured in the early Thirties?

One must be either a "labor statesman" or an imbecile to claim any benefit whatsoever from the present program of expulsion, disruption, and raiding. It is a program designed to benefit the monopolistic exploiters of every man, woman, and child in America.

These bloated hogs can now sit in their luxurious clubs, and over their glasses grin and smirk with satisfaction that at long last they have found someone inside the labor movement who is willing to bring down labor's house in ruins, rather than permit the rank and file to be masters of their own destiny.

Rank-and-file democracy is a dangerous thing to the monopolist, the labor faker, and enemies of the people. When a powerful labor union is ruled from above, the program and policy of that union reflect only the wishes of its top leadership. The needs of the rank and file are pushed aside in the interests of those who rule. But when a powerful union is controlled by its rank-and-file membership, that union's program and policy reflect the needs and desires of the men and women who pay the dues. This fact should require no argument. It is obvious even to a blind person.

This is the nub of the question. The fight now raging inside CIO is a fight to decide whether our unions are to be ruled from the top, in the interests of the top, or by the rank and file, in the interests of the rank and file.

The Red-baiting fog and smokescreen laid down by the Murray-Reuther-ACTU crowd is not as effective as they had hoped and planned. The rank and file are not as stupid as they thought, and time is not on their side. Moreover, there is one fine thing about the future—there is lots of it.

Sincerely and Fraternally,
Wyndham Mortimer
(Member of Local 32 UAW-CIO)

"MORTIMER SAYS"—COLUMNS IN *PEOPLE'S WORLD*

Los Angeles, January 3, 1951

In the December issue of *The Wage Earner,* mouthpiece of the Catholic hierarchy inside the UAW, there is an interesting article dealing with the proposed increase in dues being put forward by Pres. Walter Reuther and Secretary-Treasurer Emil Mazey.

To quote from the article:

> "That the leaders recognize the traditional reluctance of the membership to vote increased dues, was evidenced at the recent right wing caucus where the matter was handled as delicately as a lighted stick of dynamite." Again I quote: "FEAR that rank and file discussion of the matter well in advance of the convention, could solidify opposition has been expressed by some of the top brass."

So—there you have it, fellow workers. The top brass have their plans all laid to increase dues another buck a month, but—we must not know anything about it until the matter is raised at Cleveland next April.

Who's worried?

If it were a legitimate and proper proposal, why be afraid of "rank-and-file discussion"? Are they afraid that some embarrassing questions might be raised? Let us see.

This increase in dues is being asked because "There is a desire to build a $25 million defense fund," they say. Will it be a "defense fund" or a fund that must be defended? Will it be a fund that will be used to "defend" the workers, or will the auto workers have to defend the fund against some monopoly-minded injunction judge?

The recent experience of the coal miners should be enough to show that such a fund is only a convenient source of revenue to be tapped by anti-labor federal judges, who can not only levy million-dollar fines against the union, but impound the fund as well. Have we forgotten so soon that a federal judge levied a fine against the United Mine Workers of one and a half million dollars, and also impounded the union treasury?

Not money

And isn't it true, that when the miners union was heavily fined, and their funds impounded, their strike was won by the splendid spirit of solidarity shown by the American working class in steel, auto, rubber, and so forth? The American working class responded to the miners' appeal for help, in such a way, and in such a fighting mood, that monopoly capitalism was forced to capitulate.

No "defense fund," however big, has ever won a battle between capital and labor, for the very good reason that the class struggle is not fought with money. If money were the deciding factor, then our fight would be hopeless.

The great sit-down strikes were the struggles that really built our union, and they were won without any money in the international treasury at all. They were won because we relied upon something more powerful than all the money on earth. We fought and won those battles in the only way that any battle between capital and labor can ever be won.

The coal miners, the rubber workers, the clothing workers, the steel workers, all rallied to our support.

This is the way labor defends itself. This is the only way that labor can win. We will never win anything by building $25,000,000 funds for monopoly to seize and impound. The tremendous feeling of class solidarity that exists between all working people, is the only real "defense fund" we have.

—Mort.

Vanishing Power

Los Angeles, April 4, 1951

Sheer curiosity caused me to listen to Walter Reuther on "Meet the Press" a week ago Sunday. He was having a difficult time explaining to several sharp newspaper men just why "labor" had walked out of the Wage Stabilization Board.

In spite of an endless supply of clichés and wisecracks, Reuther's answers were weak and unconvincing because no real working class leader would be seen in the company of C. E. Wilson, Sidney Weinberg, Eric Johnston, and others. Among such representatives of monopoly, the presence of "labor leaders" is hard to explain.

One of the "beefs" Reuther had against the present Administration was that during the last war Sidney Hillman and Bill Knudsen held posts of equal authority, while now "labor" is relegated to a few very minor places.

What Reuther failed to mention was that during the Roosevelt Administration, there was a powerful, militant, and United CIO. Sidney Hillman held an equal position with Knudsen because the CIO spoke for six million working men and women in the basic industries of America. What does the CIO represent today? How much influence does it have?

The monopolist knows, even if the top brass of CIO does not, that the influence and power of the once great CIO has vanished into thin air, thanks to the leadership of the Reuther–Murray–Roman Catholic hierarchy.

Fifteen years ago, under the leadership of John L. Lewis, ably supported by a host of honest rank-and-file leaders, the CIO burst upon the American labor scene with an impact which the deeply entrenched and powerful corporations were unable to withstand.

The foundations were laid for labor's temple, and our future was never so bright. We were united, and an injury to one was the concern of all.

Red-baiting and witch-hunting were the exclusive monopoly of big business and the executive council of the AFL. "Join the CIO in building a Soviet America" was their cry in frantic efforts to prevent the organization of the mass industries.

Eager recruits

But this is 1951. Roosevelt has been succeeded by a Truman, while John L. Lewis has given the leadership of CIO to a Murray.

The Murray–Reuther–Roman Catholic hierarchy swallowed Harry S Truman and his Administration hook, line, and sinker, They have followed every turn and twist in the Truman Administration line faithfully, even when they knew it was determined entirely by the needs of monopoly capitalism for a blood transfusion.

They eagerly enlisted in monopoly's army set out to cripple the unity and solidarity of the world's working people. Their stooges infest all of Europe, Asia and Africa like a swarm of vermin at sixty dollars per day plus expense, and their job is to disrupt, confuse and, if possible, destroy the labor unions of these countries.

They have scuttled the once powerful CIO. They have assassinated the greatest hope American labor ever had, and have dealt the working men and women of America a cowardly blow from which they will not recover for many a long day.

They are even now busy as beavers trying to sell the working people World War III, even though they know (if they know anything) that such a war would mean the end of democracy and the free trade unions.

American labor needs unity. Their top leadership works for division and disruption. The working people need peace. Their top leadership works for war.

—*Mort.*

That Convention

Los Angeles, April 18, 1951

It appears to me, the major decisions at the UAW Cleveland convention, were about as far away from the needs and desires of the auto workers as they could get. Democracy, as it used to exist in UAW conventions, is no more. We have arrived at the place where major decisions are made in an atmosphere of witch-hunting, hysteria, and a denial of the most elementary principles of democratic trades unionism.

Certainly no one could claim that such a thing as a dues increase is in the best interests of the auto workers, or the American labor movement generally. The reasons advanced by the Reuther leadership for the additional dollar, would not stand up under a free and honest discussion by the rank-and-file, and so a referendum vote was prevented by a process of parliamentary maneuvering and trick convention rules. It would not stand up because:

The UAW was organized and built to improve the wages and living standards of the auto workers, and not to fill some bank with money. When our union accumulates a bank balance of $25 million, the bank balance becomes the thing that must be protected, not the membership. It becomes a source of easy living and high salaries for those who protect it, and their real job of improving the conditions of life for the membership, becomes very unimportant.

Reuther's claim of using the increased dues to build up a strike fund is a colossal piece of hypocrisy. Every major contract in the auto industry contains a five-year, no-strike clause.

The UAW was built and won its right to live without any money. The great struggles of 1936, 1937, and 1938 were won because the American working class supported us, and any future struggles will be won in the same way.

Trying to match monopoly capitalism's bank balance is the greatest piece of hypocrisy, and the most dangerous delusion that any fast-talking phony labor statesman ever put over on the rank and file.

Huge "strike funds" are always tied up by an injunction, and serve only as a convenient source from which an anti-labor judge can levy nice, fat, juicy fines. The United Mine Workers have such a huge fund, but Goldsborough prevented its use. Is our memory so short that we have forgotten the miners' strike was won not by a huge bank balance, but by the unity and solidarity of the working class? It was the food, clothes, and money sent by the auto workers, rubber workers, steel workers, electrical workers, and others that defeated the mine owners.[24]

Any union that spends hundreds of thousands of dollars in raiding and destroying the unions of other workers in other industries, needs less income not more.

John L. Lewis of the miners, proposed in a letter to Reuther, that the auto workers, steel workers, miners, and in fact all labor unite in a pact of defense, and offered a million dollars to the UAW in the late Chrysler strike. What was Reuther's answer? He told Lewis the UAW didn't need the money, and failed to even consider the plan of unity.

It may be argued that any discussion of the dues increase is now academic. But to point out the direction Reuther is going, is not academic. The Reuther–Murray–Roman Catholic hierarchy, has plans for us. They plan to make the American labor movement the staunch ally of monopoly capitalism in its war against the exploited and poverty stricken peoples of the world. And here at home, their witchhunting, disrupting, and raiding of other unions, is treason to the American working class.

—*Mort.*

NOTES

NOTES

1. During the Great Depression, which began with the stock market crash of October, 1929, and lasted for ten years, until war production became the pump primer which started industry going again, a number of organizations developed which sought to take care of the needs of the unemployed and the dispossessed. The Communist Party of that day, by all accounts, achieved leadership in that field. The Socialist Party, particularly its left wing, was also active. A number of individual churchmen helped to develop actions on a scattered basis. The principal organizations, of a national scope, were the Unemployed Councils and the Workers Alliance. The two eventually merged into the Workers Alliance. President Roosevelt later established government work projects for the unemployed known as the Works Projects Administration (WPA). Activity of the Workers Alliance was transferred to these projects on a sort of quasi-union basis. A by-product of these unemployment activities was the leadership which was developed both in numbers and in skill. It resulted in a ready supply at all levels when the union organization of the basic industries began rolling in 1934 and after.

Unique among these organizations was the Small Home and Landowners Federation whose activities Wyndham Mortimer describes here. Although it did not achieve national organization its pattern was adopted in many localities. Farmers used some of its methods very effectively when they were being plagued with foreclosures. When government officials showed up to foreclose a farm they would first see a number of trees with a rope and noose draped over a high branch. Then they would encounter a hostile crowd of farmers from the area. If the officials went through with their purpose the farmers would take steps to nullify the action. Often the officials were chased. And more often than not the local sheriff and his deputies yielded gracefully to the farmers' wishes.

The Roosevelt Administration, partly in response to the demands of the home owners and farmers, declared a moratorium on foreclosures. Federal Housing Administration (FHA) legislation was effected. The organizations of the unemployed began a magnificent campaign for pay for the jobless and the Unemployment Insurance Bill was enacted. Americans take these things for granted today. But they were due to the imaginative and courageous activity of the unemployed and the dispossessed.

2. Early in the twentieth century Cleveland was the city of Mayor Tom L. Johnson and his cohesive group of single-taxers and liberals. But then the Republican Party took over and maintained power for a long stretch. On a city, state, and national scale it was the party of Mark Hanna and the Big Business interests. But in Cleveland it was a strange amalgam. It had close to one hundred percent electoral support from the Negro community. In the Hungarian neighborhood the ward leader was a loyal Republican on week days and on Sundays a fervent philosophical anarchist with a printing press. The party was led by Maurice Maschke. He worked out a deal with his Democratic counterpart, Burr Gongwer, whereby political patronage—which was considerable before civil service—was distributed on a 60–40 basis. The official labor movement lined up stoutly with Maurice Maschke and the Republican Party.

3. The AFL of that period was composed largely of craft unions. Carpenters, plumbers, bricklayers, and other craftsmen were organized each into their own separate national unions (called internationals because Canadian locals were often included). During the depression the membership of the AFL declined until it hovered around the two million mark.

The AFL consistently, for a number of reasons, refused to attempt organization in the basic industries such as steel, auto, and rubber where the bulk of workers and production was now concentrated. Nevertheless the AFL maintained a sort of dog-in-the-manger jurisdiction in this area, which meant that if and when and by whomsoever these industries were organized, each individual category of workers within the plant would have to be assigned to their respective international.

The industrial union theme was that all workers in a plant, regardless of craft or job, must be organized into one single union, and that these locals in a particular industry be organized into an international union.

4. Richard Reisinger subsequently became one of the three regional directors of the UAW in Ohio. He remained in this post, and thereby a member of the International Executive Board, until the Milwaukee convention of 1949. He and Mortimer generally worked together effectively although they did not necessarily see eye to eye on all questions.

5. One takes premium pay—time-and-a-half and double time for more than eight hours in a day or forty hours in a week —for granted today. But overtime did not become comparatively universal until the Fair Labor Standards Bill of 1937 was enacted. Even today a great many employees are excluded for one reason or another.

6. The first major project of the Roosevelt Administration in its attempt to pull the nation out of the Depression was the National Recovery Act, known popularly as NRA or the Blue Eagle. (The latter because it was a symbol of compliance which adorned the walls of those business establishments which agreed voluntarily to abide by its provisions.) The Act attempted basically to establish a floor for wages and prices. The theory was that if both could be kept from plummeting further there would be no direction but up for these two components of the economy, and hence for the economy as a whole. But the theory proved to be totally non-viable. The Act was laid to rest by a Supreme Court decision on a poultry case in which a major section of the law was ruled unconstitutional. The case became known as the "sick chicken" case and the Blue Eagle was mercilessly caricatured as the "sick chicken."

7. General Motors workers in the Fisher Body Cleveland plant and the Chevrolet Toledo plant were particularly effective

in strike actions. In the Cleveland plant a full dress strike took place in the spring of 1934. "Bull" McKinnon and his co-worker, frail, bird-like Bill McWheeney, compelled them to go back to work with threats and meaningless promises, but only after a stormy jam-packed meeting at the Metal Trades Hall.

Chevy in Toledo had a completely effective strike in early March of 1935, and Francis Dillon demanded that the strikers return to work. They voted him down at an overflow meeting in the Civic Center. Dillon left the platform, returned to his hotel room, and told the strikers to call him when they were ready to comply with his orders. Meanwhile he promised that he would pull the rug from under them.

The workers met late into the night. But demoralization set in, and they finally voted to go back to work. Jim Roland was the hero of the strikers. The next morning he took up his post on a hillock in front of the plant. He exhorted the workers not to go in. Most sympathized with him, but the general feeling was that victory was elusive for the moment and must await a better day. By ten o'clock he was talking to only a handful of workers.

8. General Hugh Johnson was designated by President Roosevelt to administer the NRA. He swashbuckled into his assignment and was often enough in trouble. He advised business interests to make peace with John L. Lewis in preference to dealing with unpredictable labor leaders from the left. He misjudged John L.'s purposes.

9. Although Mortimer is probably quite right in designating this statement by Father Coughlin as one which began his uncoupling from the American people, it is interesting to note that at the very same moment Harold Ickes, President Roosevelt's Secretary of the Interior, was lamenting the fact that no one in Washington nor any substantial political figure came to the defense of the President. Coughlin enlisted the aid of some of the demagogues Mortimer mentions and others including the Rev. Gerald L. K. Smith who was presiding over the diminishing "Share-the-Wealth" organization of the assassinated Huey Long. He drew in the still-robust pension movement of gullible Dr. Francis Townsend, elements of the Farmer–Labor parties in

Iowa, Michigan, and even Minnesota (where it was the major party at the time) and agrarian and old-time Populist forces influenced by Congressman Lemke. It looked good but it fell apart because of the fascist virulence of certain of its leaders and because the American labor, farm, and middle class population was fearful of returning power to the Hoover Republicans. Formidable as it had appeared at first glance, Lemke's Union Party failed to gather even a million votes in the 1936 Presidential election.

10. David Dubinsky later joined with John L. Lewis to form the CIO. But it soon became evident that his interests lay in a different direction. Within a few years, even when the CIO was at the height of its achievements, he left that body and returned to the AFL.

11. John Brophy had had sharp differences with John L. Lewis during the mid-twenties. He broke with him, set up a Save-The-Union committee, and then formed the National Miners Union. The internecine strife became frantic. There were pitched battles, bloody strikes, and mass arrests, particularly in the East Ohio and West Virginia panhandle mining camps. But as Lewis moved toward spreading industrial unionism Brophy became one of his top lieutenants.

12. There were probably no two more polarized people in the leadership area of the CFL than Bill Finnigan and Max Hayes. Finnigan was a businessman's business agent who believed in the direct approach and the sweetheart agreement; who did his work at the race track between meets; and whose explicit definition of political action was to spread ten or fifteen thousand dollars among his political cronies at Christmas time.

With the merger of the AFL and CIO in 1955, Finnigan ran into trouble as Executive Secretary of the reunited CFL. This editor was awarded the prize for the best labor editorial of the year by the International Labor Press whose judges were working newsmen of the Nieman Fellowship of Harvard. Subject of the editorial was "Finnigan Must Go." The uproar around Finnigan compelled George Meany to remove him.

Max Hayes, on the other hand, had a radical background, had been a Socialist Vice-Presidential candidate, represented the labor thinker–theorists in the movement. He was the editor of the CFL's official organ, *The Citizen*. But in this post, he was severely circumscribed. He came to life with the beginnings of the drive for industrial unionism and supported it vigorously, but there was a growing skepticism in his support and for him this fatalism was fulfilled with the split in labor. He spent the rest of his life as the routine editor of a routine journal.

13. In early 1936, during a severe winter, the rubber workers of Akron went on strike. In themselves, they were not part of a major industry, but as an indispensable supplier to the key auto manufacturers and as a highly concentrated mass production industry, they were important. All the wrath of a boiling Jupiter descended on them, but they held fast and won. It was an important rehearsal and portended that it was not impossible to win in auto and steel.

14. Actually the term "disaffiliate" is chronologically wrong here and did not come into prominence until the 1947 Convention of the AFL. After severing relations with the CIO, Lewis re-entered the AFL; but at the 1947 convention Lewis was extremely unhappy with the acceptance of the hated Taft–Hartley Act by the AFL. This would mean that every labor official on a national or local union level would have to sign annually a non-Communist affidavit. Sitting on the convention floor after the resolution was ratified Lewis borrowed a piece of scrap paper and wrote on it:

Dear Bill,
We disaffiliate.
John

He had it handed to William Green and walked out.

15. Unlike the Ford Motor Company, which concentrated almost all its production in the gigantic River Rouge plant, where at times more than 70,000 workers were employed, General Motors, from its inception, decentralized its production in all corners of the United States and Canada. It now has close to 150 plants. In 1936 it had about half that number. GM early became partial to the system of annual model changes. This meant extensive die work for pressing or fabricating the steel which constitutes the body parts. It adopted the system of building the

body dies for the most part in the plant which was to do the fabricating. Assembly work can be moved from plant to plant with a comparatively small loss of efficiency. This is impossible in fabrication, where the presses, sub-assembly equipment, and dies are specialized to the parts to be built.

16. In 1936 Flint had 48,000 GM workers. Today it has more than 80,000. There is probably no other city in the private enterprise world which has such a large concentration of workers, in combined numbers and percentage, in one company.

17. Except for its foundries, the employment policies of General Motors prior to our involvement in World War II were almost exclusively lily-white. The Ford Motor Company, on the other hand, permitted a percentage of Negro workers in its production departments, including some even in skilled trades categories and in some of its offices. Yet these two apparently diametrically opposed policies were really two sides of the same coin. GM used its "whites only" policy to keep the white workers closer to its skirts, while Ford held out its employment of Negroes as a magnet to them, and as an unspoken threat to the white workers. The purpose of both policies was basically to handicap the organization of unions. White workers had to learn that unity circumvented these purposes. To a surprising degree they did. Some would say, however, that today, with many of their goals accomplished, there has been an evaporation of that solidarity within many unions.

18. It should be remembered that the elder Ford openly engaged in the most outrageous political projects. He was, for example, an overt anti-Semite. He owned the *Dearborn Independent* and through it carried on a virulent anti-Semitic campaign printing material like the defamatory and completely imaginary Protocols of Zion.

19. There was intense discussion within the Roosevelt Administration about the strike. At a cabinet meeting Frances Perkins, Secretary of Labor, spoke for thirty minutes about the strike, uninterrupted except for an occasional question by President Roosevelt.

Secretary of the Interior Harold Ickes thought that Lewis had hurt himself because he reminded Roosevelt that it was the efforts and the votes of labor that had re-elected him to a second term.

On the other hand Alfred Sloan, who headed the General Motors Corporation for 23 years, complained that although the "sit-down strikes were plainly illegal . . . yet President Franklin D. Roosevelt . . . exerted steady pressure upon the corporation" and upon himself personally to negotiate with the strikers who had seized their property, until finally he felt obliged to do so.

20. Dave Beck was riding high at that time, but he overreached himself. A few years later, after World War II, the Federal government moved in, and he ended by serving penitentiary terms.

21. Congressman Martin Dies of Texas enjoyed the same notoriety in prewar and World War II days later assumed by Senator Joseph McCarthy. He was the chairman of the House Un-American Activities Committee, and his antics won consistent banner headlines. They also won the hatred of the labor movement.

22. Richard Frankensteen had no real stomach for the labor movement. At the 1944 Grand Rapids convention of the union he defeated Walter Reuther for the first vice presidency, strangely enough with the aid of Mortimer and the Left. But a few years later he quit the union. He became instead a factory owner.

23. In later years Walter Reuther switched his position, and an International Executive Board post was created specifically for a Negro. At a subsequent convention a board post was created specifically for a woman.

24. In the postwar period the coal miners went on strike for pensions and shorter hours. The courts ordered them back to work but they disobeyed the order. Federal Judge Goldsborough then ordered their treasury confiscated. Local 45 of the UAW in Cleveland loaded a van of food to Yorkville in the East Ohio coal fields. Ford Local 600 of the UAW with more than 60,000 members at the River Rouge plant sent six huge moving vans to the same area. The movement caught on and trucks rolled into the mine fields. The miners ate and they won the strike.

INDEX

INDEX